◆ DIVIDED WE GOVERN

◆ DIVIDED WE GOVERN

PARTY CONTROL,

LAWMAKING, AND

INVESTIGATIONS,

1946 – 2002

SECOND EDITION

DAVID R. MAYHEW

YALE UNIVERSITY PRESS

NEW HAVEN ◆ LONDON

First published 1991 by Yale University Press.
Second Edition published 2005 by Yale University Press.

Printed in the United States of America
Library of Congress Control Number: 2004117534

ISBN 978-0-300-10288-8 (pbk. : alk. paper)

A catalogue record for this book is available from the British Library.

The paper in this book meets the guidelines for permanence and durability of
the Committee on Production Guidelines for Book Longevity of the Council on
Library Resources.

10 9 8 7 6 5 4 3

CONTENTS

CONTENTS

TABLES AND FIGURES

TABLES

FIGURE

PREFACE TO
THE SECOND EDITION

I put the finishing touches on the original edition of *Divided We Govern* in early 1991. At that time, divided party control of the American national government was a topic of rising awareness and alarm. For ten years in a row—a span of five consecutive Congresses under Ronald Reagan and George H. W. Bush—neither party had ever simultaneously controlled the House, the Senate, and the presidency. Those ten split years were an American record, and they were not the only instance of split control within easy memory.

Granted, the nearest recallable instance then of *unified* party control, that under Jimmy Carter in 1977–80, was scarcely remembered as the gold standard in effective government. Even so, it was widely speculated by 1990, aren't things going awfully wrong? Isn't divided government basically unworkable? Especially in the legislative realm, doesn't it keep the government from doing anything at all, even when action is cried for—as many thought was the case around 1990? I remember chewing over these questions in the fall of 1990, book manuscript in hand, as I watched the saga of Bush's effort to enact a half-trillion-dollar deficit-reduction plan play out day after day on television. This was the president's top priority, and the stakes were high. The measure finally did pass, but it might as easily have failed. The route was as rocky and as full of surprises as a Florida recount or a California recall election. What would George Mitchell do next? What would Newt Gingrich do next? Wasn't there a better way?

Fast forward to 2005. One point is even clearer today. Whether or not we approve of divided party control, it has become an abundant fact of life. It is true that the Republican party, by winning the Senate, ascended to unified party control after the 2002 midterm, and there was no telling then what the future would bring. Yet consider the span of twenty-two years from Reagan's first election in 1980 through the 2002 midterm.

Only two years and five months of that time span featured unified party control — Clinton's first Congress in 1993–94 and the early months of George W. Bush's first Congress in 2001 before Senator James Jeffords defected from Republican ranks, giving the Senate to the Democrats. Until the 2002 midterm, I was encountering undergraduates and even young graduate students who seemed to view unified party control as a rare event on the order of an eclipse of the moon.

There is another development since 1980. This book, like most treatments of the subject, addresses party control as a yes-or-no matter. That makes good sense. It must be the case that either a) one party simultaneously controls all three national elective institutions, or b) one party controls two of them and the other party controls the third.[1] For most analytic purposes, a yes-or-no coding is the way to go. Yet it is also true that *eight* possible conditions, not just the conventional two, arise if we take into account which party controls which institutions. If the presidency, House, and Senate are arrayed in order, the possibilities are respectively DDD, DDR, DRD, RDD, RRD, RDR, DRR, and RRR. How many of those eight patterns have appeared since 1980? The answer is now *six*, which shows the surprising versatility of the regime that has unfolded in recent decades. The only exceptions are DDR (the Republicans have not controlled *just* the Senate since 1885–89) and DRD (the Republicans have not controlled *just* the House since 1859–61).[2]

Clearly, divided party control remains a subject to reckon with. Intricacies aside, sticking to a yes-or-no formulation, the paramount questions have been and of course remain: What difference does it make whether party control of the government is unified or divided? Why should we care? *Divided We Govern,* in its original 1991 edition, tackled these questions by addressing certain strands of historical reality between 1946 and

1. At least we thought that was true until "power sharing" came along in the Senate during the early months of 2001 when the Republicans and Democrats both had fifty members. Vice President Dick Cheney could break ties. Power sharing may deserve an asterisk.

2. Wrong, a graduate student fired back at me when I recently presented this material to a seminar at the University of Wisconsin. Technically, a DRD pattern existed for a couple of weeks in January 2001, between the start of the new 107th Congress and the inauguration of George W. Bush. During this interval, outgoing Vice President Al Gore could break ties in the new 50–50 Senate. Fleetingly, the outgoing president was a Democrat, the new House was Republican, and the new Senate was precariously Democratic. Later it occurred to me that a DDR pattern existed briefly for comparable reasons in January 1981. Technically, then, *all eight* patterns have appeared at least briefly since the late 1970s.

1990. In this new edition I have opted to leave the original text of that edition intact. Save for a few corrections, nothing has been changed in the original chapters one through seven. Instead, I have updated the book as best I could by contributing a new epilogue chapter that continues the original data, discussion, and analysis from January 1991 through December 2002.

In terms of real political life, that means adding a new span of six Congresses in the shape of a Bush-Clinton-Bush sandwich—the last two years of the Bush 41 presidency in 1991–92, then all eight years of the Clinton presidency in 1993–2000, then the first two years of the Bush 43 presidency in 2001–02.

It may help to recall the highlights of those twelve years. The 102nd Congress under Bush 41 approved the Persian Gulf Resolution, which authorized the war against Iraq that quickly ensued, but then bogged down in demoralizing and largely inconsequential maneuvers. The Democrats after the 1992 election, exuberantly possessing the Senate, House, and presidency, aimed for another New Deal or Great Society. It was to be 1933 or 1965 all over again. The saga of Clinton's budget, another half-trillion-dollar plan to reduce the deficit, ended in a considerable victory in August 1993 notwithstanding a vexed legislative history as in 1990. A few other party measures passed. The North American Free Trade Agreement (NAFTA) was approved. Yet Clinton's ambitious health-care plan went down to disastrous defeat along with other aspirations in a particularly nasty, partisan environment in 1994. The Democrats lost both houses of Congress in the 1994 midterm.

Enter the Gingrich-led Republicans in 1995, who aimed as high in legislative terms and missed their target by as much. The party's "Contract with America" passed the House but ran into trouble in the Senate and the White House. The party's ambitious omnibus budget drive—don't let them "cut Medicare," the Democrats framed it as—brought on a showdown over shutting down the government between Gingrich and Clinton that Clinton won. Yet in 1996 the parties settled into a mode of bipartisan lawmaking that generated, among other results, welfare reform. In the 105th Congress in 1997, the two sides reached a deal to balance the budget in five years. Otherwise, that Congress was notable for the House's impeachment of Clinton in 1998. The 106th Congress of 1999–2000 during Clinton's last two years was largely post-impeachment aftermath and pre-election warmup.

Enter Bush 43, under whom the 107th Congress enacted the president's sizable tax cut in early 2001 and several other domestic items, including campaign finance reform, yet also reacted energetically to the terrorist attack of September 11, 2001. A flurry of enactments including a "use of force" resolution and the USA Patriot Act followed that attack in short order, and in late 2002 another Iraq resolution cleared Congress. At the outer edges of the Bush slices of the twelve-year sandwich were resolutions authorizing war in Iraq — those of January 1991 and October 2002.

That is the relevant recent history, briefly stated.[3]

In lawmaking terms, does unified versus divided party control make a difference? More specifically, to introduce the main question addressed in this book, does the government produce more major enactments under one condition than the other? Strip away the promises, the programs, the schemes, the sagas, and the pyrotechnics, and what do we see? What does the government actually do? Central to an answer is a time-series dataset documenting major enactments. In the 1991 edition I identified 267 of those for the 80th Congress of 1947–48 through the 101st Congress of 1989–90. In an epilogue to this new edition, relying this time entirely on journalists' "wrapup" stories written at the ends of congressional sessions, I add another 66 enactments for 1991 through 2002. I introduce, discuss, and analyze this new dataset and place it in the longer context of post–World II history. I touch on such matters as the ideological content of legislation during 1991–2002, the level of roll-call conflict during that time, and the prominence of major congressional investigations. A new Appendix C is a list of the wrap-up sources for 1991–2002. A new Appendix D is a brief theoretical and methodological discussion centering on the "Sweep Two" ingredient of the 1991 edition — that is, the use of retrospective judgments by policy experts to identify important legislation.

The gist of the case? In the 1991 edition, I challenged the conventional claim that unified party control has been legislatively more productive than divided party control. At least during modern times, I judged that claim to be "wrong, or at least mostly or probably wrong" (see page 3). I have not found any good reason in the record of 1991 through 2002 to challenge that judgment.

---

3. Ending in December 2002, the analysis misses some now familiar enactments of calendar 2003 — another Bush tax cut, a ban on partial-birth abortion, and the new Republican program for prescription drugs through Medicare.

ACKNOWLEDGMENTS

For help with research on this project, I am grateful to Matthew Berger, Rogan Kersh, David Kinsella, Grant Reeher, and Christopher Soper. For thoughtful reactions to an early draft—though I very likely ignored too much good advice—I am indebted to Bruce Ackerman, R. Douglas Arnold, Charles M. Cameron, Robert A. Dahl, James Fesler, Morris Fiorina, John Gilmour, Loch Johnson, Frederick M. Kaiser, Joseph LaPalombara, Robert Peabody, Grant Reeher, Francis E. Rourke, Byron Shafer, Rogers Smith, Patricia Sykes, and Richard Valelly. For helpful discussions, I thank John Mark Hansen, Herbert Kaufman, William Keech, Philip Klinker, J. Morgan Kousser, Peter Schuck, and H. Bradford Westerfield. For his invaluable criticism as the manuscript's anonymous referee, I am indebted to Frank J. Sorauf. I relied on the fine libraries at Boston University, the California Institute of Technology, and Yale University, and on the Library of Congress. The last phase of the work was supported by a Sherman Fairchild Fellowship at the California Institute of Technology.

I ✦ INTRODUCTION

Since World War II, divided party control of the American national government has come to seem normal. Between the 1946 and 1990 elections, one of the two parties held the presidency, the Senate, and the House simultaneously for eighteen of those years. But control was divided for twenty-six years, it is divided right now, and we may see more such splits. Some opinion studies suggest that today's voters prefer divided control on principle: Parties jointly in power are seen to perform a service by checking each other.[1]

Of course, divided control is not a new phenomenon. During a twenty- two-year stretch between 1874 and 1896, to take the extreme case, the two parties shared control of the government for sixteen years.[2] But after that, the country settled into a half-century habit of unified control broken only by two-year transitions from one party's monopoly to the other's that closed out the Taft, Wilson, and Hoover administrations. It is against this immediate background that the post–World War II experience stands out.

Should we care whether party control is unified or divided? That depends on whether having one state of affairs rather than the other makes any important difference. Does it? Much received thinking says yes. The political party, according to one of political science's best-known axioms about the American system, is "the indispensable instrument that [brings] cohesion and unity, and hence effectiveness, to the government as a whole by linking the executive and legislative

1. See Everett Carll Ladd, "Public Opinion and the 'Congress Problem,' " *Public Interest* 100 (Summer 1990), 66–67, and Morris P. Fiorina, "An Era of Divided Government" (MS, 1989), pp. 16–18.

2. Evidently, the 1873 depression and reactions against Reconstruction lowered the Republicans from their post–1860 dominance to rough electoral equality with the Democrats. The 1893 depression and the McKinley-Bryan election of 1896 elevated them again.

branches in a bond of common interest."[3] In the words of Woodrow Wilson, "You cannot compound a successful government out of antagonisms."[4]

At a concrete level, this means at least that significant lawmaking can be expected to fall off when party control is divided. "Deadlock" or "stalemate" will set in. Variants of this familiar claim could be cited endlessly. Randall B. Ripley argued in a 1969 study, for example: "To have a productive majority in the American system of government the President and a majority of both houses must be from the same party. Such a condition does not guarantee legislative success but is necessary for it."[5] V. O. Key, Jr., wrote: "Common partisan control of executive and legislature does not assure energetic government, but division of party control precludes it."[6] Ripley argued again in 1983: "In general, not much legislation is produced in [circumstances of divided control], particularly on domestic matters. What domestic legislation does pass is likely to be bland and inconsequential."[7] Lloyd N. Cutler concluded in a recent piece attacking divided control: "Putting . . . aside [Reagan's tax cut in 1981 and tax reform in 1986], there has never been in modern days any successful domestic legislative program at a time of divided government."[8] These authors do not

3. James L. Sundquist presents this crystallization of the familiar party-government view in "Needed: A Political Theory for the New Era of Coalition Government in the United States," *Political Science Quarterly* 103 (Winter 1988–89), 614. At pp. 616–24, Sundquist undertakes an especially useful review of the theoretical case for unified party control.

4. Quoted in ibid., p. 618.

5. Randall B. Ripley, *Majority Party Leadership in Congress* (Boston: Little, Brown, 1969), p. 168, and more generally pp. 11–18 and chap. 5. This seems to be the only serious empirical study of the effects of unified versus divided party control.

6. V. O. Key, Jr., *Politics, Parties, and Pressure Groups*, 5th ed. (New York: Crowell, 1964), p. 688, and more generally pp. 656, 687–88.

7. Randall B. Ripley, *Congress: Process and Policy* (New York: W. W. Norton, 1983), p. 355, and more generally pp. 347–56.

8. Lloyd N. Cutler, "Some Reflections about Divided Government," *Presidential Studies Quarterly* 18 (1988), 490. See also Cutler, "The Cost of Divided Government," *New York Times*, November 22, 1987, p. IV:27; Hedrick Smith, *The Power Game: How Washington Works* (New York: Random House, 1988), chap. 17 ("Divided Government: Gridlock and the Blame Game"); and James L. Sundquist, "The Crisis of Competence in Our National Government," *Political Science Quarterly* 95 (1980), 183–208. "At such times [that is, of divided

argue that unified party control always generates large collections of notable legislation. But they can be read to predict that it should generate, over a long period of time when contrasted with divided control, considerably more such legislation.

Another familiar claim has to do with congressional oversight. It is that Congress acting as an investigative body will give more trouble to the executive branch when a president of the opposite party holds power. That propensity can be viewed as bad or good. Woodrow Wilson might say that accelerated probing of the executive provides just another kind of unfortunate "antagonism." From another perspective, it can be expected to keep presidents and bureaucrats in line better. Either way, what causes the effect is a predicted difference between unified and divided control. Morris S. Ogul has written, "A congressman of the president's party is less likely to be concerned with oversight than a member of the opposition party."[9] Republican leaders of the Eightieth Congress under Truman were said, perhaps apocryphally, to follow a strategy of "open with a prayer and close with a probe." Seymour Scher concluded, after studying congressional oversight of the regulatory agencies in 1958–61: "When the leadership of the majority party in Congress believes it can cause sufficient embarrassment, with accompanying profit for itself, to a past or current opposition president who is held responsible for the performance of his agency appointees, committee oversight tends to be used for this purpose."[10]

I shall argue in this work that the above claims are wrong, or at least mostly or probably wrong. They do not, to be sure, address the

government], the normal tendency of the U.S. system toward deadlock becomes irresistible. Harmonious collaboration, barring national crisis, is out of the question. The president and Congress are compelled to quarrel. No presidential proposal can be accepted by the legislature without raising the stature of the president as leader. Similarly, no initiative of Congress can be approved by the president without conceding wisdom to his enemies. The conflict, bickering, tension, and stalemate that characterized the fourteen years of divided government [under Eisenhower, Nixon, and Ford] were inevitable." Sundquist, p. 192.

9. Morris S. Ogul, *Congress Oversees the Bureaucracy: Studies in Legislative Supervision* (Pittsburgh: University of Pittsburgh Press, 1976), p. 18.

10. Seymour Scher, "Conditions for Legislative Control," *Journal of Politics* 25 (1963), 541. A committee of a Democratic House grilled Eisenhower's regulatory appointees, but after the 1960 election, "members of both parties on the committee were agreed that the prospect was remote of a Democratic

only differences that one might expect to find between unified and divided control. Other claims, such as that divided party control generates fiscal disorder or other kinds of "incoherence," will be taken up in the concluding chapter. But the main argument in the following pages will be that unified as opposed to divided control has not made an important difference in recent times in the incidence of two particular kinds of activity. These are, first, high-publicity investigations in which congressional committees expose alleged misbehavior in the executive branch: Such extravaganzas seem to go on regardless of conditions of party control. And second, the enactment of a standard kind of important legislation: From the Taft-Hartley Act and Marshall Plan of 1947–48 through the Clean Air Act and $490 billion deficit-reduction package of 1990, important laws have materialized at a rate largely unrelated to conditions of party control. To see this pattern, one has to peer through a Capitol Hill haze that can feature delay, suspense, party posturing, ugly wrangling, and other presentations. One has to look at actual enactments. There, the pattern is as stated.

Not to be taken up here is the question of whether a separation-of-powers regime like the American can be expected to generate its own distinctive kind of investigative or lawmaking activity. That is a separate matter. Also separate is the question of whether Democrats and Republicans push in opposing ideological directions when they make laws. Of course they often do. Ideological direction will enter the argument here in chapters 4 and 6, and partisan as well as other causes of it will be discussed. But the basic concern in this work, as regards lawmaking, is not with direction but with motion—whether much gets done at all.

My method will be simply to compare what took place in investigating and lawmaking, in circumstances of unified as opposed to divided party control, from the Eightieth Congress of 1947–48 through the 101st Congress of 1989–90. That is, I compare some reality with other reality; I do not hold up reality against some abstract model of how government ought to work. I classify each two-year inter-election period between 1946 and 1990 as "unified" or "divided"— one or the other. The "unified" segments include two years of Republican rule under Eisenhower in 1953–54, and sixteen years of Democratic rule under Truman in 1949–52, Kennedy and Johnson in 1961–68, and

majority continuing its inquiry into agency relations with their regulated clientele once the new [Kennedy] administration's appointees began to appear in the agencies' top positions" (p. 538).

Carter in 1977–80. The "divided" times include two years of a Democratic president facing a Republican Congress under Truman in 1947–48; eighteen years of a Republican president facing a Democratic Congress under Eisenhower in 1955–60, Nixon and Ford in 1969–76, Reagan in 1987–88, and Bush in 1989–90; and six years of a Republican president along with a Republican Senate and Democratic House under Reagan in 1981–86.

Does the unique 1981–86 pattern require special handling? Under a limiting-case assumption, the answer is no for legislating but yes for investigating. It takes the assent of all three institutions—Senate, House, and presidency—to pass a bill. If one assumes that each party unanimously opposes the other, any institution run by one party can and will block bills favored by the other two run by the other party. This holds for an odd-man-out blocking House (as in 1981–86) just as for an odd-man-out blocking presidency (as under Nixon). (The argument assumes that a president is not completely immobilized by having to confront veto-proof two-thirds majorities of the opposite party in both houses of Congress; no president ever faced an opposition like that between 1946 and 1990.) Thus for lawmaking purposes, 1981–86 is formally just like any other divided time. In undertaking investigations, however, each house of Congress ordinarily runs its own enterprise. Hence more probes of the executive might be expected when both houses confront an odd-man-out president (as under Nixon) than when just one house confronts a president of the opposite party (as in 1981–86 under Reagan).

Why choose to examine 1946 through 1990? First, as a matter of research design, the period's mix of "unified" and "divided" segments affords a good contrast. The segments are not far apart in number and they are rather well scattered across the four decades. And each party had at least one spell of complete rule and one of controlling the presidency but not Congress. Second, forty-two years is a long span over which many sorts of idiosyncrasy should iron out. Generalizations accordingly gain strength. Third, the post–World War II era seems to constitute, in some relevant background respects, a natural modern unit. The New Deal and the war raised the government to heights of activity from which it never entirely came down. Basic U.S. commitments in foreign and defense policy date to the late 1940s. The Employment Act of 1946 officially made macroeconomic management the government's job. With these commitments, it seems a good bet that the country's resulting busy and non-stop agendas in the areas of defense, foreign policy, and economics have affected relations between presidents and Congresses, even if one cannot be certain exactly how. In addition, Franklin Roosevelt strengthened the presidency as an independent institutional actor in the 1930s and 1940s. The custom of presenting "the president's program" as a comprehensive annual legislative agenda dates to Truman's administration in the late 1940s.[11] The La Follette-Monroney Act of 1946 helped to equip Congress as a counterpart of the modern presidency (even if most of the massive growth in Capitol Hill staffing came later). Finally, the televising of particularly newsworthy congressional investigations began in 1948.[12]

If these arguments are valid, can conclusions about unified versus divided control during 1946 through 1990 be extrapolated to any time beyond that era? Perhaps to coming decades more safely than to periods before the 1940s, though what would emerge from a suitable study of earlier times is an open question. A treatment of lawmaking in chapter 6 will suggest that at least some patterns during the second half of the twentieth century look a lot like ones during the first half.

This study requires, above all, some plausible ways of identifying important investigations and laws. My decision rules for doing so are set out in considerable, though I think necessary and readily understandable, detail in chapters 2 and 3. I hope the resulting uses of data will be a contribution. Surprisingly, for all the work done on legislative behavior, laws and investigations are seldom tackled in a way that is reasonably systematic yet tries to sort out the significant from the trivial.[13] That is because, to do so, a line has to be walked between being unconvincingly anecdotal on the one hand, and being irrelevantly indiscriminate and safe in quantifying evidence on the other. I have tried to walk that line. I have undertaken to select, compare, and for some purposes add up items of evidence that cannot be subjected to these treatments in any indisputable way. As one conse-

11. Richard E. Neustadt, "Presidency and Legislation: Planning the President's Program," *American Political Science Review* 49 (1955), 980–1021.

12. The first televised hearing featured a House Un-American Activities Committee interrogation of Alger Hiss. See Allen Weinstein, *Perjury: The Hiss-Chambers Case* (New York: Alfred A. Knopf, 1978), p. 44.

13. A classic work that makes such an effort is Lawrence H. Chamberlain, *The President, Congress, and Legislation* (New York: Columbia University Press, 1946).

quence, I hedge my conclusions. As another, in chapters 2 and 4, I rely heavily on the technique of presenting large displays of material that will be generally familiar to the reader, so as to enlist reader participation in judging what claims are valid.

The plan of the book is as follows. In chapter 2, I outline a methodology for selecting, and then present, a list of particularly well publicized postwar investigations of alleged executive misbehavior. Discussion ensues about the incidence of such probes in times of unified as opposed to divided party control. Chapters 3 and 4 taken together provide a comparable treatment of important postwar statutes; the methodology appears in chapter 3 and the presentation and discussion in chapter 4. Chapters 5 and 6 are a two-part speculative discussion aimed at explaining the non-patterns detected earlier. Why, that is, has unified versus divided control not seemed to cause any appreciable difference in the incidence of such probes and enactments? A number of possible explanations are introduced and considered. Turned upside down, these become positive accounts of what arguably *does* occasion investigations and lawmaking. Chapter 7 brings some parting order to this discussion and then briefly takes up five additional differences that unified versus divided control might be thought to make. Again I argue, if inconclusively, that it probably does not.

2 ◆ HIGH-PUBLICITY INVESTIGATIONS

Beyond making laws, Congress probably does nothing more consequential than investigate alleged misbehavior in the executive branch. Consider the Teapot Dome investigation of the 1920s, Senator Joseph McCarthy's search for Communists in the Army and State departments in 1953–54, the Watergate inquiries of 1973–74, and the Iran-Contra hearings of 1987. All these investigations attracted the media. When that happens, a probe can sometimes gain the attention of the public, weigh down the White House, trigger resignations of leading officials, and register a long-term impact on public opinion and government policy. Occasionally a probe leads to a dramatic confrontation that seems to decide something or frame an important question or issue. Thus in 1948, in a House Un-American Activities Committee (HUAC) probe spearheaded by Richard Nixon, Whittaker Chambers confronted Alger Hiss about whether Hiss had been a spy. Attorney Joseph Welch shamed Senator McCarthy in a televised hearing in 1954. Senator J. William Fulbright and Secretary of State Dean Rusk tangled on camera about Vietnam in 1966. Senator Sam Ervin dealt Old-Testament fashion with Nixon's various lieutenants in 1973. And Oliver North reacted feistily to questioners John Nields, Jr., and Arthur Liman in 1987.

This chapter addresses undertakings such as these—congressional committee "exposure probes" of the executive branch that draw considerable publicity. Clearer specification is needed. An "exposure probe," let us say, is a committee investigation that dwells on the alleged misbehavior of some person, group, or organization. Many congressional oversight enterprises do not have that kind of concern and hence do not qualify as "exposure probes." Also, much committee oversight that does dwell on misbehavior draws little media attention. That large universe of activity has no relevance here either. The objective is to zero in on a category of investigations that gain a kind of political importance exactly because they *do* draw considerable publicity. Finally, some congressional probes of misbehavior that do succeed in attracting a lot of media attention have targets other than the executive branch. In recent decades those have included union racketeers, Hollywood Communists, organized crime, drug firms, General Motors, and disk jockeys who took payola. That kind of probe is irrelevant here too. So this chapter deals with only one class of events that fall under the rubric of congressional oversight activity. It is not a representative class, but it is a particularly important one.

Note also that, since high publicity is one threshold, the events at issue here stemmed from media decisions about what was hot "news" as well as from congressional action. That has to be borne in mind. The media organ I rely on in this chapter, the *New York Times*, seems to have adhered to more or less the same "news sense" during, say, fifteen- or twenty-year intervals from 1946 through 1990, though not throughout the entire period. The *Times*'s changes in coverage routines do not impede the analysis much, but they will be discussed. At any time, of course, members of congressional committees have to take steps to make "newsworthy" items available for there to be anything to report.

Precisely how should we recognize a relevant probe? An investigation enters this chapter's data set if it generated a specified kind of content in one or more *New York Times* front-page stories, on at least twenty days (not necessarily consecutive), during any Congress between 1946 and 1990. The test for content is as follows. A front-page story becomes relevant if it featured a committee-based charge of misbehavior against the executive branch, or an executive response to such a charge.

Committee-based means that someone or some set of people involved in or accommodated by a committee investigation made the charge. It might have been the full committee (as in a report), a committee member, a committee's party majority or minority, a committee staff member, a witness who testified (including a member of the executive branch who criticized part of that branch), or even an outsider who wrote a smoking-gun letter that a committee member disclosed. According to this criterion, note that a committee might have generated charges even if its leaders or party majority preferred not to. By stipulation, any senator or House member's preliminary call for an investigation also counts as relevant story content, as in "Senator Jones Demands Full Probe of Justice Department."

To continue with terms, *misbehavior*, as applied to the conduct of executive or administrative affairs, means any of a wide variety of kinds of behavior that members of Congress and the public commonly regard as improper or incompetent. The offenses might include treason, disloyalty, usurpation, corruption, conflict of interest, other illegalities, maladministration, bad policy planning, bad faith, or simply making mistakes. In the sector of foreign and defense policy, where the executive enjoys constitutional leeway, the offenses might include unconstitutional, deceptive, ill-conceived, or ill-managed use of that leeway. It makes no difference here whether allegations of any of the various offenses from 1946 through 1990 were in fact valid, partly valid, or fantasy. Some were evidently fantasy. Excluded, in principle, are congressional criticisms that addressed the executive's policy positions rather than its past or present conduct. The aim is to confine the analysis to oversight processes and stay away from relations between the branches as co-participants in lawmaking. This distinction turned out to be rather easy to enforce, though there were some close calls.

Against the executive branch means against some unit, or a past or present official(s) or employee(s), of the executive branch. That includes the armed services and the regulatory agencies. Alger Hiss is the signal instance of a past rather than present official who drew investigation. Hiss left the State Department in December 1946. HUAC went after him in August 1948. Targeting Hiss was, among other things, a way to assault the policy-making apparatuses of both the Roosevelt and Truman administrations.

An executive response is a reply to a committee-based charge by some relevant past or present executive official. Here is a clear instance: "Secretary Smith Calls Jones Corruption Charge Outrageous." Some responses were delivered in committee testimony, some in news conferences, speeches, or other settings. Whether executive acts or utterances qualified as responses to committee charges was often a matter of judgment. Eisenhower, for example, spoke in above-the-fray abstractions about McCarthyism, but it seems quite clear that responding to the senator is what he was doing.[1] Proximity in time between a charge and an executive expression was one sensible qualifying test. If sources besides congressional committees—judges, the

1. See Fred I. Greenstein, *The Hidden-Hand Presidency: Eisenhower as Leader* (New York: Basic Books, 1982), pp. 175–76, 189–212.

media, or non-committee politicians, for example—had also been leveling charges against the executive, and the executive responded to somebody but it was not clear who that somebody was, I shied away from deciding that it was a committee. The congressional units often had important company in pursuing executive misbehavior.

Finally, *a story featured.* This means, in practice, that the *New York Times Index*'s summary squib about a story that began on the front page included at least one item about a pertinent charge or response.

One point remains about processing evidence. Ordinarily one committee provoked all the stories connected with an investigation. But sometimes a narrative of charges and responses moved among two or more committees as the *Times* wove it from day to day. In the case of the House's probe of the intelligence agencies in 1975, for example, much went on in other quarters before Otis Pike's select committee finally assumed control. Sometimes one committee had good command of an investigation but others briefly interfered. In two instances, a commodity speculation probe in 1947–48 and the Billy Sol Estes probe in 1962, handoffs occurred between a House committee and a Senate committee. The decision rule in such cases was to go along with the *Times* narrative. If an investigation was functionally a multi-committee enterprise, so be it.

Thirty-one investigations between 1946 and 1990 met the above criteria.[2] Table 2.1 lists these under the headings of "divided" and

2. What were the near misses? Six investigations inspired front-page stories for at least fifteen but fewer than twenty days. In 1949, the House Armed Services Committee aired the military's (chiefly the Navy's) complaints about Secretary of Defense Louis Johnson's moves to unify the services. In 1955, a Senate Government Operations subcommittee went after Secretary of the Air Force Harold Talbott, who had kept business connections, for conflict of interest. Talbott resigned. In 1962, a Senate Armed Services subcommittee headed by Stuart Symington pursued former Eisenhower administration officials for waste and conflict of interest in the stockpiling of war-related materials. Also in 1962, a Senate Armed Services subcommittee voiced and listened to objections that Secretary of Defense Robert McNamara had outlawed anti-Communist indoctrination in the military. Senators John Stennis and Strom Thurmond figured in the stories. In 1973, the Senate Armed Services Committee revealed, and channeled criticism of the fact, that the Nixon administration had secretly bombed Cambodia in 1969–70. And in late 1986, the Senate Intelligence Committee got in some early licks about the Iran-Contra affair. Two of these six probes occurred during times of divided party control. Four occurred during unified control, if one includes the Republican Senate versus the Reagan administration in 1986 as an instance

"unified" party control. Presented for each is the number of days it generated relevant front-page coverage, the charges, which committee or committees conducted it, who chaired it, and also some phrases about what took place during it. Table 2.1 contains this chapter's chief supply of basic information about the thirty-one probes.

A variety of concerns and topics drove these investigations. Fifteen dwelt at least partly on alleged corruption, conflict of interest, favoritism, or an administration's handling of such a charge. Under Truman the charges were of improperly awarded airplane contracts, insider commodity speculation, influence peddling by "five-percenters," dubious transactions in the Reconstruction Finance Corporation (RFC) and the Bureau of Internal Revenue, and the Justice Department's incompetence in policing corruption.[3] Under Eisenhower came allegations of improper influence in arranging the Dixon-Yates power contract and in the regulatory agencies.[4] Under Kennedy, it was questions of favoritism toward grain-storage dealer Billy Sol Estes and in awarding the TFX fighter-plane contract.[5] Nixon's time featured an allegation of suspicious dealings between the Justice Department and the International Telephone and Telegraph Corporation (ITT).[6] Under Carter, questions arose about budget director Bert Lance's earlier bank transactions and Billy Carter's $220,000 fee from the Libyan government. Under Reagan it was charges of conflict of interest (as well as general mismanagement) in the Environmental Protection Agency (EPA), and under Bush, accusations of wholesale

---

of that. But in one of the four unified instances (stockpiling in 1962), the target was an earlier administration run by the other party.

3. The "five-percenters" were figures with White House connections who were said to have procured government contracts for outsiders at a price of 5 percent of each contract. See Andrew J. Dunar, *The Truman Scandals and the Politics of Morality* (Columbia: University of Missouri Press, 1984), chap. 4. On the RFC: ibid., chap. 5. On the Bureau of Internal Revenue, which was the agency's name then: ibid., chap. 6.

4. On Dixon-Yates: Aaron Wildavsky, *Dixon-Yates: A Study in Power Politics* (New Haven: Yale University Press, 1962), chaps. 16, 17. For an insider's account of the probe of the regulatory agencies, see Bernard Schwartz, *The Professor and the Commissions* (New York: Alfred A. Knopf, 1959), chaps. 3, 4.

5. Robert J. Art, *The TFX Decision: McNamara and the Military* (Boston: Little, Brown, 1968), Introduction.

6. Anthony Sampson, *The Sovereign State of ITT* (New York: Stein and Day, 1973), chap. 10.

TABLE 2.1

Congressional Investigations Critical of the Executive Branch that Generated *New York Times* Front-page Stories on Twenty or More Days, 1946–1990

	Divided party control		Unified party control	
	n days of NYT stories	The charges and the investigations	n days of NYT stories	The charges and the investigations
1947–48 Truman R Cong	29	*Improper influence in airplane contracts.* Senate War Investigations Committee. Chaired by OWEN BREWSTER, R-ME; at subcommittee level by HOMER FERGUSON, R-MICH. Featured Elliot Roosevelt, Howard Hughes, generals, Hughes's flying boat. 1947.		
	27	*Inside-info commodity speculation by government officials.* Senate Appropriations Committee, chaired by STYLES BRIDGES, R-NH; and subsequent House Select Committee to Investigate Commodity Transactions, chaired by AUGUST ANDRESEN, R-MINN. Featured allegations against Edwin Pauley, dispute over release of list of traders. 1947–48.		

TABLE 2.1 (*continued*)

Divided party control	Unified party control
90 *Disloyalty and espionage in or near government ranks.* House Un-American Activities Committee. Chaired by J. PARNELL THOMAS, R-NJ; spearheaded on Hiss by RICHARD NIXON, R-CALIF. Featured Dr. Edward Condon, Elizabeth Bentley, William Remington, Whittaker Chambers, Alger Hiss, Hiss's typewriter, the pumpkin papers. 1948.	
	1949–50 26 *Mismanagement and security problems at the Atomic Energy Commission.* Joint Atomic Energy Committee. Chaired by Sen. BRIEN MCMAHON, D-CONN; animated by Sen. BOURKE HICKENLOOPER, R-IA. Featured defense of AEC by David Lilienthal. 1949.
Truman D Cong	
	26 *Influence peddling by and around the White House staff.* Subcommittee of the Senate Committee on Expenditures in the Executive

TABLE 2.1 (continued)

Divided party control		Unified party control
		Departments. Chaired by CLYDE HOEY, D-NC; energized by KARL MUNDT, R-SD, and JOSEPH MCCARTHY, R-WIS. Featured "five-percenters" label, Harry Vaughan, John Maragon, deep freezers. 1949.
	67	*Disloyalty in the State Department.* Special subcommittee of the Senate Foreign Relations Committee, set up to investigate charges by JOSEPH MCCARTHY, R-WIS. Chaired by MILLARD TYDINGS, D-MD; dominated by non-member McCarthy. Featured controversy over release of government files, McCarthy charges against Philip Jessup, John Stewart Service, Owen Lattimore. 1950.
1951–52 Truman D Cong	55	*Maladministration and favoritism in the Reconstruction Finance Corporation.* Subcommittee of the Senate Banking and Currency Committee. Chaired by

(continued)

TABLE 2.1 (*continued*)

Divided party control		Unified party control
		J. WILLIAM FULBRIGHT, D-ARK. Featured White House aides, dubious loans, mink coats. 1951.
	53	*Truman Administration misconduct of the Korean War.* Joint probe by Senate Armed Services and Foreign Relations Committees. Chaired by RICHARD RUSSELL, D-GA. Featured criticism by Gens. Douglas MacArthur (just fired), Albert Wedemeyer, Patrick Hurley; defense by Secretary of State Dean Acheson, Defense Secretary George Marshall, Gens. Omar Bradley and J. Lawton Collins. 1951.
	34	*Disloyalty in making of China policy.* Internal Security Subcommittee of Senate Judiciary Committee. Chaired by PAT MCCARRAN, D-NEV. Featured assaults against Owen Lattimore, Philip Jessup, John Carter Vincent, and other China hands. 1951–52.

TABLE 2.1 (continued)

Divided party control	Unified party control
	58 *Corruption in the Bureau of Internal Revenue* (then its title). Subcommittee of the House Ways and Means Committee. Chaired by CECIL KING, D-CAL. Featured T. Lamar Caudle, Henry "the Dutchman" Grunewald, city machine operatives as revenue collectors. 1951–52.
	29 *Maladministration in the Justice Department.* Subcommittee of the House Judiciary Committee. Chaired by FRANK CHELF, D-KY. Featured resignation of Attorney General J. Howard McGrath. 1952.
1953–54 Eisenhower R Cong	25 *Soviet spy rings operating under Truman.* Internal Security Subcommittee of the Senate Judiciary Committee. Chaired by WILLIAM JENNER, R-IND. Featured charges against Harry Dexter White. 1953.

TABLE 2.1 (continued)

	Divided party control		Unified party control	
			203	*Subversion in the State Department and the Army.* Investigative Subcommittee of the Senate Government Operations Committee. Chaired by JOSEPH MCCARTHY, R-WIS. Featured probes of the Voice of America, overseas libraries, Fort Monmouth laboratories; Cohn and Schine; who promoted Peress?; McCarthy vs. Joseph Welch in televised hearings. 1953–54.
1955–56 Eisenhower D Cong	25	*Improper influence in Dixon-Yates power contract.* Subcommittee of the Senate Judiciary Committee. Chaired by ESTES KEFAUVER, D-TENN. 1955.		
	21	*Inadequate air-power planning.* Special subcommittee of the Senate Armed Services Committee. Chaired by STUART SYMINGTON, D-MO. Featured Defense Secretary Charles		

TABLE 2.1 (*continued*)

	Divided party control		Unified party control
	Wilson, open interservice rivalry, charges of falling behind the Soviets. 1956.		
1957–58 Eisenhower D Cong	106		
	Improper influence in the regulatory agencies. Special subcommittee of the House Commerce Committee. Chaired by MORGAN MOULDER, D-MO, then OREN HARRIS, D-ARK. Featured FCC Commissioner Richard Mack, Bernard Goldfine, vicuna coat, Oriental rug, dethroning of Eisenhower aide-in-chief Sherman Adams. 1958.		
1959–60 Eisenhower D Cong	None		
		1961–62 Kennedy D Cong	26
			Agriculture Department favoritism toward shady grain-storage dealer Billy Sol Estes. Subcommittee of the Senate Government Operations Committee, chaired by JOHN MCCLELLAN, D-ARK; and subcommittee of the House

(*continued*)

TABLE 2.1 (*continued*)

Divided party control		Unified party control
		Government Operations Committee, chaired by L. H. FOUNTAIN, D-NC. 1962.
	25	*Favoritism in award of TFX fighter-plane contract to General Dynamics, rather than Boeing.* Subcommittee of the Senate Government Operations Committee. Chaired by JOHN MCCLELLAN, D-ARK. 1963.
1963–64 Kennedy and Johnson D Cong		
	26	*Misguided Indochina policy.* Senate Foreign Relations Committee. Chaired by J. WILLIAM FULBRIGHT, D-ARK. Featured testimony by critics George Kennan and Gen. James Gavin, defenders Secretary of State Dean Rusk and Defense Secretary Robert McNamara. Early 1966.
1965–66 Johnson D Cong		
	27	*Disastrous and deceptive Indochina policy.* Senate Foreign Relations Committee. Chaired by J. WILLIAM FULBRIGHT, D-ARK. Featured charge that Johnson
1967–68 Johnson D Cong		

(continued)

TABLE 2.1 (*continued*)

	Divided party control	Unified party control
		Administration misled Congress on nature of 1964 Tonkin Bay encounter. 1967–68 (sporadic).
1969–70 Nixon D Cong	31 *Continued U.S. overinvolvement in Indochina.* Senate Foreign Relations Committee. Chaired by J. WILLIAM FULBRIGHT, D-ARK. Featured strong reaction against invasion of Cambodia in spring 1970. 1969–70 (sporadic).	
1971–72 Nixon D Cong	28 *Justice Department awarded ITT a favorable antitrust settlement in exchange for a $400,000 campaign contribution.* Senate Judiciary Committee. Chaired by JAMES EASTLAND, D-MISS; energized by PHILIP HART, D-MICH, and EDWARD KENNEDY, D-MASS. Featured Deputy Attorney General Richard Kleindienst, ITT document shredding, damaging memo by fugitive witness Dita Beard. 1972.	

TABLE 2.1 (*continued*)

	Divided party control	Unified party control
1973–74 **Nixon and** **Ford** **D Cong**	187	*Watergate break-in and cover-up.* Senate Select Committee on Presidential Campaign Activities. Chaired by SAM ERVIN, D-NC. Featured L. Patrick Gray, John Dean, James McCord, H. R. Haldeman, John Ehrlichman, John Mitchell, the plumbers, hush money, the tapes, executive privilege. 1973–74 (mainly 1973).	
	149	*Watergate break-in and cover-up.* House Judiciary Committee. Chaired by PETER RODINO, D-NJ. Ended in vote to impeach President Nixon. 1973–74 (mainly 1974).	
1975–76 **Ford** **D Cong**	69	*Dubious covert operations by U.S. intelligence agencies.* Select Senate Committee to Study Government Operations with Respect to Intelligence Activities. Chaired by FRANK CHURCH, D-ID. Featured CIA, FBI; reports of moles in the media, secret dossiers and	

TABLE 2.1 (*continued*)

	Divided party control		Unified party control
	wiretaps, mail surveillance, burglaries of leftist offices, and plots to assassinate foreign leaders. 1975–76.		
46	*Dubious covert operations by U.S. intelligence agencies.* House Select Committee on Intelligence. Chaired by OTIS PIKE, D-NY. Featured CIA, FBI, reports of files on domestic dissidents and members of Congress. 1975–76.	1977–78 Carter D Cong 26	*Old shady bank dealings by Bert Lance, Director of the Office of Management and Budget.* Senate Governmental Affairs Committee. Chaired by ABRAHAM RIBICOFF, D-CONN. Featured Ribicoff call for Lance to resign, Lance's resignation. 1977.
		1979–80 Carter D Cong 21	*Dubious use of President's brother Billy Carter as intermediary to Libyan government.* Special Subcommittee of the Senate Judiciary

TABLE 2.1 (*continued*)

		Divided party control	Unified party control
			Committee. Chaired by BIRCH BAYH, D-IND. Featured report of $220,000 Libyan fee to Billy Carter, criticism of Administration policy processes. 1980.
1981–82		None	
Reagan			
R Senate			
D House			
1983–84	28	*Political favoritism, conflict of interest, and general laxness in toxic-waste cleanup by the Environmental Protection Agency.* Subcommittee of the House Energy and Commerce Committee. Chaired by JOHN DINGELL, D-MICH. Featured struggle over access to agency files, resignation of EPA director Anne Burford. 1983.	
Reagan			
R Senate			
D House			
1985–86		None	
Reagan			
R Senate			
D House			

TABLE 2.1 (continued)

	Divided party control		Unified party control
1987–88 Reagan D Cong	95	*Ill-advised arms-for-hostages deal with Iran.* Select Senate and House committees acted as one unit. Chaired by Sen. DANIEL INOUYE, D-HAW, and Rep. LEE HAMILTON, D-IND. Featured Robert McFarlane, John Poindexter, Oliver North, testimony on covert funding of the Nicaraguan Contras. 1987.	
1989–90 Bush D Cong	23	*Corruption in Reagan's Department of Housing and Urban Development.* Subcommittee of House Government Operations Committee. Chaired by TOM LANTOS, D-CAL. Featured Samuel R. ("Silent Sam") Pierce, Jr., former HUD Secretary. 1989–90.	

corruption in Reagan's Department of Housing and Urban Development (HUD).

Six probes dealt at least partly with loyalty or security. In 1948, HUAC pursued Dr. Edward Condon, Alger Hiss, and others in an espionage inquiry.[7] In 1949, members of the Joint Atomic Energy Committee claimed to have unearthed security problems at the Atomic Energy Commission (AEC). In 1950, in an inquiry chaired by Senator Millard Tydings to look into McCarthy's charges of disloyalty in the State Department, McCarthy managed to dominate the proceedings and win ample new publicity for his charges.[8] In 1951–52, Senator Pat McCarran dug after disloyalty among framers of U.S. policy toward China.[9] In 1953, Senator William Jenner looked into spy rings that had allegedly operated under Truman.[10] And in 1953–54, Senator McCarthy capped it all with his long-running probe of subversion in the State Department and the Department of the Army that culminated in his televised confrontation with Joseph Welch.[11]

Eight probes addressed military, foreign policy, or intelligence matters (although the loyalty probes at least indirectly did that also). In 1951, after Truman fired General Douglas MacArthur, Senator Richard Russell chaired an inquiry into the administration's conduct of the Korean war.[12] In 1956, Senator Stuart Symington looked critically into the Eisenhower administration's airpower planning. In 1966, Senator Fulbright began his episodic, five-year-long investigation of the Indochina war.[13] In 1975–76, in the wake of Watergate, both a Senate

7. Walter Goodman, *The Committee: The Extraordinary Career of the House Committee on Un-American Activities* (New York: Farrar, Straus and Giroux, 1964), chap. 8.

8. Robert Griffith, *The Politics of Fear: Joseph R. McCarthy and the Senate* (Lexington: University Press of Kentucky, 1970), pp. 65–114.

9. Earl Latham, *The Communist Controversy in Washington: From the New Deal to McCarthy* (Cambridge: Harvard University Press, 1966), pp. 296–314.

10. Ibid., pp. 371–73.

11. Griffith, *Politics of Fear*, pp. 207–20 and chap. 8.

12. John W. Spanier, *The Truman-MacArthur Controversy and the Korean War* (Cambridge: Harvard University Press, 1959), chaps. 12, 13.

13. Eugene Brown, *J. William Fulbright: Advice and Dissent* (Iowa City: University of Iowa Press, 1985), pp. 74–79, 97–100; Lee Riley Powell, *J. William Fulbright and America's Lost Crusade: Fulbright's Opposition to the Vietnam War* (Little Rock, Ark.: Rose Publishing, 1984), chaps. 8, 9; William C. Berman,

committee chaired by Frank Church and the House unit headed by Otis Pike ran inquiries into dubious covert operations by the intelligence agencies.[14] And in 1987 came the Iran-Contra hearings.[15]

In a class by themselves are the Watergate inquiries conducted by Ervin's special Senate committee and Peter Rodino's House Judiciary Committee in 1973–74.[16]

Obviously, some of these probes were more important than others, however one judges importance. Watergate or McCarthyism is one thing, commodity speculation or Bert Lance quite another. The tabulation of days on the front page shown in table 2.1 is suggestive. McCarthy's probe of the State Department and Army in 1953–54 leads the list with 203 days, followed by the Ervin fact-finding phase of Watergate with 187 days, the Rodino impeachment phase with 149, the 1958 probe of Eisenhower's regulatory agencies with 106, the Iran-Contra hearings with 95, HUAC's 1948 probe with 90, the 1975–76 Senate intelligence probe with 69, the Tydings committee's 1950 State Department investigation with 67, the 1951–52 internal revenue probe with 58, the 1951 RFC probe with 55, the 1951 Korean war hearings with 53—on down through the 1956 airpower and 1980 Billy Carter probes with 21 each.[17]

Almost all the thirty-one enterprises, however, gave a president some real trouble. It is no fun, and it eats up time, energy, authority, and sometimes personnel, to have a committee go after oneself or one's subordinates on the front pages week after week. The two probes during Carter's time, for example, centering on Bert Lance and Billy

---

William Fulbright and the Vietnam War: The Dissent of a Political Realist (Kent, Ohio: Kent State University Press, 1988), chaps 4–8.

14. On the Church probe: Loch K. Johnson, *A Season of Inquiry: The Senate Intelligence Investigation* (Lexington: University Press of Kentucky, 1985).

15. See Frederick M. Kaiser, "Causes and Conditions of Inter-Branch Conflict: Lessons from the Iran-Contra Affair" (Paper delivered at the 1989 Annual Meeting of the American Political Science Association).

16. On the Ervin committee: James Hamilton, *The Power to Probe: A Study of Congressional Investigations* (New York: Vintage Books, 1977). On the Rodino committee: J. Anthony Lukas, *Nightmare: The Underside of the Nixon Years* (New York: Viking, 1976), chaps. 15, 16.

17. The two Watergate probes produce a count of 324 days if they are added together to comprise one investigation. This is because the Ervin and Rodino narratives shared the same front page on 12 days. So, 187 + 149 − 12 = 324. By the same logic, the 1975–76 House and Senate intelligence investigations, if conflated into one probe, produce a count of 101 days.

Carter, were scarcely historic undertakings. But they helped to exhibit the outsider status and cronyism of Carter's Georgia connection. And the Billy Carter probe preoccupied the White House at a vulnerable time in 1980.

Officials who lost their positions at least partly because of committee probes ranged from the many victims of loyalty investigations in the 1940s and 1950s through Truman's attorney general J. Howard McGrath owing to the Justice Department probe in 1952, Eisenhower's chief aide Sherman Adams as an upshot of the regulatory agencies probe in 1958, Bert Lance in 1977, Reagan's EPA director Anne Burford in 1983, and former investigator Richard Nixon himself in 1974.

Not quite all the investigations proved to be more cost than benefit to an incumbent administration. The Korean war inquiry in 1951 gave Truman's critics yet another forum, and it used up his top officials' time. But the officials made convincing arguments, chairman Russell presided dispassionately, and the overall effect was apparently not unfavorable to Truman.[18] The real outlier among the thirty probes was Jenner's 1953 investigation of 1940s spy rings. That was the only instance where a committee focused on past executive officials of the party not currently holding the presidency. Those can be easy targets. The new Eisenhower administration more or less waved the effort along. McCarthy also pursued some holdover Truman administration personnel in 1953–54. But he seems to have wanted to assault the continuing national-security establishment regardless of party or administration, and he ultimately clashed with Eisenhower.

How about patterns of incidence over time? The first thing one notices in table 2.1 is decline. Sixteen of the thirty-one probes took place under Truman and Eisenhower, ten under Kennedy-Johnson and Nixon-Ford, and only five under Carter, Reagan, and Bush. Has the genre been falling on hard times? Notwithstanding Watergate and Iran-Contra, the answer may be yes. If so, one likely reason is that the *Times* (as well as other media organs) has altered its coverage routines. Transmitting what senators and witnesses said day after day about executive misbehavior has partly given way to using other sources. In the 1960s and 1970s, the development of "investigative journalism" brought not only "deep throats" but such moves as using the newly enacted Freedom of Information Act to get hold of exec-

18. See Robert J. Donovan, *Tumultuous Years: The Presidency of Harry S Truman, 1949–1953* (New York: W. W. Norton, 1982), p. 370.

utive documents.[19] Probably one result has been to cut down on ex-posure stories based on congressional sources. Also, *Times* reporters have come to rely more on thick analytic reports—such as ones by the General Accounting Office—to track official misbehavior. Not only can this cut down on Congress-based stories but it also works to compress scandals into one-shot revelations as opposed to long-running dramas.[20]

In addition, one gets the sense that the executive branch, perhaps as a reaction to Watergate, has gotten more deft at fending off congressional inquiries. Often now when confronted by disaster or embarrassment, a president himself sets up a pre-emptive investigation run by well-credentialed experts. Thus in 1986, presidential commissions quickly materialized after both the *Challenger* disaster and the first Iran-Contra revelations. In the latter case, that body was the Tower commission. A move like this can help to stave off or at least delay congressional probes. And it can demote press coverage to the back pages while study occurs, de-emphasize blame in favor of impersonal causes, and on the whole limit damage to executive interests. Use of special prosecutors, although it was Congress that prescribed that procedure, tends also to move executive embarrassments off the front pages and off Congress's own agenda in the early days when public interest is keen.

High-publicity congressional exposure probes, in short, may have had better days. If so, that is worth noting. Against odds, given the records of many of its personnel, the Reagan administration ran eight years and drew only one corruption probe—the 1983 EPA inquiry—that made the threshold here. (The HUD scandal did not break until 1989 under Bush.) In retrospect, it is striking that no congressional unit promoted savings-and-loan regulation into a major front-page

19. For example, use of the FOIA fleshed out a 1989 story on the HUD scandal: Philip Shenon with Leslie Maitland, "Files Show Pierce Helped Friends and the G.O.P.: Letters Offer Strongest Evidence to Contradict Previous Testimony," *New York Times*, August 4, 1989, pp. A1, A9. The FOIA was enacted in 1966 and amended importantly in 1974.

20. Down a few pegs in importance, it is worth noting that the *Times* redesigned its front page in 1976 so that it now has six columns rather than the traditional eight. Some stories had to go, and perhaps ones about investigations figured among them.

scandal during the 1980s.[21] All it takes is one aggressive subcommittee chairman. But the decline in incidence of high-publicity probes does not hobble the analysis in this chapter. Since spells of both unified and divided government occurred during early, middle, and late phases of the 1946–90 period, analytic leverage is still available.

Another pattern surfaces in table 2.1. There are two clusters of probes into national-security affairs, broadly defined, although the second requires some interpretation to see it. Conservatives from about 1948 through 1954, and liberals from about 1966 through 1975, waged assaults against U.S. national-security policy and the central state apparatus that presidents had been using to conduct it. Both times investigations figured as a major opposition tactic. In the earlier period, Nixon's Hiss probe scored a breakthrough in 1948, and after that it was one loyalty probe after another through 1954.[22] All of them had a broader, policy-related subtext. Also, the MacArthur side made its case during the Korean war hearings in 1951.[23] There was accompanying legislative activity. In 1954, Senate conservatives came within one vote of putting through John Bricker's constitutional amendment to curb the president's treaty-making powers.[24] The aim was to rule out more Yaltas.

In the later period, liberals used investigative tactics against the Johnson, Nixon, and Ford national-security records or apparatuses during four Congresses. Fulbright's hearings on Indochina sprawled across three—from 1966 through 1970. The Church and Pike probes of the CIA and FBI came later in 1975–76. Considerable liberal energy between 1969 and 1975 went into legislating rather than investigating—as in promoting the Hatfield-McGovern and Cooper-Church

21. See David E. Rosenbaum, "How Capital Ignored Alarms on Savings," *New York Times*, June 6, 1990, p. A1.

22. Of course, not all the headlines about disloyalty derived from investigations. In the early months of 1950, Senator McCarthy captured attention just by making speeches.

23. See David R. Kepley, *The Collapse of the Middle Way: Senate Republicans and the Bipartisan Foreign Policy, 1948–1952* (Westport, Conn.: Greenwood Press, 1988), pp. 125–31.

24. See Duane Tananbaum, *The Bricker Amendment Controversy: A Test of Eisenhower's Presidential Leadership* (Ithaca, N.Y.: Cornell University Press, 1988), chaps. 5–10. Technically, the one-vote outcome occurred on a watered-down version of Bricker's proposal.

amendments to curb Nixon's options in Indochina. The War Powers Act of 1973 was designed to constrain presidential power more generally and, unlike the Bricker amendment twenty years earlier, it passed. There was also Watergate. Interpretations of it vary, but for many in Congress it was at least a windfall opportunity to rein in a runaway "imperial presidency." The foreign policy implications were clear enough, even though the House Judiciary Committee finally dropped Nixon's secret Cambodian bombings as an impeachment offense. In this indirect sense, the Watergate probes belong in a 1966–75 cluster with the Fulbright, Church, and Pike investigations.[25]

To move to the crux of the analysis, one pattern that decisively does *not* come to light in table 2.1 is a relation between the incidence of exposure probes and whether party control was unified or divided. Table 2.2 presents some summary data for the forty-four years. Whether driven by corruption or other matters, high-publicity exposure probes occurred about as often under one background condition as the other. Perhaps the House leaned toward shooting or holding fire according to partisan criteria. Eight out of eleven, or 73 percent, of the House probes occurred when the other party held the presidency—the state of affairs 59 percent of the time. But these numbers are too small to tell much. The Senate, which attracted much more media coverage, ran twenty-two probes without showing any such partiality.

At the level of individual presidents, Truman drew at least as much investigative fire per year from the Democratic Eighty-first and Eighty-second Congresses as from the Republican Eightieth. Of all the postwar presidents, Truman probably suffered the worst from corruption probes, and the ones that damaged him most were staged by Democratic Congresses.[26] Eisenhower had major problems with the Republican Eighty-third Congress, which gave McCarthy a committee chairmanship and turned him loose, and the Democratic Eighty-fifth, which rolled up the regulatory agencies and then Sher-

25. In the "near miss" category, there was also the Senate Armed Services Committee's 1973 exposure of Nixon's covert Cambodian bombings of 1969–70.

26. Dunar, *Truman Scandals*, chap. 8. All three issues highlighted by the Republicans in the 1952 election campaign—Communism, corruption, and Korea—had gotten investigatory workouts during the Democratic Congresses of 1949–52.

TABLE 2.2
Numbers of High-publicity Investigations during Times of Unified and
Divided Party Control

	During unified party control (18 yrs)	During divided control: pres vs. Congress (20 yrs)	During divided control: pres & Senate vs. House (6 yrs)
Total[a]	15	14	1
About corruption	8	6	1
About other matters	7	8	
By House committees[b]	3	7	1
By Senate committees[b]	13	9	

[a]This leaves out the Jenner committee's 1953 spy hunt.

[b]The probes about commodity speculation in 1947–48, Billy Sol Estes in
1962, and Iran-Contra in 1987 count for both House and Senate.

man Adams.[27] Eisenhower's other two Democratic Congresses were
quiet by comparison. Senator Fulbright, once he decided to move on
Vietnam, challenged fellow Democrat Johnson and then Nixon without any regard for party. So far as one can tell, he did more damage
to Johnson.[28] Nixon had to endure the Watergate inquiries, which
are hard to match. Ford had the Church and Pike investigations. But
in more recent times, Carter encountered about as much investigative
trouble per year as have Reagan and Bush.

But how about weighing investigations for importance? In particular, shouldn't Congress's Watergate probes, which took place during
a time of divided party control, weigh more heavily than anything
else? No doubt they should. But if we take into account the overall
impact of investigations on policy making, international relations, domestic political conflict, public careers, the tone of public life, and

27. On the level of attention Eisenhower had to give to McCarthy in 1953–
54—it was high—see Greenstein, *Hidden-Hand Presidency*, chap. 5.

28. "During the 1966 Vietnam hearings the Foreign Relations Committee
transferred its respectability to the opposition against the Vietnam war, and
began the discrediting of President Johnson's policies which eventually contributed to his decision not to seek re-election in 1968." Powell, *Fulbright:
America's Lost Crusade*, p. 178.

even national folklore, there is a good case for the loyalty probes of 1948–54 as at least a solid second. Those took place mostly under unified control. It was not that party control made no difference at all. After the 1948 election, House Democratic leaders moved HUAC off the front pages by changing the committee membership.[29] Senate Democrats set up the 1950 Tydings inquiry to contain McCarthy's charges, not to amplify them. But amplify them it did: Week after week of well-publicized disloyalty charges resulted. Accused China hand Owen Lattimore became a household name. Republican Senators injected the same kind of headline-catching, anti-administration aggressiveness into the AEC and influence-peddling probes of those years. The Democratic side had its own resourceful disloyalty hunter, Pat McCarran of Nevada. That was the way things worked. Of Joe McCarthy's use of Senate committees to attack the executive branch, not the least to be said is that he did every bit of it under conditions of unified party control. He turned Democratic instruments against Democrats under Truman. Once a committee chairman himself, he waged his own campaign against Eisenhower.[30]

29. Goodman, *Committee*, pp. 269–74.

30. Earl Latham came to a similar judgment about the era's loyalty investigations. (His analysis begins with the Martin Dies committee in 1938 and ends in 1954. That is an appropriate choice of years, although the 1948 Hiss probe greatly raised the stakes and the publicity level.) Latham's conclusion: "Second, party identification does not explain the vigor of the congressional investigations either. From 1938 to 1947, it was the Democratic Martin Dies and a committee with a Democratic majority that investigated possible subversion in a Democratic administration. From 1949 to 1953, it was the Democratic Pat McCarran with a Democratic committee that investigated the suspected delinquencies of the Democratic administrations of the 1940s. The Democratic Francis Walter was no less fervent a chairman of the House Committee on Un-American Activities than the Republican J. Parnell Thomas. The Republican Senator Joseph McCarthy gave the Republican administration of President Eisenhower trying times in the investigations of Fort Monmouth and the Department of State, and in the controversy over the Department of the Army. It was the lame duck Republican Eighty-third Congress that condemned McCarthy. Great majorities from both parties regularly voted funds to continue the investigations. The only partisan investigation—in which the Democrats and the Republicans were on opposite sides—was the Tydings inquiry in 1950, when the Democratic Tydings defended the Democratic Department of State from accusations by McCarthy." *Communist Controversy in Washington*, p. 374. McCarthy nonetheless *used* the Tydings committee. Headlines are headlines.

3 ◆ LAWMAKING

SELECTING THE LAWS

I n the legislative realm, what happened during the first two years of the New Deal that is worth remembering? Here are some of the laws passed during Roosevelt's "hundred days" of 1933: the Emergency Banking Act, the National Industrial Recovery Act, the Agricultural Adjustment Act (AAA), the Federal Emergency Relief Act, the Home Owners' Loan Act, the Securities Act, and measures creating the Civilian Conservation Corps (CCC), the Federal Deposit Insurance Corporation (FDIC), and the Tennessee Valley Authority (TVA). A measure to legalize low-alcohol-content beer cleared Congress. In 1934 came the Reciprocal Trade Agreements Act, the Taylor Grazing Act, the Indian Reorganization Act, and measures setting up the Securities and Exchange Commission (SEC), the Federal Communications Commission (FCC), and the Federal Housing Administration (FHA). The list could go on.[1]

In short, many important laws were passed. That, in principle, is the standard that will be used here to judge Congresses from 1946 through 1990: Were many important laws passed?

This is not the only kind of standard that could be used to estimate legislative effectiveness, productivity, or success. Analysts often reach for a quotient measure—some actually-did-pass numerator over some all-that-were-possibilities-for-passage denominator. Perhaps the best known of these is the "presidential box-score," which can be calculated

1. See William E. Leuchtenburg, *Franklin D. Roosevelt and the New Deal, 1932–1940* (New York: Harper and Row, 1963), chap. 3 and pp. 85–86, 90–91, 135, 203–05.

for a year or a full Congress and which divides number of presidential requests enacted by number of presidential requests.[2]

For two reasons, presidential scores of this sort will be side-stepped here. First, to weigh a great many requests or enactments equally— the understandable norm in such calculations—can distort political reality too much. Consider 1981–82. As a legislative achievement, the "Reagan revolution" came down to just two enactments— the sizable tax cut of 1981 and the omnibus spending cut of 1981 (Gramm-Latta II) that trimmed a wide range of programs. In turn, each of these two enactments hinged on one showdown roll-call vote in the House. "Many important laws" came bundled together, in effect, in just two packages. That is the gist of what took place in 1981–82.

Second, why should we care whether presidents got what they wanted? That is not the appropriate question. For purposes here, the question should be: Is the system capable of generating important legislation? Such accomplishment might come at the president's request, through his acquiescence, or over his vehement opposition. In principle it does not make any difference. To take probably the extreme case in American history, a "presidential box-score" for Andrew Johnson in 1865–69 might be interesting but it would be useless as anything like an index of system performance. Congress undertook Reconstruction without him.[3] From 1946 through 1990, scores of important laws were enacted at the initiative of Congress—some with a president's very grudging assent or over vetoes. Those that survived vetoes included the Taft-Hartley Labor-Relations Act of 1947, the McCarran-Walter Immigration Act of 1952, the War Powers Act of 1973, and South Africa sanctions in 1986. Some Congresses during this period resembled the Thirty-ninth and Fortieth Reconstruction Congresses more than one might think. But laws are laws. System production should be the final test, not whether presidents happened to get what they wanted.

Once past a president's request list, however, it is very difficult to see what a denominator for a Congress—an agenda of potential en-

2. See Stephen J. Wayne, *The Legislative Presidency* (New York: Harper and Row, 1978), pp. 168–72; George C. Edwards III, *Presidential Influence in Congress* (San Francisco: W. H. Freeman, 1980), chap. 1; and Edwards, "Measuring Presidential Success in Congress: Alternative Approaches," *Journal of Politics* 47 (1985), 667–85. The "boxscore" is one of a family of measures.

3. For an account, see Howard P. Nash, Jr., *Andrew Johnson: Congress and Reconstruction* (Rutherford, N.J.: Fairleigh Dickinson University Press, 1972).

actments—might be. "As demanded by the needs of the time," per-haps, in some sense, as in the case of the Depression needs of 1933? That would be hopeless to administer. And at any rate, many acts of even Franklin Roosevelt's first Congress had no obvious connection to demands or needs of exactly that time as opposed to, say, five years before or five years later. The TVA, for example, had been an agenda item for a long time; now in 1933, because support crystallized, it could pass. That is the pattern with many important acts of Congress, perhaps most of them. Unquestionably some acts do follow rather quickly from agenda-setting events—aid to Greece and Turkey in 1947, for example, or the bailout of Chrysler in 1979.[4] Fortunately for the analysis here, there does not seem to be any relation from 1946 through 1990 between the incidence of such quick triggering by events and whether party control of government was unified or divided.

There are other, more tangible possibilities for usable agendas. Sometimes the opposition's agenda upstages a president's, as hap-pened with Senator Robert Taft's in 1947–48, Senate Majority Leader Lyndon Johnson's in the late 1950s, and Speaker Jim Wright's in 1987–88. But just as often, proposals bubble up from Congress's de-centralized committee system. Beyond that, since any member may introduce bills, perhaps a Congress's agenda should be thought of as all proposals introduced by all Senate and House members, plus the president's. As a matter of principle that is not a bad idea, though of course it would be cumbersome to work with.[5] Perhaps, for any Con-gress, an agenda could be assembled for research purposes out of proposals that make it to the "much talked about" stage. Medicare and federal aid to education did that in 1961–62, for example, causing comment when they finally did *not* pass. Something like this will be undertaken briefly and informally at the close of chapter 4, in defer-ence to natural reader curiosity about what did not happen as well as did during these various Congresses.

But the main analysis here will address what did pass—no quotients or denominators, just numerators. Did a Congress generate a New Deal–like harvest of legislation or not? An inventory of "important

4. See the discussion in chapter 6.

5. Peter VanDoren adroitly takes into account all relevant congressional pro-posals in a recent study of energy policy. See "Congress and Energy Policy, 1945–1976" (Ph.D. diss., Yale University, 1985).

laws enacted" will be presented for each Congress from 1946 through 1990. In principle, the term "important" will connote both innovative and consequential—or if viewed from the time of passage, thought likely to be consequential. These inventories, which sum to 267 enactments in all, or an average of 12 per Congress, result from two sweeps through the history of the forty-four years. The first picks up judgments that close observers of each Congress made at the time about what enactments, without regard for policy area, were particularly notable. The second picks up retrospective judgments that policy specialists have made, looking back over many Congresses, about what enactments in their own policy areas have been particularly notable.

Needless to say, preparing an inventory like this cannot be done as cleanly and surely as isolating a chemical element. But it can be done as systematically as the material permits. The methodologies used in the two sweeps will be presented in some detail.

SWEEP ONE: CONTEMPORARY JUDGMENTS

The best source of such judgments is the journalist's annual end-of-session wrapup story, ordinarily written as a Congress is adjourning. Especially useful is the sort of detailed appraisal that has been developed and routinized over the years by the *New York Times*'s John D. Morris, John W. Finney, Martin Tolchin, and Steven V. Roberts, and the *Washington Post*'s Robert C. Albright, Richard L. Lyons, Spencer Rich, and Helen Dewar. Wrapup writers undertake exactly the task of trying to judge the importance of a session's enactments. They ordinarily review one year's record in an odd year and a Congress's full two-year record in an even year. In reaching for absolute judgments, they draw comparisons across the current Congress's enactments, regardless of what policy areas the bills were in, and across the records of current and past Congresses. *Times* and *Post* writers normally say about the same thing. One supposes that they apprehend the Washington community's collective sense of what happened and then present it, no doubt with their own spin.

Here is a report on the extraordinary 1965 session that put in place most of Johnson's Great Society:

> The session lasted nine and one-half months and produced more major legislation than at any other session since the first years of the New Deal.

... Included in this seminal legislation were measures to provide hospital care for the elderly under Social Security, to supply Federal aid for primary and secondary education, to create a Department of Housing and Urban Development, to guarantee Negro voting rights through Federal registrars, to attack the problems of poverty in urban areas and Appalachia, to end or reduce most excise taxes, to set up regional medical centers for combating heart disease, cancer and stroke and to beautify the highways.[6]

By contrast, the 1960 session during Eisenhower's last year brought "slim legislative accomplishment," and that of 1963 under Kennedy a "paucity of legislative accomplishments."[7] It was said of the 1951 session under Truman: "Legislatively, there has been nothing in the way of initiation, no new ideas."[8] The 1985 session, at the start of Reagan's second term, was "one of the least productive and most frustrating in recent memory, many members of Congress from both parties say."[9] But Eisenhower's Congress of 1957–58 was "certain to be remembered by future generations for two achievements [the 1957 Civil Rights Act and Alaska statehood]."[10] In 1972, "Among top achievements were approval of President Nixon's revenue sharing with state and local governments, water pollution control legislation, a 20 per cent increase in Social Security benefits, and constitutional amendments to permit 18-year-olds to vote ... and to secure equal legal rights for women and men."[11] In 1986, "The 99th Congress adjourned last night with a record of accomplishment that could leave a profound mark on the nation—from its taxes, debt and foreign policy to its landscape and even the faces, accents, and heritage of its people [through immigration reform]."[12] Two years later, "Overshad-

6. E. W. Kenworthy, "Congress Passes Last Major Bills and Ends Session," *New York Times*, October 23, 1965, pp. 1, 28.

7. On 1960: John D. Morris, "1960 Congress Yielded Little Major Legislation, Frustrating Democratic Leadership," *New York Times*, September 2, 1960, p. 10. On 1963: John D. Morris, "Slow Pace Marks Congressional Session," *New York Times*, December 22, 1963, p. 27.

8. "82d, 1st Session," *New York Times*, October 21, 1951, p. IV:2.

9. Steven V. Roberts, "Many in Congress Say Session of '85 Was Unproductive," *New York Times*, December 22, 1985, p. I:1.

10. John D. Morris, "Alaska and Rights Session's Top Bills," *New York Times*, August 24, 1958, p. I:1.

11. Richard L. Lyons and Spencer Rich, "92d Congress: Mixed Bag of Accomplishments," *Washington Post*, October 15, 1972, p. A1.

12. Helen Dewar, " 'Productive' Congress Goes Home: Wide-Ranging Rec-

owed for six years by a popular and aggressive President, Congress regained its voice in the 1987–88 sessions, enacting ground-breaking legislation in areas as diverse as trade policy and welfare, civil rights and arms control."[13] Bush's first Congress of 1989–90 drew the head-line: "The 101st: A Solid—Not a Great—Record."[14]

These excerpts give a sense of the coverage. Note the highlighting of enactments thought to be particularly significant, and the constant explicit or implicit resort to absolute standards—largely supplied by history—as grounds for deciding.

The newspaper sources were supplemented where possible by books or articles that discuss the overall legislative records of particular Congresses and, in doing so, pick up or embody judgments that ob-servers or participants expressed during those Congresses about the importance of enactments.[15] For the analysis here, such judgments were blended with those by the contemporary journalists. Especially helpful were Susan M. Hartmann's book on the Eightieth Congress and Gary W. Reichard's on the Eighty-third.[16] In general, the earlier the Congress, the heavier the reliance here on non-journalistic sources. This is partly because historians tend to let a generation or so go by before treating a subject, and partly because *Times* and *Post* coverage had soft spots before the now standard wrapup formula took hold around 1960.

In practice, using the sources came down to teasing out of them

---

ord of Major Changes Includes Taxes, Aliens," *Washington Post*, October 19, 1986, p. A1.

13. Susan F. Rasky, "Congress Regains Its Voice on Policy in 1987–88 Ses-sions," *New York Times*, October 24, 1988, p. A1.

14. Helen Dewar, "The 101st: A Solid—Not a Great—Record," *Washington Post National Weekly Edition*, November 5–11, 1990, p. 8. Beyond the much-discussed deficit-reduction act, six measures enacted in 1990 were judged "major," "landmark," or "far-reaching" by one or more wrapup writer. These were in the areas of immigration, air pollution control, housing, child care, agriculture, and rights of the disabled. See ibid.; Richard L. Berke, "101st Congress Wraps Up Work Belatedly and a Little Battered," *New York Times*, October 29, 1990, p. A1; and Paul Houston, "101st Congress: Mixed Record of Achievement," *Los Angeles Times*, October 28, 1990, p. A1.

15. See appendix A for these as well as the newspaper sources.

16. Susan M. Hartmann, *Truman and the Eightieth Congress* (Columbia: Uni-versity of Missouri Press, 1971); Gary W. Reichard, *The Reaffirmation of Re-publicanism: Eisenhower and the Eighty-third Congress* (Knoxville: University of Tennessee Press, 1975).

yes-no judgments about individual enactments that they at least mentioned. Did contemporary observers think a new law was particularly important or not? That was the key question. For any enactment, the evidence tests included what claims the sources made or imparted about it, how much attention or emphasis they gave it, and how regularly they mentioned it. Did both the *Times* and *Post*, for example, dwell on it? Many enactments, such as Medicare in 1965, made the yes list easily. Others, such as the Portal-to-Portal Act of 1947, made it closer to the cutpoint. That, in principle, was located low enough to provide fairly large Congress-by-Congress inventories of "particularly important" acts for listing and examination.

Constitutional amendments and Senate treaty ratifications could count as enactments. Excluded, however, even if the sources dwelt on them, were congressional resolutions, appropriations acts, very-short-term measures (such as a one-year extension of rent control in 1947), statutory amendments taken by themselves, and extensions or re-authorization acts that seemed to me to offer little new. But by stipulation, multi-year extensions of foreign trade law and the 1965 Voting Rights Act, both of which ordinarily drew fanfare, could count regardless of their novelty. Hikes or coverage expansions of Social Security or the minimum wage could count and routinely did.[17]

17. In a few cases I fudged on these rules so as to include items that contemporary observers (or Sweep Two's retrospective analysts, yet to be discussed) addressed *as if* they were important, single, free-standing statutory achievements even though, strictly speaking, they were not. One had to examine the fine print to find out that they were not. Measures making the enactment list this way were the Point Four foreign aid initiative of 1950, which passed as part of an omnibus foreign aid bill; Kennedy's Alliance for Progress in 1961, which piggybacked on an appropriations bill; the Economic Stabilization Act of 1970, which passed as part of the Defense Production Act of 1970; a 1969 Social Security hike that nested in a tax reform; Social Security hikes in 1971 and 1972, as well as the Gramm-Rudman-Hollings Act of 1985, which were attached to bills raising the debt ceiling; and the child care package of 1990, which won enactment as part of that year's deficit-reduction instrument. In two instances of the above eight—Social Security in 1969 and child care in 1990—the parent instruments also made it onto the enactment list, independently. Also in the spirit of "as if," I counted the two Panama Canal treaties of 1978 and a pair of closely related 1963 mental health bills as just one free-standing enactment in each case, because that is the way contemporary observers wrote about them. There is a kind of political truth to these coding variances, even if they are a bit messy. Note that, for what it is worth, they do not extend to including independently any items that observers have sized up and written about as "amendments," regardless of their importance.

That is the methodology for Sweep One. Here are some comments about it that emphasize its vulnerabilities.

First, it obviously singles out one kind of legislative action and ignores others. It looks for the major, direct innovative thrust, probably our prevailing cultural ideal of what legislating should amount to. But it overlooks the practices and logics of the appropriations process, imaginatively placed amendments, and incrementalism by way of many small bills.

Second, partly for the above reasons, the methodology works better in some policy areas than in others. It does best in areas where occasional major enactments establish binding new rules. Among such areas are taxes, labor-management relations, civil rights, immigration, regulation, deregulation, social insurance, reorganization of the government, and treaties. When addressed to spending programs—housing, for instance—the methodology can miss appropriations erosion as well as changes that come about through re-authorization processes. It sags in the cases of farm subsidies and foreign aid, where the inevitable renewal acts tend to look bland and all alike. It does poorly with defense, where it misses spending moves—for example, the 1950–51 Korean war buildup—as well as new weapons. The only new weapons system that made it unambiguously into an enactment inventory was the ABM in 1969, and this was thrown out on the ground that including none at all made more sense. Losing defense issues from the data set is unfortunate, although it might be added that the standard case against divided party control scarcely hinges on defense policy, which tends to draw bipartisan support.[18]

In the area of foreign relations, the methodology misses some important resolutions and statutory amendments. Among these are the authority-granting resolutions that presidents used to extract rather easily from Congresses during the decade or so of policy consensus after the Korean war—Eisenhower's on Formosa in 1955 and the Middle East in 1957, and Johnson's on the Tonkin Gulf in 1964. All these were approved by Democratic Congresses. Missing also are the restraining amendments that Congresses have come to use against presidents in more recent, controversial times—notably the Cooper-Church amendment on Indochina in 1970 and the Boland provisions

18. During this century, Franklin Roosevelt's struggle against congressional isolationists just before World War II probably stands out as the chief instance of governmental "stalemate" or "deadlock" on defense initiatives. That was a time of unified party control.

on Central America in the 1980s. Note that these two kinds of instrument seem to sort by era—before and after Vietnam arose as an
issue—rather than by unified versus divided party control.[19]

Third, by crediting appraisals by contemporaries, the methodology
of course picks up many acts that looked important on paper but later,
for various reasons, fell short. The "demonstration cities" act of 1966,
for example, never lived up to its promotional copy. The Equal Rights
Amendment (ERA) to the Constitution, approved by Congress in 1971,
failed to win ratification by the state legislatures. Carter's 1980 synfuels
program has dropped from sight. A drug-abuse measure passed in
1988 was stingily financed afterward.[20] On the other hand, the methodology misses some laws that had more impact than observers
thought they would when they were being passed. The National Environmental Policy Act, for example, seems to have gone through in
1969 without rousing awareness that its requirement of "environmental impact statements" would tie government processes in knots.[21]
A food additives act passed in 1958 rose to public attention several
years later when it triggered a ban on saccharin. Still, even though
they often over- or under-predict, appraisals reached at the time of
passage probably deserve respect as one gauge of "importance." A
system cannot escape making public choices in the present based on
current information.

Fourth, the methodology obviously puts an emphasis on the highly
public. It tends to select acts whose passage took time, spurred considerable deliberation in Congress, drew media coverage, and engaged at least a fairly broad public outside Washington—not just
interest groups. Attention, in effect, helps to index "importance." But
perhaps it should. According to the standards of civic republicanism
and some theories of democracy, lawmaking efforts take on a certain

19. If so, the post-Vietnam era may be over. Congress's resolution of January
1991 granting Bush authority in the Persian Gulf looks like a throwback to
Eisenhower's time, even though the measure's margin of victory in the Senate
was only 52–47.

20. Paul M. Barrett, "Federal War on Drugs Is Scattershot Affair, With Dubious Progress: Money Is Disbursed Slowly and With Varying Aims and
Bureaucratic Snarls," *Wall Street Journal*, August 10, 1989, p. A1.

21. See David Vogel, *Fluctuating Fortunes: The Political Power of Business in
America* (New York: Basic Books, 1989), p. 67, and John C. Whitaker, *Striking
a Balance: Environment and Natural Resources Policy in the Nixon-Ford Years*
(Washington, D.C.: American Enterprise Institute, 1976), p. 48.

significance exactly because they do provoke such attention and deliberation. They are a system's instances of *public* choice. One can argue that an inventory of important enactments, whatever else it includes, should pick up acts of such conspicuousness.

Fifth, for better or worse, the methodology tends to zero in on the controversial.

Sixth, even though the sources ordinarily frame a Congress's enactments by drawing on absolute or historical standards, they may end up assigning "importance" more equally across Congresses than one would like. It would be a natural tendency. Surely *this* session had its important acts? Here they are.

Seventh, the methodology sags somewhat in addressing the 1980s, when omnibus budgetary acts such as "deficit reduction" measures came to be vehicles for many items of substantive legislation. This happened, for example, in the health area.[22] The model of major free-standing enactments that are specific to policy areas applies less well after the 1970s.[23]

Eighth, before about 1970 the sources focused more than one would like on presidents' agendas. Perhaps too many of Congress's own initiatives went unnoticed as a result, though not all did.

Finally and fortunately, the methodology does not show signs of ideological bias, despite its heavy reliance on the *Times* and *Post*. One does not have to like a statute to write that it was important. It will not come as a surprise that liberal initiatives dominate many of the enactment lists between 1946 and 1990, but conservative ones appear too. Under Truman, for example, Congress passed the McCarran Internal Security Act of 1950 as well as the Taft-Hartley and McCarran-Walter acts. Pat McCarran was a formidable legislator as

22. Julie Rovner, "Reconciliation Dominates Policy-Making Process," *Congressional Quarterly Weekly*, April 29, 1989, pp. 964–68. "Once upon a time, Congress made health policy one bill at a time.... Then came the 1980s and legislating 'by the numbers.' Today, nearly all major changes in health policy are made at a single swoop, as part of the budget-reconciliation process" (p. 964).

23. On the general point see Roger H. Davidson, "The New Centralization on Capitol Hill," *Review of Politics* 50 (1988), 352–54; Steven S. Smith, *Call to Order: Floor Politics in the House and Senate* (Washington, D.C.: Brookings Institution Press, 1989), pp. 52–56. As explained earlier, I did count child care in 1990 as a free-standing statute, even though it passed as part of an omnibus budgetary measure.

well as investigator.[24] To take the 1950s, Eisenhower promoted measures to shape the organization and infrastructure of the private economy. Thus the Atomic Energy Act of 1954 laid the basis for the private
nuclear-power industry. The St. Lawrence Seaway finally won authorization in 1954. The Federal-Aid Highway Act of 1956 ushered
in the interstate highway system.[25] The old idea that liberals do the
initiating and conservatives the resisting needs considerable qualification.[26]

Sweep One yielded 211 enactments altogether. Johnson's Great
Society Congress of 1965–66 ranked first with nineteen. The Congress
of 1959–60 ranked last with four; in those two final Eisenhower years,
Democratic House and Senate majorities beefed up by the 1958 election tried to put through an ambitious program but got nowhere.

SWEEP TWO: RETROSPECTIVE JUDGMENTS

The second search complements the first. By drawing on long-term
perspectives of policy specialists about what enactments have counted
most in their areas, it adds a dimension of expertise. (The Sweep One
sources were generalists.) It pursues the effects of laws, not the promise attached to them when they were passed. Its sources are not greatly
concerned whether enactments drew publicity, provoked controversy,
ensued from presidential sponsorship as opposed to congressional

24. Conservative legislative entrepreneurs tend to get underplayed in academic accounts. Among the notable ones during 1946–90 were Pat McCarran,
the senior Robert Taft, and Phil Gramm.

25. On passage of the Atomic Energy Act: Reichard, *Reaffirmation of Repub-
licanism*, pp. 153–63. On the St. Lawrence Seaway: ibid., pp. 164–74. On the
Highway Act: Mark H. Rose, *Interstate: Express Highway Politics, 1941–1956*
(Lawrence: Regents Press of Kansas, 1979), chaps. 6, 7.

26. Nelson W. Polsby writes in a study of the 1946–65 period: "During the
era from which our cases are drawn, liberals were doing most of the initiating,
and conservatives were, on the whole, resisting." *Political Innovation in America:
The Politics of Policy Initiation* (New Haven and London: Yale University Press,
1984), p. 10. Before 1961, this claim is not obviously valid. To give another
example, the management-oriented Landrum-Griffin labor reform act stands
out among laws passed by the Eighty-sixth Congress of 1959–60. On the
enactment of that law, see R. Alton Lee, *Eisenhower and Landrum-Griffin: A
Study in Labor-Management Politics* (Lexington: University Press of Kentucky,
1990).

initiatives, or took place in a Congress that enacted few laws or many. Also, it manages to sort out agriculture and foreign aid.

But Sweep Two uses the results of Sweep One as a starting point. And it carries over Sweep One's implicit judgments about the relative significance of whole policy areas. It does this by accepting, at least approximately, the distributive standards derivable by seeing how much space each of various policy areas managed to take up on Sweep One's full list of 211 enactments. There are 21 laws about taxes, for example, 16 about the environment, 13 about Social Security, ten about agriculture, seven about foreign trade, four about immigration, two about campaign finance, and one about the post office. Perhaps the best way to explain Sweep Two is to present a set of directions for carrying it out. Hence the following.

1. First, examine the 211 laws from Sweep One to see what policy areas, if any, each might be said to belong to—taxes, agriculture, transportation, Social Security, poverty, environment, and so forth. The areas do not need to be mutually exclusive. Both "health" and "Social Security," for example, can accommodate the Medicare act of 1965. Nor do they have to be exhaustive. There is no point in straining to find one to cover, for example, the District of Columbia home rule act of 1973.

2. For each such promising policy area, try to find one or more works by policy specialists that discuss the enactments in it during the last few decades with an eye for their relative importance. Make the works as up-to-date as possible so as to cover, if it can be done, at least some laws passed in the 1980s. Usable sources came to light in forty-three policy areas.[27] The tax area, for example, features works by Joseph A. Pechman, James M. Verdier, and John F. Witte.[28] Immigration has a work by Michael C. LeMay, energy one by Richard

27. See appendix B for a list of these areas and their sources. I could not find good sources for two areas in which most of the notable laws have passed quite recently—narcotics and crime.

28. Joseph A. Pechman, *Federal Tax Policy*, 5th ed. (Washington, D.C.: Brookings Institution Press, 1987); James M. Verdier, "The President, Congress, and Tax Reform: Patterns over Three Decades," *Annals of the American Academy of Political and Social Science* 499 (September 1988), 114–23; John F. Witte, *The Politics and Development of the Federal Income Tax* (Madison: University of Wisconsin Press, 1985).

H. K. Vietor.[29] Foreign aid has one work by Robert A. Pastor and another by Elliott R. Morss and Victoria A. Morss.[30]

3. Ignore, for a moment, the contents of the Sweep One enactment list. Canvass the specialist sources in each of the forty-three policy areas for *their* judgments about which enactments of recent decades have proven particularly important in their areas. It makes no difference whether these appraisals duplicate those of Sweep One. Tease out such judgments by taking into account attention and emphasis given to laws, explicit evaluations, and in instances where there is more than one source, by testing source against source.

4. Press the sources for defensible cutpoints—that is, ones that reasonably clearly dichotomize an area's enactments into more important and less important. A policy area may offer alternative cutpoints. In agriculture, for example, one plausible cut distinguishes just two particularly notable acts from all others—the Hope-Aiken Act of 1948, which inaugurated the basic postwar dialogue about flexible versus rigid price supports, and the Agriculture and Consumer Protection Act of 1973, which ushered in "target prices."[31] After that, though special mention might be made of the acts of 1949 and 1954, comparisons get difficult for quite awhile as a lot of multiyear subsidy measures compete for attention.[32] The next good cut seems to come after 13 acts—the above four plus the acts of 1956, 1961, 1964, 1965, 1970, 1973, 1977, and 1981, and Food for Peace 'n 1954. (The sources do not reach the recent acts of 1985 and 1990.)

9. Michael C. LeMay, *From Open Door to Dutch Door: An Analysis of U.S. Immigration Policy since 1820* (New York: Praeger, 1987); Richard H. K. Vietor, *Energy Policy in America since 1945: A Study of Business-Government Relations* (New York: Cambridge University Press, 1984).

30. Robert A. Pastor, *Congress and the Politics of U.S. Foreign Economic Policy, 1929–1976* (Berkeley: University of California Press, 1980); Elliott R. Morss and Victoria A. Morss, *U.S. Foreign Aid: An Assessment of New and Traditional Development Strategies* (Boulder, Colo.: Westview Press, 1982).

31. See especially Kenneth J. Meier, *Regulation: Politics, Bureaucracy, and Economics* (New York: St. Martin's Press, 1985), chap. 5 ("Regulating Agriculture"). I am indebted also to a conversation with John Mark Hansen on this subject.

32. On the 1949 and 1954 acts: U.S. Department of Agriculture, Economic Research Service, *History of Agricultural Price-Support and Adjustment Programs, 1933–84: Background for 1985 Farm Legislation*, Agriculture Information Bulletin #485 (Washington, D.C., December 1984), 17–36.

None of these judgments is unassailable but each, given the sources, can be defended.[33]

5. Now make some decisions. Choose each policy area's optimal collection of enactments for purposes of Sweep Two. In each case, that is the collection that satisfies the following three conditions: (a) It consists of all the enactments, and just those, on the "more important" side of some defensible Sweep Two cutpoint. (b) It includes at least two-thirds as many enactments as its policy area's Sweep One enactment list.[34] This is to keep the lists of Sweep Two enactments from getting too small. We can learn more about a policy area if its Sweep Two collection is big enough to admit at least some acts unreached by Sweep One.[35] (c) Without violating the constraints set out by (a) and (b), it matches as closely as possible the size— that is, the number of enactments—of its policy area's Sweep One list.[36] Applying these three conditions produces a unique Sweep Two solution for each policy area.[37]

33. Besides Meier and the Department of Agriculture publication, the sources are: Willard W. Cochrane and Mary E. Ryan, *American Farm Policy, 1948–1973* (Minneapolis: University of Minnesota Press, 1976), chaps. 2, 3; D. Gale Johnson, Kenzo Hemmi, and Pierre Lardinois, *Agricultural Policy and Trade: Adjusting Domestic Programs in an International Framework* (New York: New York University Press, 1985), pp. 60–66; Luther G. Tweeten, "Agriculture Policy: A Review of Legislation, Programs, and Policy," in Conference on Food and Agricultural Policy, *Food and Agricultural Policy* (Washington, D.C.: American Enterprise Institute, 1977), pp. 29–42; and Graham K. Wilson, *Special Interests and Policymaking: Agricultural Policies and Politics in Britain and the United States of America, 1956–70* (New York: John Wiley and Sons, 1977), pp. 60–72.

34. Ignoring Sweep One laws passed too recently to be appraised by Sweep Two sources.

35. Though note that, in principle, a Sweep Two list does not need to include any acts generated by Sweep One.

36. Again ignoring recent laws.

37. I violated the set of conditions in handling two policy areas. "Internal security" produced two laws in Sweep One—the McCarran Internal Security Act of 1950 and the Communist Control Act of 1954. One defensible Sweep One cutpoint singles out just the 1950 act, but I could not decide where the next cutpoint should come. So, for Sweep Two purposes, I went with just the 1950 act even though that produced a list less than two-thirds as long as Sweep One's. On this subject, see Robert Justin Goldstein, *Political Repression in Modern America: From 1870 to the Present* (New York: Schenkman, 1978). The policy area of "employment opportunity" produced just one law in Sweep One—the Civil Rights Act of 1964. (This ignores the Americans with Dis-

Note that one effect of these moves is to generate three categories of enactments. Some laws that surfaced in Sweep One now also make it onto Sweep Two lists: They are "validated," in a sense, by Sweep Two. Some laws that surfaced in Sweep One are *not* thus "validated." And some laws now come to notice for the first time by making it onto Sweep Two lists.

Another effect is inflationary. Sweep Two lists tend, as expected, to be longer than their companion Sweep One lists.[38] The two-thirds and everything-above-a-cutpoint conditions nudge the sizes up. In agriculture, for example, the optimal Sweep Two collection proves to be the thirteen laws, not the two or four. The area's Sweep One list had eight acts (those of 1949, 1954, 1956, 1958, 1961, 1964, 1973, and 1977).[39] The Sweep Two list accommodates all those eight, as it happens, and adds five more (Hope-Aiken, Food for Peace, and the acts of 1965, 1970, and 1981). Similarly in foreign aid, the Sweep Two list accommodates all five Sweep One acts and adds four more. In the environment area, the Sweep Two list accommodates eight out of twelve Sweep One acts (through 1980), and adds nine more to total seventeen. In housing, the Sweep Two list picks up seven Sweep One acts (through the mid-1980s), fails to pick up one (a rather weak 1959 act), and adds on the acts of 1954 and 1974. But not all policy areas expand in Sweep Two. Immigration, for example, features the same three major acts of 1952, 1965, and 1986.[40] Social Security shrinks:

abilities Act of 1990, which passed too recently for Sweep Two sources to reach it.) And a good Sweep Two cutpoint singles out just this 1964 law. But another quite good cutpoint yields this law plus three others—the Equal Pay Act of 1963, the Age Discrimination Act of 1967, and the Equal Employment Opportunity Act of 1972. I decided to go along with the set of four for Sweep Two, even though doing that violates condition 3. It seemed to me that Sweep One seriously underselected in this area, probably because some of the statutes in question were not very thick. On this subject, see Sar A. Levitan, Peter E. Carlson, and Isaac Shapiro, *Protecting American Workers: An Assessment of Government Programs* (Washington, D.C.: Bureau of National Affairs, 1986), chap. 4.

38. Appendix B indicates which acts appear on each policy area's Sweep Two list.

39. As well as the acts of 1985 and 1990, which passed too late for Sweep Two's sources to reach them.

40. Leaving aside the newly passed Immigration Act of 1990.

TABLE 3.1
Numbers of Important Enactments Produced by Sweep One and
Sweep Two

	Contemporary Sweep One enactment inventory	Retrospective Sweep Two enactment inventory	Total Acts
Sweep One acts validated by Sweep Two	147	147	147
Sweep One acts that passed too recently to be covered by Sweep Two sources	30		30
Sweep One acts that passed early enough but did not fit into any Sweep Two policy-area categories	19		19
Sweep One acts that passed early enough, fit into policy areas, but did not make it into Sweep Two enactment sets	15		15
Acts added to the mix by Sweep Two		56	56
Total	211	203	267

Nothing new bids to be added, and the twelve acts of Sweep One (through 1983) give way to eight in Sweep Two through the demotion of four evidently secondary laws passed in 1952, 1954, 1961, and 1973. That reflects what seems to be the compelling cutpoint.

Of Sweep One's 211 enactments, 147 win validation in one or more policy areas in Sweep Two (see table 3.1). (Acts such as Medicare could win validation in more than one policy area.) Thirty, including all twenty-one enactments of the Congresses of 1987–88 and 1989–90, passed too recently to receive Sweep Two appraisals. Nineteen acts did not inhabit workable policy areas. Fifteen could be tested for Sweep Two validation but failed. Sweep Two, meanwhile, yields the

147 validated enactments plus 56 newcomers. Altogether, Sweep Two generates a total of 203 enactments that made it onto the lists of one or more of its policy areas. This is just 8 lower than the forty-four-year summary figure produced by Sweep One.[41]

41. Policy area by policy area, the Sweep Two lists are nonetheless longer (on average) than their counterpart Sweep One lists for times covered by Sweep Two sources. Sweep Two's 203 laws are perhaps best thought of as counterparts to Sweep One's 162 laws that both (a) fit into one or more of Sweep Two's forty-three policy areas, and (b) passed during spans of time covered by Sweep Two's specialty literatures.

4 ◆ LAWMAKING

THE ANALYSIS

L aws, or programs created by them, often enter our consciousness by way of catchphrases, initials, or their sponsors' names.
The record since World War II has a rich list of such shortcuts.
Catchphrases associated with the era's enactments include urban renewal, the Truman Doctrine, 90 percent of parity, Point Four, national origins quotas, Food for Peace, depressed areas, community
action programs, wilderness areas, food stamps, model cities, rent
supplements, Medicare, Medicaid, open housing, emissions standards,
environmental impact statements, Amtrak, Conrail, revenue sharing,
Pell grants, block grants, freedom of information, the oil depletion allowance, language minorities, Superfund, synfuels, budget reconciliation, deficit reduction, welfare reform, catastrophic health insurance,
and child care.

Sponsors' names that have attached to laws include Taft-Hartley,
McCarran-Walter, Landrum-Griffin, Kerr-Mills, Magnuson-Moss,
Gramm-Latta, Gramm-Rudman-Hollings, and Goldwater-Nichols.
Initials associated with enactments include NATO, CIA, DOD, ERP,
NASA, AID, ACDA, COMSAT, OEO, VISTA, HUD, ESEA, DOT, WIN, PBC,
OSHA, SSI, ABM, ERA, FEC, CDBG, HMO, ERDA, INF, and HOPE. We
have witnessed NSF grants, NDEA fellowships, VRA renewals, RICO
powers, and CETA jobs. Policy specialists write matter-of-factly about
FIFRA, RTAA, MDTA, NEPA, ERISA, FLPMA, NFMA, JTPA, OBRA, and
IRCA.

All these items and many more appear in table 4.1, a display of the
267 postwar enactments selected as important by chapter 3's methodological maneuvers. I urge the reader to examine the material in
this display, which continues for several pages. Listed, Congress by
Congress, are all enactments generated either by Sweep One's contemporary evidence or Sweep Two's retrospective evidence. An

TABLE 4.1
Lists of Important Enactments by Congress, 1946–1990

Divided party control	Unified party control

1947–48
Truman
R Cong

#**TAFT-HARTLEY LABOR-MANAGEMENT RELATIONS ACT OF 1947.* Major anti-union rollback of Wagner Act. Enacted over Truman's veto.

#**Greece and Turkey aid (Truman Doctrine).* 1947.

**Portal-to-Portal Act of 1947.* Warded off back-wages claims against employers for travel time, etc.

#**National Security Act of 1947.* Military services unified under one Defense Secretary. CIA established.

**22nd Amendment: Two-term limit for presidents.* 1947.

Federal Insecticide, Fungicide, and Rodenticide Act (FIFRA) of 1947. Basic pesticides statute.

#**MARSHALL PLAN (EUROPEAN RECOVERY PROGRAM).* 1948.

#**Income tax cut.* GOP-inspired. Over Truman's veto. 1948.

Water Pollution Control Act of 1948. The ancestral law.

Hope-Aiken Agricultural Act of 1948. 90% of parity for basic crops for one more year, then shift to flexibles.

TRUMAN, 80th

1949–50
Truman
D Cong

#**HOUSING ACT OF 1949.* Basic post–New Deal charter for urban redevelopment, public housing.

#**NATO TREATY RATIFIED.* 1949.

#**Minimum wage increase.* To 75 cents. 1949.

TABLE 4.1 (*continued*)

Divided party control	Unified party control
	#**Mutual Defense Assistance Act of 1949*. $1.3 billion in military aid to allies.
	#**Agricultural Act of 1949*. Replay of 1948 Hope-Aiken Act.
	#**Point Four foreign aid program*. Beginning of economic aid to underdeveloped countries. 1950.
TRUMAN, 81st (Fair Deal) ⟶	#**Social Security expansion*. Benefits up 70%; 10 million new beneficiaries. 1950.
	# *National Science Foundation Act of 1950*. NSF established.
	#**McCarran Internal Security Act of 1950*. Communist and front groups to register. Emergency detention powers. Deport or exclude subversive aliens. Over Truman's veto.
	#**Defense Production Act of 1950*. Wartime economic control powers to president.
	#*Tax increase. To finance Korean War. 1950.
	# *Excess Profits Tax of 1950*. More war revenue.
	1951–52 #**Mutual Security Act of 1951*. Coupled foreign
	Truman economic and military aid in new agency.
	D Cong #**Reciprocal trade act extension*. For 2 years; tariff-cutting authority curbed. 1951.
TRUMAN, 82nd (Korean War) ⟶	#*Tax increase. For wartime defense buildup. 1951.
	**Social Security increase*. Benefits up modestly. 1952.
	#**McCarran-Walter Immigration and Nationality Act of 1952*. National origins quotas reaffirmed. Provisions to
	(*continued*)

TABLE 4.1 (*continued*)

Divided party control	Unified party control
	exclude subversives. Enacted over Truman's veto.
	# *Japanese Peace Treaty ratified.* 1952.
	1953–54 * *Tidelands oil act.* Turned submerged tidelands
	Eisenhower over to coastal states. 1953.
	R Cong #* *Tax schedule revision.* Major overhaul. 1954.
	* *Social Security expansion.* Benefits raised; 10
	million new people covered. 1954.
	* *St. Lawrence Seaway approved.* After 33-year effort. 1954.
	* *Communist Control Act of 1954.* Communist party
	outlawed. A Democratic party move.
	#* *Atomic Energy Act of 1954.* Laid basis for private atomic
	energy industry, cooperation abroad.
	#* *Agricultural Act of 1954.* Victory for flexible price
	supports between 82.5 and 90% of parity.
	# *Housing Act of 1954.* Urban renewal; city plans required.
	# *Food for Peace program.* To sell U.S. agricultural surpluses
	abroad. 1954.
EISENHOWER, 83rd ———▶	
	◀——— **EISENHOWER, 84th**
1955–56 #* *Reciprocal trade act extended.* For 3 years with	
Eisenhower reformulated presidential authority. 1955.	
D Cong #* *Minimum wage increase.* To 90 cents. 1955.	
#* *Agricultural Act of 1956.* New soil bank plan.	
#* *Disability insurance.* Added to Social Security. 1956.	
#* *Federal-Aid Highway Act of 1956.* $33 billion for 42,000	
miles to be built over 13 years. The basic instrument.	

TABLE 4.1 (continued)

Divided party control	Unified party control
#*Upper Colorado River Project authorized. Four-state, $760 million river-harnessing plan. 1956.	

1957–58   #*CIVIL RIGHTS ACT OF 1957. First since
Eisenhower   1870s. Federal injunctive powers on voting
D Cong   rights. Civil Rights Commission established.
              # Price-Anderson nuclear industry indemnity act.
      Insurance against damage claims for accidents. 1957.
    *Alaska statehood. 1958.
#*National Aeronautics and Space Administration Act of 1958.
    NASA established.
#*National Defense Education Act (NDEA) of 1958. After
    Sputnik. Loans to college students, grants to schools.
#*Reciprocal trade act extended. For 4 years. 1958.
#*Defense Department reorganized. Strengthened Defense
    Secretary vs. the services. Eisenhower's plan. 1958.
#*Agricultural Act of 1958. GOP victory. Corn, cotton, and
    rice supports might fall to 65% of parity.
#*Social Security increase. Benefits up 7%. 1958.
  # Transportation Act of 1958. Help for the railroads.
  # Food Additives Amendments of 1958. Flat ban on additives
    that cause cancer in laboratory rats. (Delaney clause.)

— EISENHOWER, 85th

1959–60   #*Landrum-Griffin Labor Reform Act of 1959.
Eisenhower   Curbs on union violence, corruption,
D Cong   power abuses.

(continued)

TABLE 4.1 (*continued*)

Divided party control	Unified party control

EISENHOWER, 86th →

Housing Act of 1959. Modest compromise measure after two Eisenhower vetoes.

Hawaii Statehood. 1959.

#**Civil Rights Act of 1960.* Voting rights protection, criminal penalties for bombings.

Kerr-Mills aid for the medically needy aged. AMA-backed grant program to ward off looming Medicare. 1960.

← KENNEDY, 87th
(New Frontier)

1961–62
Kennedy
D Cong

#**Housing Act of 1961.* Urban open spaces, middle-income housing, community facilities.

#**Minimum wage increase.* To **$1.25**. Coverage for 3.6 million new workers. 1961.

Social Security increase. Benefits raised. 1961.

#**Area Redevelopment Act of 1961.* Grants and loans for economically depressed areas.

#**Peace Corps established.* 1961.

#**Agricultural Act of 1961.* New acreage retirement programs for wheat and feed grains.

#**Arms Control and Disarmament Agency (ACDA) created.* 1961.

Alliance for Progress. Aid to Latin America. 1961.

Foreign Assistance Act of 1961. Emphasis shifted to loans for underdeveloped countries. AID established.

#**TRADE EXPANSION ACT OF 1962.* Gave president unprecedented tariff-cutting powers. 5-year authorization.

TABLE 4.1 (*continued*)

Divided party control	Unified party control
	#**Manpower Development and Training Act of 1962.* To retrain workers with obsolete or inadequate skills.
	#**Communications Satellite Act of 1962.* Authorized private corporation to develop and run system.
	#**Drug regulation.* Post-thalidomide. Tightened regulation of medical products for safety and effectiveness. 1962.
	#**Revenue Act of 1962.* Investment tax credits for business.
	#**Public Welfare Amendments of 1962.* Beefed up federal support for state assistance programs.
	1963–64 #**NUCLEAR TEST BAN TREATY RATIFIED.* 1963.
	Kennedy and Johnson D Cong #**Higher Education Facilities Act of 1963.* Funds to build college classrooms, libraries, etc.
	#**Aid for mentally ill and retarded.* For research and treatment centers. 1963.
	#**Aid to medical schools.* Student loans, buildings. 1963.
	#**Clean Air Act of 1963.* Expanded federal role.
	#**Equal Pay Act of 1963.* Outlawed gender discrimination.
	#**CIVIL RIGHTS ACT OF 1964.* Banned discrimination in public accommodations, employment, publicly owned facilities, federally funded programs.
	#**ECONOMIC OPPORTUNITY ACT OF 1964.* Johnson's anti-poverty program. Job Corps, community action programs, VISTA.

KENNEDY/JOHNSON, 88th ➡

(*continued*)

TABLE 4.1 (*continued*)

Divided party control	Unified party control
KENNEDY/JOHNSON, 88th ⟶	#*TAX CUT. Kennedy's (delayed) Keynesian-inspired cut to promote economic growth. 1964.
	#**Urban Mass Transportation Act of 1964*. Federal grants.
	#**Wilderness Act of 1964*. Set up a national Wilderness System of lands free from intrusion.
	#**Food Stamp Act of 1964*. Program made permanent. Result of Johnson logroll with cotton and wheat interests.
	#**Cotton-wheat commodity programs*. Logroll result. 1964.
1965–66 Johnson D Cong	#**MEDICAL CARE FOR THE AGED.* Medicare for the aged via Social Security. Medicaid for the medically indigent. 1965.
	#**VOTING RIGHTS ACT OF 1965.* The major statute: federal registrars to police southern elections.
	#**ELEMENTARY AND SECONDARY EDUCATION ACT (ESEA) OF 1965.* For the first time, broad federal aid to schools.
	#**Department of Housing and Urban Development (HUD)* established. 1965.
	#**Appalachian Regional Development Act of 1965.* $1 billion for 12-state region.
	**Regional medical centers for heart disease, cancer, and stroke.* Federal grants. 1965.

TABLE 4.1 (continued)

Divided party control

Unified party control

JOHNSON, 89th ⟶
(Great Society)

#*Highway Beautification Act of 1965. Lady Bird Johnson's project. Ban on billboards.

#*Immigration reform. Ended national origins quotas. 1965.

#*National Foundation on the Arts and Humanities established. 1965.

#*Higher Education Act of 1965. Scholarships and insured loans for college students.

#*Housing and Urban Development Act of 1965. Omnibus measure featuring rent supplements.

#*Excise Tax Reduction Act of 1965.

Motor Vehicle Air Pollution Control Act of 1965. HEW to set emissions standards for new cars.

Water Quality Act of 1965. States to impose standards.

Food and Agriculture Act of 1965. 4-year subsidy plan.

#*Department of Transportation established. 1966.

#*Clean Waters Restoration Act of 1966. Subsidies to locales to control water pollution.

*Air pollution control. Aid to states and locales. 1966.

#*Traffic Safety Act of 1966. New Nader-inspired standards.

*Fair Packaging and Labeling Act of 1966. Truth-in-packaging standards for labels.

#*Minimum wage increase. To $1.60, with 9.1 million new workers covered. 1966.

#*Demonstration cities program. For coordinated attack on blight in selected "model cities." 1966.

(continued)

TABLE 4.1 (*continued*)

Divided party control	Unified party control
	1967–68 #*Social Security increase. 13% hike; new work- Johnson requirement (WIN) curb on welfare. 1967. D Cong

	*Public Broadcasting Act of 1967. Set up
	       corporation to aid educational TV and
	       radio.

	*Air Quality Act of 1967. Stepped-up pollution regulation.
	#*Wholesome Meat Act of 1967. Improved meat inspection.
	# Outer space treaty ratified. To promote peaceful exploration, rule out nuclear weapons. 1967.
	# Age Discrimination Act of 1967. Banned in employment.

	#*OPEN HOUSING ACT OF 1968. Ban on discrimination
	    in sale or rent of housing. First such act in the 20th
	    century.

	#*Housing and Urban Development Act of 1968. To provide 1.7 million new or rehab units for low-income families.
	*Gun Control Act of 1968. Ban on mail sales of long guns.
	#*Omnibus Crime Control and Safe Streets Act of 1968. Law- enforcement aid to states and locales.
	#*Income tax surcharge. Johnson anti-inflation move. 1968.
	#*Central Arizona Project authorized. $1.3 billion; largest reclamation project ever authorized in one bill. 1968.
	*National scenic trails system established. 1968.
	*National Gas Pipeline Safety Act of 1968. Set standards.
	#*Wholesome Poultry Products Act of 1968. More inspection.
	*Truth-in-Lending Act of 1968. Required disclosure of information to consumers in credit transactions.

JOHNSON, 90th →

TABLE 4.1 (continued)

Divided party control	Unified party control
1969–70 #*Coal mine safety act. New standards.	
Nixon #* Compensation for black lung disease. 1969.	
D Cong #*Social Security increase. 15% hike. 1969.	
*Draft lottery system. 1969.	
#*Tax Reform Act of 1969. Said to be most comprehensive revision of tax schedule in U.S. history.	
# Nuclear Nonproliferation Treaty ratified. 1969.	
# National Environmental Policy Act (NEPA) of 1969. The source of "environmental impact statements."	
*Organized Crime Control Act of 1970. Unprecedented federal authority (including RICO powers) vs. mobsters.	
#*Postal Reorganization Act of 1970. Set up U.S. Postal Service as independent agency.	
#*Voting Rights Act extension. For 5 years. Coverage beyond the South. Gave suffrage to 18 year-olds (upheld by courts only for federal elections). 1970.	
#*Clean Air Act of 1970. Uniquely ambitious. Set specific deadlines for reduction of auto emissions.	
*Water Quality Improvement Act of 1970. Aimed at oil spills, sewage.	
*Ban on cigarette advertising on radio and TV. Also strengthened warning label on packages. 1970.	
#*Occupational Safety and Health Act (OSHA) of 1970. New on-the-job standards plus enforcement mechanism.	
#*Rail Passenger Service Act of 1970. Set up Amtrak.	

⟶ NIXON, 91st

(continued)

TABLE 4.1 *(continued)*

Divided party control	Unified party control
Omnibus Crime Control Act of 1970. $3.5 billion for LEAA to aid state and local programs.	
Narcotics control act. Revised penalties, stiffened enforcement, expanded treatment. 1970.	
# *Agricultural Act of 1970.* Subsidy programs continued. "Set aside" plan to cut production.	
# *Airport and Airway Development Act of 1970.* Trust fund.	
# *Urban Mass Transportation Assistance Act of 1970.* Federal funding greatly expanded. $12 billion plan.	
# *Economic Stabilization Act of 1970.* Nixon given unwanted power to impose wage-price controls; he used it in 1971.	
# *Food stamps program expanded.* National standards. Multiplied funding. 1970.	
# *Unemployment compensation expanded.* Extended benefits, 4.8 million more potential beneficiaries. 1970.	
1971–72 #**Social Security increase.* 10% hike. 1971.	
Nixon #**Tax reduction.* To spur the economy. Included	
D Cong $1 checkoff for campaign finance. 1971.	
#**National Cancer Act of 1971.* $1.6 billion.	
#**Emergency Employment Act of 1971.* $2.25 billion for public-service jobs. First such plan since New Deal.	
**18-year-old voting age as constitutional amendment.* Soon ratified by the states. 1971.	

TABLE 4.1 (continued)

Divided party control	Unified party control
#*Federal Election Campaign Act of 1972. Ceilings on radio and TV spending for ads; rigorous disclosure rules.	
#*Water pollution control act. Uniquely comprehensive and expensive. New standards; $24 billion to build sewage treatment plants, etc. Over Nixon's veto. 1972.	
#*State and Local Fiscal Assistance Act of 1972. Nixon's general revenue sharing plan. $30 billion for 5 years.	
#*Social Security increase. Major 20% hike, plus automatic tie of future hikes to cost-of-living index. 1972.	
*Equal rights amendment to the constitution (ERA). Against gender discrimination. 1972. Not ratified by states.	⟵ NIXON, 92nd
#*Pesticide Control Act of 1972. Comprehensive program.	
#*ABM treaty ratified. Limit on U.S. and Soviet anti-ballistic missile systems. 1972.	
#*Consumer Product Safety Act of 1972. New commission to set and enforce safety standards for consumer products.	
# Equal Employment Opportunity Act of 1972. Added enforcement powers to 1964 Civil Rights Act, extended coverage to state and local governments.	
# Supplemental Security Income (SSI) program approved. New income floor for the aged, blind, disabled. 1972.	
# Higher Education Act of 1972. $25 billion package; new Pell grants as aid floor for lower-income students.	

(continued)

TABLE 4.1 (continued)

Divided party control	Unified party control

1973–74   #*WAR POWERS ACT OF 1973. Limited
Nixon and   president's authority to commit U.S. troops
Ford   in combat. Enacted over Nixon's veto.
D Cong   #*Federal Aid Highway Act of 1973. Opened up
     Highway Trust Fund to mass-transit
     projects.
#*Agriculture and Consumer Protection Act of 1973. Shift to
     "target price" formula to subsidize commodity
     growers.
#*Comprehensive Employment and Training Act (CETA) of
     1973. Reorganized manpower programs via Nixonian
     block grants. Continued public-service employment as
     CETA jobs.
*Social Security increase. Two-step 11% hike. 1973.
*District of Columbia home rule. Mayor and council. 1973.
#*Trans-Alaskan pipeline authorized. 1973.
# Foreign Assistance Act of 1973. Major shift in direction. 	
     Aid to go to poorest populations in poorest countries.
# Regional Rail Reorganization Act of 1973. Bankrupt 	
     northeastern-quadrant railroads consolidated into
     Conrail.
# Aid for development of Health Maintenance Organizations 	
     (HMOs). Also defined their form and activities. 1973.
# Emergency Petroleum Allocation Act of 1973. Called for a 	
     mandatory allocation program for oil and oil products.	

TABLE 4.1 (*continued*)

Divided party control	Unified party control
#*Trade Act of 1974. Major rewrite. For 5 years. Free Jewish immigration to be a bargaining point with USSR.	→ NIXON/FORD, 93rd (Watergate)
#*Employment Retirement Income Security Act (ERISA) of 1974. Landmark guarantee of pension rights in private systems.	
#*Federal Election Campaign Act of 1974. The basic law: limits on contributions and spending, full disclosure, public funding of presidential elections, the FEC.	
#*Minimum wage increase. To $2.30 in 3 stages, plus coverage of 7 million new workers. 1974.	
#*Congressional Budget and Impoundment Control Act of 1974. New congressional budget system, curbs on impoundment.	
*Freedom of Information Act Amendments of 1974. Beefed up earlier act to insure public access to government records—e.g., FBI files. Enacted over Ford's veto.	
# Nuclear Regulatory Commission (NRC) and Energy Research & Development Administration (ERDA) created. AEC killed.	
# Magnuson-Moss product warranty act. Gave FTC power to set industry-wide rules vs. unfair business practices. 1974.	
# National Health Planning and Resources Development Act of 1974. New national network of local planning agencies.	

TABLE 4.1 (*continued*)

Divided party control	Unified party control
# *National Mass Transportation Assistance Act of 1974.* $11 billion. Funds for operating costs, for first time.	
# *Housing and Community Development Act of 1974.* Switch to block grants, direct rent subsidies.	

1975–76
Ford
D Cong

Energy Policy and Conservation Act of 1975. Oil price control now, but phased decontrol later.

#* *Voting Rights Act extension.* For 7 years; language minorities added to coverage. 1975.

#* *New York City bailout.* $2.3 billion in federal loans to stave off default. 1975.

* *Repeal of fair-trade laws.* That is, 40-year-old state laws allowing manufacturer-dealer price fixing. 1975.

Tax Reduction Act of 1975. Anti-recession move. Repealed the oil depletion allowance (for large firms).

Securities Act Amendments of 1975. Broad reform of securities regulation; some deregulation.

#* *Unemployment compensation overhaul.* Revised finances; coverage for 8.5 million new workers. 1976.

#* *Copyright law revision.* Major rewrite, to cover photo-copying, cable-TV royalties, etc. 1976.

#* *Toxic substances control act.* Required chemical firms to test risky products. Banned PCBs. 1976.

⟶ FORD, 94th

TABLE 4.1 (*continued*)

Divided party control	Unified party control
#*Tax Reform Act of 1976.* Concerted rewrite of schedule.	
# *Railroad Vitalization and Regulatory Reform Act of 1976.* New subsidies and a move toward deregulation.	
# *National Forest Management Act of 1976 (NFMA).* Commitment to strenuous planning. Rules about clear-cutting.	
# *Federal Land Policy and Management Act (FLPMA) of 1976.* Gave Bureau of Land Management permanent authority to manage public lands. A cause of Sagebrush Rebellion.	
# *Resource Conservation and Recovery Act of 1976.* Cradle-to-grave EPA regulation of hazardous wastes.	

CARTER, 95th ⟶

1977–78	#*Social Security tax increase.* To raise additional
Carter	$227 billion over 10 years. 1977.
D Cong	#*Tax cut.* 3-year stimulus package. 1977.
	#*Minimum wage hike.* To $3.35 in 4 stages. 1977.
	#*Surface Mining Control and Reclamation Act of 1977.* New standards for strip mining.
	#*Food and Agriculture Act of 1977.* Higher commodity subsidies; revised and expanded food stamp program.
	# *Clean Water Act of 1977.* Standards relaxed. $24.5 billion more for sewage treatment construction.
	# *Clean Air Act Amendments of 1977.* Standards relaxed.

(*continued*)

TABLE 4.1 (continued)

Divided party control	Unified party control
	#**Tax revision.* Cut corporate, capital-gains taxes. 1978.
	#**Comprehensive energy package.* Conservation provisions; phased decontrol of natural gas prices. A shadow of Carter's April 1977 omnibus plan. 1978.
	**Panama Canal treaties ratified.* U.S. control to end. 1978.
	#**Civil Service Reform Act of 1978.* Extensive revamping. Carter plan to inject merit into pay system.
	#**Airline deregulation.* Decontrol of routes, fares. 1978.
	1979–80 **Chrysler Corporation bailout.* **$3.5 billion aid**
	Carter package to ward off bankruptcy. 1979.
	D Cong #**Foreign trade act extension.* Approved Tokyo Round non-tariff barrier reductions. 1979.
	**Department of Education established.* 1979.
	#**Depository Institutions and Monetary Control Act of 1980.* Banking deregulation. Removed most distinctions between commercial banks and savings-and-loans units.
	#**Trucking deregulation.* Greater pricing freedom, end of some antitrust immunities. 1980.
	#**Staggers Rail Act of 1980.* More deregulation.
	#**Windfall profits tax on oil.* Carter's plan; to bring in **$227** billion over a decade. 1980.
	#**Synthetic fuels program.* Carter's **$88 billion** plan to spur development of a private industry. 1980.

CARTER, 96th ⟶

TABLE 4.1 (continued)

Divided party control	Unified party control
	#**Alaska lands preservation.* Curbed future development of over 100 million acres of federal holdings. 1980.
	#**Toxic wastes Superfund.* \$1.6 billion fund, largely from levies on industry, to clean up chemical dumps. 1980.

1981–82 #**ECONOMIC RECOVERY TAX ACT OF 1981.*
Reagan   Reagan's plan. Largest tax cut in U.S.
R Senate   history: \$749 billion over 5 years.
D House   Individual income tax cuts of 5%, 10%,
    and 10% over three years; indexing of tax
brackets to offset inflation; cuts in corporate taxes.

#**OMNIBUS BUDGET RECONCILIATION ACT OF 1981*
(OBRA; GRAMM-LATTA II). Stockman plan to slash
domestic spending, permanently, by revising
authorization blueprints. Cuts for fiscal 1982 to total
\$35.2 billion. To affect disability benefits, Medicare,
Medicaid, AFDC payments, subsidized housing, health
programs, food stamps, unemployment insurance,
CETA jobs, student loans, Pell grants, impacted areas
aid, school lunches, medical education, sewer grants,
postal subsidies, trade adjustment assistance, small
business loans, mass transit systems, highway funds,
Conrail, Amtrak, and more.

REAGAN, 97th
(Tax cut, Gramm-Latta II)

\# *Agriculture and Food Act of 1982.* 4-year subsidy plan.

(continued)

TABLE 4.1 (continued)

Divided party control	Unified party control

#*Transportation Assistance Act of 1982.* $71 billion for highway construction, road repairs, mass transit. Raised the gasoline tax.

#*Tax Equity and Fiscal Responsibility Act of 1982.* 3-year deficit-reducing plan to raise taxes by $98.3 billion, cut welfare and entitlements spending by $17.5 billion.

#*Voting Rights extension.* For 25 years. 1982.

Nuclear waste repository act. Underground dumps. 1982.

Garn-St. Germain Depository Institutions Act of 1982. Part deregulation, part support of savings and loans.

Job Training Partnership Act of 1982. Dan Quayle's bill.

1983–84	*Martin Luther King's birthday declared a legal holiday.* 1983.
Reagan	
R Senate	#*Social Security Act Amendments of 1983.* $170 billion bipartisan package of tax increases and benefit cuts to stave off system insolvency.
D House	

Anti-recession jobs measure. $4.6 billion. 1983.

#*Anti-crime package.* Criminal code revision addressing insanity defense, sentencing procedures, pretrial detention, computer tampering, credit card fraud, etc. 1984.

#*Deficit reduction measure.* Spending cuts of $13 billion, new taxes worth $50 billion, through fiscal 1987. 1984.

→ REAGAN, 98th

TABLE 4.1 (*continued*)

Divided party control	Unified party control
# *Trade and Tariff Act of 1984*. Extension of authority.	
# *Cable Communications Policy Act of 1984*. Rearrangement of cable-TV regulation.	

1985–86 Reagan / R Senate / D House

#* *Gramm-Rudman-Hollings anti-deficit act*. Move to balance the budget by 1990 through automatic spending cuts. 1985.

* *Food Security Act of 1985*. Record commodity subsidies—$52 billion over 3 years.

#* *TAX REFORM ACT OF 1986*. Sweeping revision. 14 tax brackets collapsed into 2; many breaks eliminated; rates sharply cut; shift from individual to corporate taxes.

#* *Immigration Reform and Control Act of 1986 (IRCA)*. Hiring of illegal aliens outlawed. Amnesty offered to illegals in U.S. since 1982.

* *South Africa sanctions*. Banned all new U.S. investment there, some key imports. Over Reagan's veto. 1986.

* *Anti-narcotics measure*. $1.7 billion for enforcement, education, treatment. Stiffer penalties. 1986.

* *Cleanup of toxic waste dumps*. Major expansion of Superfund. New standards, new taxes, $9.6 billion. 1986.

* *Omnibus water projects act*. First such act since 1976. $16.3 billion, 262 projects, users to share costs. 1986.

⟶ REAGAN, 99th

(*continued*)

TABLE 4.1 (continued)

Divided party control	Unified party control

#*Goldwater-Nichols Reorganization Act of 1986 (Defense Department). Authority shifted from the services to coordinators—e.g., chairman of the Joint Chiefs.

1987–88   *Water Quality Act of 1987. $18 billion to
Reagan   sewage treatment plants, etc. Over
D Cong   Reagan's veto.

     *Surface Transportation Act of 1987. $88 billion
for highways, mass transit. Over Reagan's veto.
*Deficit reduction measure. 2-year $40 billion package of
spending cuts, tax increases, sales of assets. 1987.
*Housing and community development act. First housing
authorization since 1980. $30 billion. 1987.
*McKinney Homeless Assistance Act of 1987. $443 million for
shelter, health, food, etc.
*Catastrophic health insurance for the aged. Major costs to be
paid for by insurance premiums. 1988.
*Family Support Act of 1988. Welfare reform. Aimed tc
ease taking jobs, support families of those who do.
*Omnibus foreign trade measure. 5-year authority. 1988.
*Anti-drug-abuse act. Funds for policing and treatment;
new drug czar; death penalty for drug kingpins. 1988.
*Grove City civil rights measure. Overturned 1984 court
decision; reasserted that civil rights laws reach whole

⟵——————— REAGAN, 100th

TABLE 4.1 (continued)

Divided party control	Unified party control

BUSH, 101st →

institutions receiving federal aid, not just particular programs. Enacted over Reagan's veto. 1988.

*Intermediate-Range Nuclear-Force (INF) treaty ratified. 1988.

*Japanese-American reparations. $1.25 billion to those interned during World War II. 1988.

1989–90
Bush
D Cong

*Minimum wage hike. To $4.25 in 1991. New training wage for teenagers. 1989.

*Savings-and-loan bailout. $50 billion to sell off or close down insolvent banks. 1989.

*DEFICIT REDUCTION PACKAGE. Bipartisan deal; $490 billion in tax hikes and spending cuts over 5 years. Fall 1990.

*Americans with Disabilities Act of 1990. To guarantee job rights and access to public facilities.

*Clean Air Act of 1990. To curb acid rain, airborne toxics, urban smog.

*Child care package. $22.5 billion; tax credits and state grants for children of working parents. 1990.

*Immigration Act of 1990. 40% increase in annual intake; new emphasis on occupational skills.

*National Affordable Housing Act of 1990. New block grants to expand stock; new HOPE program to sell off public housing projects to tenants.

*Agriculture act. 15% cut in subsidized acreage. 1990.

asterisk (*) appears alone in front of each Sweep One act that Sweep Two, for whatever reasons, did not reach or validate. Both a number sign and an asterisk (#*) precede each Sweep One act that Sweep Two did validate. And just a number sign (#) precedes each act that Sweep Two added to the mix. So Sweep One's 211 laws are the ones that exhibit at least an asterisk, and Sweep Two's 203 are the ones that exhibit at least a number sign. Printed in capital letters are 19 acts, including the Marshall Plan, the Voting Rights Act of 1965, and Reagan's 1981 tax cut, that Sweep One sources seemed to think reached beyond being important to being historically important. Brief explanatory squibs appear in most entries. It should be said that these often reflect an act's promise when it was passed rather than its eventual effects.[1]

Looked at chronologically, the display starts with the Republican Eightieth Congress, which produced the Taft-Hartley Act and the Marshall Plan.[2] In 1949–50 came the most energetic phase of Truman's Fair Deal, which yielded among other things the ambitious Housing Act of 1949. Both Congress and the president gave much of their attention to the Korean war during 1951–52. Eisenhower had Republican congressional majorities in 1953–54, then coexisted rather harmoniously with Democratic ones led by Sam Rayburn and Lyndon Johnson from 1955 through 1960. Kennedy pursued his New Frontier in 1961–63 and then Johnson his Great Society from 1964 through about 1966. Nixon in turn proposed a New Federalism. But taglines have not adhered as well to legislative enterprises pursued under Nixon and Ford, and that, as we shall see, is not a minor point. Later,

1. A word is in order on the titles of acts. When an official or customary title of an act proved to be available, brief, and to the point, I used it in table 4.1. The form for these is "National Security Act of 1947" or "McCarran-Walter Immigration and Nationality Act of 1952." Otherwise, listings take a form such as "Comprehensive energy package" or "Deficit reduction measure," with dates of passage presented separately.

2. Readers may wonder about the absence of some other laws that passed just after World War II. Much productive legislating took place in 1946 when Truman was still dealing with the Democratic Congress elected in 1944. Among that year's enactments were Senator Brien McMahon's Atomic Energy Act, the Administrative Procedure Act, the Hill-Burton Act providing grants for hospital construction, the Employment Act setting up the Council of Economic Advisers (CEA), the La Follette-Monroney Legislative Reorganization Act, and a measure creating the Fulbright exchange program.

an emphasis on deregulation and energy in the late 1970s under Carter gave way to Reagan's agenda of tax and spending cuts in 1981. Resulting budgetary problems slowed down most lawmaking efforts until about 1985, but after that, as Reagan seemed to lose interest, bipartisan or Democratic coalitions on Capitol Hill put through quite a few notable laws. Those included tax and immigration reform in 1986, and several items of Speaker Wright's domestic agenda in 1987–88. Under Bush, who began with a meager program, deficit reduction highlighted the legislative record during 1989–90.

What are the general patterns? For one thing, some Congresses contributed much more to table 4.1 than others. With Sweep Two's acts now included, the low producers with five, six, or seven laws are the Congresses of 1951–52 under Truman, 1955–56 and 1959–60 under Eisenhower, and 1983–84 under Reagan. The top producers with twenty-two laws apiece are those of 1965–66 under Johnson, 1969–70 under Nixon, and 1973–74 under Nixon and Ford. Sweep Two shored up especially the Nixon or Ford Congresses of 1969–70, 1973–74, and 1975–76. This happened repeatedly through such judgments as: If a selection of environmental laws above some cutpoint is to include the toxic wastes Superfund act of 1980 (a Sweep One law), then it needs to include also the National Environmental Policy Act of 1969 (not a Sweep One law).[3] If the food stamps act of 1964, then the food stamps act of 1970.[4] If just about anything on housing, then the Housing and Community Development Act of 1974.[5] If the Wilderness Act of 1964 as a public lands measure, then also both the Federal Land Policy and Management Act (FLPMA) of 1976 and the National Forest Management Act (NFMA) of 1976.[6]

3. The judgment is based on Kenneth J. Meier, *Regulation: Politics, Bureaucracy, and Economics* (New York: St. Martin's Press, 1985), chap. 6.

4. Based on Robert X. Browning, *Politics and Social Welfare Policy in the United States* (Knoxville: University of Tennessee Press, 1986), pp. 95, 110–11, 142–48; Timothy Conlan, *New Federalism: Intergovernmental Reform from Nixon to Reagan* (Washington, D.C.: Brookings Institution Press, 1988), pp. 81–82.

5. Based on R. Allen Hays, *The Federal Government and Urban Housing: Ideology and Change in Public Housing* (Albany: State University of New York Press, 1985), p. xiv and chaps. 4–8; Eugene J. Meehan, *The Quality of Federal Policymaking: Programmed Failure in Public Housing* (Columbia: University of Missouri Press, 1979), chap. 2.

6. Based on Tom Arrandale, *The Battle for Natural Resources* (Washington, D.C.: Congressional Quarterly Press, 1983), pp. 7–9 and chap. 3.

For another thing, the forty-four-year record bulges in the middle. The average number of laws per Congress starts with 9.3 under Truman and 7.8 under Eisenhower, surges to 16.5 under Kennedy and Johnson and 18.5 under Nixon and Ford, then falls to 11.0 under Carter and 9.2 under Reagan and Bush. Is this pattern believable? In its favor is that it corresponds to one that Roger H. Davidson has recently found in indicators of Congress's postwar legislative workload: There was a swing up in the mid-1960s and a swing down in the late 1970s.[7] In the case of the 1960s, a surge in virtually any indicator of legislative activity would be easy to accept. If we know anything about the history of that time, it is that lawmaking accelerated in many policy areas. Whether the later swing downward is "real" is more problematic. At least in the 1980s, as noted earlier, omnibus budgetary acts came to accommodate some initiatives that earlier would have emerged as free-standing bills. But such displacement is probably not the whole story. It is hardly novel to discern a lack of legislative drive under Carter or some doldrums under Reagan.

What does not emerge from table 4.1, however, is any relation worth crediting between the incidence of important laws and whether party control was unified or divided. If all 267 laws are counted equally, the nine "unified" two-year segments average 12.8 acts, and the thirteen "divided" segments average 11.7. The difference is trivial, and since the 1980s was all "divided," that decade's shift to the use of omnibus budgetary measures can probably account for it, so to speak, entirely. In particular, Reagan's package of Gramm-Latta II and the 1981 tax cut figures as just two acts. Also worth noting is that the number of laws per Congress varies much more within the universes of unified and divided times than it does between them. The "unified" two-year segments range from six laws in 1951–52 during the Korean war to the twenty-two in 1965–66 under Johnson. The "divided" ones range from five laws in 1959–60 to the twenty-two apiece in 1969–70 and 1973–74. The Vietnam war proceeded at full tilt in 1969–70: So much for the immobilizing effects of wars.[8]

7. Roger H. Davidson, "The New Centralization on Capitol Hill," *Review of Politics* 50 (1988), 349–50. "In the years since World War II, overall House and Senate workload indicators have been marked by a gradual build-up, then an era of extraordinary legislative activity, and more recently a sudden and striking contraction" (p. 352).

8. Consider also the ample legislative record during the Civil War.

But there is no escape from examining table 4.1 for nuances. Some of its measures are obviously more important than others. Beyond just reflecting about the contents of the table, one way to proceed is the following. Let us consider some policy areas in which particularly notable laws passed at several points throughout the four decades, and in which innovation was ordinarily "unforced." That is, it was not brought on quickly by such events as oil crises or railroad bankruptcies. When did the laws pass? When were the major policy junctures? Of interest here are the exceptionally important enactments—the set of two in agriculture, for example, rather than the set of thirteen. For easy reference below, UNI or DIV will serve as shorthand for unified or divided party control.

The leading foreign aid acts, according to one account, were the Marshall Plan of 1948 (DIV), which aimed at rebuilding Western Europe; the Mutual Security Act of 1951 (UNI), which set a Cold War pattern for military aid; the Foreign Assistance Act of 1961 (UNI), which placed a new emphasis on economic development in poorer countries; and the Foreign Assistance Act of 1973 (DIV), which shifted to a socially oriented strategy for poorer countries.[9] (The first two of these were arguably "forced," but not the others.) The signal foreign trade measures, before 1980 at any rate, were those enacted under Kennedy in 1962 (UNI) and Nixon in 1974 (DIV), with side-mention of one under Eisenhower in 1955 (DIV).[10] All three of these were antiprotectionist victories that enhanced presidential authority. In the arms control area, the Senate ratified major U.S.-Soviet treaties under Kennedy in 1963 (UNI), Nixon in 1972 (DIV), and Reagan in 1988 (DIV).

Paramount among immigration acts were the McCarran-Walter Act of 1952 (UNI), which confirmed a system of national origins quotas and set new security standards; the 1965 reform (UNI) that repealed the quotas; and the Immigration Reform and Control Act of 1986 (DIV) that centered on illegal aliens.[11] In agriculture, as mentioned,

9. Robert A. Pastor, *Congress and the Politics of U.S. Foreign Economic Policy, 1929–1976* (Berkeley: University of California Press, 1980), chap. 9.

10. Ibid., chaps. 3–5.

11. Michael C. LeMay, *From Open Door to Dutch Door: An Analysis of U.S. Immigration Policy since 1820* (New York: Praeger, 1987), chaps. 5, 6. The Immigration Act of 1990 (DIV), which passed after LeMay's work was published, seems to be about as significant as the three earlier measures.

the Hope-Aiken Act of 1948 (DIV) and the Agriculture and Consumer Protection Act of 1973 (DIV) arguably stood out. The 1973 act's "target prices" resembled the Brannan Plan idea that Truman could not get through a Democratic Congress in 1949. The key measures in labor-management relations—both management victories—were the Taft-Hartley Act of 1947 (DIV), passed by a Republican Congress over Truman's veto; and the Landrum-Griffin Act of 1959 (DIV), championed by Eisenhower and voted by a lopsidedly Democratic Congress.[12] Union-oriented Democrats tried to move labor-management law in their direction at party high tides during Truman's administration in 1949–50, Johnson's in 1965–66, and Carter's in 1977–78, but they never had much luck.[13]

In the sphere of Social Security, once past a significant consolidating act in 1950 (UNI), the program's three "major expansions" came with disability insurance in 1956 (DIV), Medicare in 1965 (UNI), and a "quantum increase" in cash benefits in 1969–72 (DIV). Important acts aimed at squaring the program's revenue with its spending passed later in 1977 (UNI) and 1983 (DIV).[14] Another expansion came with catastrophic health insurance in 1988 (DIV), though the financing of that proved unpopular and repeal followed a year later.[15] As for tax revision, evidently the leading acts were a comprehensive Republican rewrite of the code in 1954 (UNI), the Democratic party's Keynes-inspired rate reduction in 1964 (UNI), a comprehensive Democratic measure to close loopholes that Nixon signed in 1969 (DIV), another Democratic bill that Ford signed in 1976 (DIV), Reagan's major rate reduction in 1981 (DIV), and the bracket-streamlining Tax Reform Act of 1986 (DIV).[16]

12. Betty W. Justice, *Unions, Workers, and the Law* (Washington, D.C.: Bureau of National Affairs, 1983), pp. 15–19.

13. "Taft-Hartley proved to be a surprisingly enduring piece of legislation, which set the terms and conditions of labor-management relations for more than forty years." Michael Barone, *Our Country: The Shaping of America from Roosevelt to Reagan* (New York: Free Press, 1990), p. 193.

14. Martha Derthick, *Policymaking for Social Security* (Washington, D.C.: Brookings Institution Press, 1979), chaps. 10, 15–17, 19, quotations at p. 296; Paul Light, *Artful Work: The Politics of Social Security Reform* (New York: Random House, 1985).

15. See Martin Tolchin, "How the New Medicare Law Fell on Hard Times in a Hurry," *New York Times*, October 9, 1989, pp. A1, A10.

16. John F. Witte, *The Politics and Development of the Income Tax* (Madison: University of Wisconsin Press, 1985), chaps. 7–11; James M. Verdier, "The

So far, the case that "unified" times excel in productivity is faring badly, to say the least. Civil rights, at first glance, looks like a plus for unified control. Of arguably the four main postwar acts, three passed during Johnson's presidency when the Democrats held Congress also—those addressing public accommodations in 1964, voting rights in 1965, and open housing in 1968. (The other was enacted under Eisenhower in 1957-DIV).[17] But it would be an odd call to credit the civil rights laws of the 1960s to unified party control—or for that matter more particularly to unified Democratic control. The most intense opposition, from the white South, came from Democrats also. Eisenhower and a Democratic Congress proved a better formula for actually passing laws than did Kennedy and a Democratic Congress. Because of the Senate filibuster, broad cross-party majorities were needed to put through bills. In all three major victories of the 1960s, roughly two-thirds of both Republican and Democratic Senators supported the cloture resolutions on which action hinged. Finally, the breakthrough acts of 1964 and 1965 seem to have required triggering events to win passage—violence in Birmingham and Selma, respectively, along with resulting changes in public opinion.[18]

The best cases for unified control, still with an eye for policy areas where major acts passed at several junctures, may be minimum wages and housing, although the patterns are not clear-cut. These are partisan subjects on which Republicans ordinarily prefer no action at all

President, Congress, and Tax Reform," *Annals of the American Academy of Political and Social Science* 499 (September 1988), 114–23. Now the deficit-reduction measure of 1990 (DIV) might merit addition to the list.

17. On postwar civil rights legislation, see James L. Sundquist, *Politics and Policy: The Eisenhower, Kennedy, and Johnson Years* (Washington, D.C.: Brookings Institution Press, 1968), chap. 6; Theodore Eisenberg, *Civil Rights Legislation: Cases and Materials* (Indianapolis, Ind.: Bobbs-Merrill, 1981), pp. 1–3; Gary Orfield, *Congressional Power: Congress and Social Change* (New York: Harcourt Brace Jovanovich, 1975), chaps. 5, 6; Abigail M. Thernstrom, *Whose Votes Count? Affirmative Action and Minority Voting Rights* (Cambridge: Harvard University Press, 1987); and Hugh Davis Graham, *The Civil Rights Era: Origins and Development of National Policy, 1960–1972* (New York: Oxford University Press, 1990), pp. 3–5 and chaps. 5, 6, 10, 14, 17.

18. On Birmingham and Selma as keys to 1964 and 1965 legislative action, see Paul Burstein, *Discrimination, Jobs, and Politics: The Struggle for Equal Employment Opportunity in the United States since the New Deal* (Chicago: University of Chicago Press, 1985), chaps. 3–5, 8, and Harvard Sitkoff, *The Struggle for Black Equality, 1954–1980* (New York: Hill and Wang, 1981), chaps. 5, 6.

and Democrats have a custom of marking an election victory by promptly passing a new law. Four out of seven postwar minimum wage increases came at times when the Democrats held both Congress and the presidency—the ones in 1949, 1961, 1966, and 1977—though not those in 1955, 1974, and 1989 (all DIV).[19] Ford signed a major housing bill in 1974 (DIV)—the switch to block grants—and Nixon presided over an immense expansion of federal housing during 1969–72 (DIV). Still, the lineage of major postwar housing initiatives comes down through the presidencies of Truman (second-term), Kennedy, and Johnson—all conducted under conditions of unified Democratic control. No other policy area seems to have a successful legislative history as closely associated with those three presidencies.

These are lean pickings. In general, the eleven policy areas just discussed acquired landmark acts about as frequently per year in "divided" as in "unified" times. Most remarkable, perhaps, is the co-incidence of Watergate turmoil in 1973–74 with major policy departures in foreign aid, foreign trade, agriculture, and housing.

Nonetheless, one might respond, even if this analysis is legitimate, doesn't it miss something? It plausibly considers policy areas one by one. Following the blueprints set out for this work, it dwells in principle on legislative motion—on whether the system generates important laws, regardless of ideological direction. But would these techniques do justice to the New Deal? Do they to Johnson's Great Society? Don't we somehow *know* that the Great Society was the leading instance of legislative action during recent decades? Probably most people would agree that it was, and for two reasons. First, there was a great deal of legislative motion. Notable laws were passed in the areas of, not to make an exhaustive list, education, civil rights, poverty, medical care, area redevelopment, the environment, immigration, and housing. But second, there was a holistic effect. The various legislative moves shared an ideological direction; taken together, they summed to one powerful policy thrust of a uniform or at least common ideological tendency. That sort of holistic effect seems to need addressing. If we wish to understand change via government action in the American system—particularly large-scale change—it does not seem

19. See Sar A. Levitan, Peter E. Carlson, and Isaac Shapiro, *Protecting American Workers: An Assessment of Government Programs* (Washington, D.C.: Bureau of National Affairs, 1986), chap. 5, especially the charts that appear on pp. 81 and 87.

possible to analyze legislative motion sensitively without taking into account ideological patterning across laws.

Keeping the Great Society in mind, the analysis that follows will address ideological commonality across laws—or, to extend the scope somewhat, proposed laws. For reasons to become evident as the discussion proceeds, it seems worthwhile to explore two distinct variants of such commonality rather than just one. The first might be called an "ideological surge"—that is, a spell of high-energy lawmaking that exhibits a unifying ideological thrust, has results in many policy areas, and continues for several years. During a period with a beginning and an end, though observers may disagree about exactly when those occur, laws of a common ideological tendency keep getting passed. We can look back and see that. One example is the record of the Reconstruction era, which lasted roughly a decade if one carries it through the Civil Rights Act of 1875. Another is the record at combined national, state, and local levels during the Progressive era, which also lasted about a decade.

The second, quite familiar variant of ideological commonality is a presidential program calling for enactment of an ideological vision. More specifically, it is an ambitious program of legislative proposals that exhibits a unifying ideology and excites the core activists of a party, and that the president of that party claims a mandate for and undertakes to make the country's domestic agenda. Such a program often attracts a label like New Freedom, Fair Deal, or New Frontier. Not every president presents one. The emphasis here is on the president as agent (in a "surge," by contrast, agency may be scattered or in question), on simultaneous presentation (a "surge" is a long sequence of events), and on proposals (a "surge" is a record of completed enactments). Obviously, as with the Great Society or Woodrow Wilson's New Freedom, a president's "ideological program" may help to cause or sustain an "ideological surge." But the two phenomena merit separate analysis. They will be taken up here in turn, and "surges" will receive more attention in chapter 6.

Johnson's Great Society now seems to have been, for one thing, part of an ideological surge. It came at the beginning or upswing of one that lasted a surprisingly long time. From start to finish, table 4.1's legislative bulge of the 1960s and 1970s consists principally of enactments that advanced a liberal agenda. In specialist works about policy areas, nothing comes through more emphatically than the persistence of liberal legislative energy and success from Johnson's accession to the presidency in late 1963 right up through 1975 or 1976. In general, the record is of one long state-enhancing thrust toward greater expenditure and regulation, although attention shifted over time among policy areas, and efforts to restructure relations between Congress and the president did not join the agenda until the early 1970s. In retrospect, it seems in order to speak of a joint age of Johnson and Nixon. Johnson's role is familiar. Nixon acted variously as initiator, acquiescer, footdragger, and outright vetoer. But the bills kept getting passed under him and, later, Ford even though party control switched from unified to divided.

To take expenditure, Robert J. Lampman demarcates 1965 through 1976 as the time when the country's striking postwar surge in social welfare spending occurred. The totals rose from 11.2 percent of gross national product early in Johnson's tenure to an all-time peak of 19.3 percent late in Ford's.[20] Many of Johnson's initiatives had delayed effects, but it would be a considerable mistake to credit the post-1968 part of the spending surge just to that lag.[21] For one thing, new social programs kept getting created. As table 4.2 shows, using data prepared by Robert X. Browning, the Nixon and Ford years ran a strong second to those of Kennedy and Johnson as postwar origin points of such programs—although after 1968 the initiative for most of them shifted to Capitol Hill.[22]

For another thing, it is easy to point to specific post–1968 enactments that drove up the budget. Food-stamp outlays rose tenfold

20. Robert J. Lampman, *Social Welfare Spending: Accounting for Changes from 1950 to 1978* (New York: Academic Press, 1984), pp. 8–9. The figures are for federal, state, and local governments combined, but the federal government took the lead during these years.

21. A general comment on the Nixon administration's spending record: "This active domestic spending contrasts sharply with the Nixon administration's general reputation for budgetary penury. In many ways this reputation was undeserved. It was based almost entirely on the administration's efforts to slow—not reverse—the growing costs of annually appropriated programs. Elsewhere [notably in entitlements], Nixon's record for fiscal activism bears surprising similarity to that of his Democratic predecessors." Conlan, *New Federalism*, p. 81. See also Jodie T. Allen, "Last of the Big Spenders: Richard Nixon and the Greater Society," *Washington Post*, February 24, 1983, p. A15.

22. Browning, *Politics and Social Welfare Policy*, pp. 79–83.

TABLE 4.2
New Social Programs and Regulatory Moves under Eight
Postwar Presidents

	New social programs 1946–82	New agencies regulating business 1964–77	New statutes regulating business 1962–74	New statutes regulating state & local governments 1947–80
Truman	11			0
Eisenhower	13			0
Kennedy	16		3	0
Johnson	77	2	14	8
Nixon	} 44	6	18	14
Ford		1	2	7
Carter	13	1		5
Reagan	3			

Sources:
(New social programs) Robert X. Browning, *Politics and Social Welfare Policy
in the United States* (Knoxville: University of Tennessee Press, 1986),
pp. 79–83.
(New agencies regulating business) David Vogel, "The 'New' Social
Regulation in Historical and Comparative Perspective," in Thomas K.
McCraw, ed., *Regulation in Perspective: Historical Essays* (Cambridge, Mass.:
Harvard University Press, 1981), p. 161.
(New statutes regulating business) Murray L. Weidenbaum, *Business,
Government, and the Public* (Englewood Cliffs, N.J.: Prentice-Hall, 1977),
pp. 5–10.
(New statutes regulating state & local governments) Advisory Commission
on Intergovernmental Relations, *Regulatory Federalism: Policy, Process, Impact
and Reform* (Washington, D.C.: U.S. Government Printing Office, #A-95,
February 1984), pp. 19–21. In some cases, two or more of these ACIR
"statutes" prove to be provisions of one omnibus act.

between 1969 and 1974, largely owing to a 1970 act promoted by
Nixon that federalized standards for benefits and eligibility.[23] The
Supplementary Security Income (SSI) program of 1972 broke new
ground by establishing an income floor for the aged, blind, and dis-

23. See Conlan, *New Federalism*, p. 82; Browning, *Politics and Social Welfare
Policy*, pp. 95, 110–11, 142–48. Growth in food and nutrition assistance under
Nixon "is not a latent effect of the Johnson programs. Nixon sought major
expansions in the food stamp program." Browning, p. 111. Program growth
"was very slow until the expansion proposed by President Nixon" (p. 145).

abled.[24] Publicly financed jobs for the unemployed re-emerged for the first time since the New Deal in the Emergency Employment Act (EEA) of 1971 and then the Comprehensive Employment and Training Act (CETA) of 1973.[25] Expansion of unemployment insurance, not achievable by previous presidents, took place under both Nixon in 1970 and Ford in 1976.[26] An unprecedented 1969–72 surge in housing expenditures owed mostly to Johnson's programs, but authorization acts in 1969 and 1970 and HUD Secretary George Romney's policies played a role; and although Nixon imposed a moratorium on housing spending in 1973, the Housing and Community Development Act of 1974 brought on a second, no less costly surge that lasted into the 1980s.[27]

In addition, funding for urban mass transit soared as a result of authorization acts in 1970, 1973, and 1974.[28] Control of water pollution became an expensive cause that drew $24 billion over a Nixon veto in 1972. The Higher Education Act of 1972 created new "Pell grants" to insure minimum funding for college students from lower-income families.[29] Nixon's $30 billion revenue-sharing plan to help

24. James T. Patterson, *America's Struggle against Poverty, 1900–1985* (Cambridge: Harvard University Press, 1986), pp. 197–98; Browning, *Politics and Social Welfare Policy*, pp. 110–11; Conlan, *New Federalism*, pp. 81–82.

25. Sar A. Levitan and Robert Taggart, eds., *Emergency Employment Act: The PEP Generation* (Salt Lake City: Olympus Publishing, 1974); Grace A. Franklin and Randall B. Ripley, *CETA: Politics and Policy, 1973–1982* (Knoxville: University of Tennessee Press, 1984).

26. "Nixon succeeded in another area which had eluded every previous president. Unemployment benefit coverage was expanded. Some expansion had been recommended by every president annually from Truman to Johnson." Browning, *Politics and Social Welfare Policy*, p. 161. Under Ford: Congressional Quarterly, *Congress and the Nation, 1973–1976* (Washington, D.C.: Congressional Quarterly Press, 1977), p. 709.

27. On Johnson's programs: Browning, *Politics and Social Welfare Policy*, pp. 110–11. On the 1969 and 1970 authorizations: Nathaniel S. Keith, *Politics and the Housing Crisis since 1930* (New York: Universe Books, 1973), pp. 206, 220–21. On Romney: Hays, *Federal Government and Urban Housing*, pp. 110–11. On the 1974 act: Hays, pp. 150–53.

28. Robert C. Lieb, *Transportation: The Domestic System* (Reston, Va.: Reston Publishing, 1978), pp. 260, 409–11.

29. Lawrence E. Gladieux and Thomas R. Wolanin, *Congress and the Colleges: The National Politics of Higher Education* (Lexington, Mass.: D. C. Heath, 1976), p. xi and chaps. 5, 8–10; Philip Brenner, *The Limits and Possibilities of Congress*

fund state and local governments passed by way of an odd 1972 coalition that included many northern Democratic liberals.[30] Most striking of all, perhaps, was an "explosion of social security benefits" that resulted from a sequence of enactments in 1969, 1971, and 1972. Benefit levels, controlling for inflation, rose 23 percent.[31]

In the regulatory area, Nixon's years produced more legislation than any period since the New Deal. What David Vogel calls the "new social regulation" of American industry came about during the years roughly from 1964 through 1977. The peak reform years were 1969 through 1974.[32] Ten new federal regulatory agencies were established, seven of them under Nixon and Ford (see table 4.2). The campaign for consumer protection, after spurring several enactments under Johnson, carried into the 1970s to generate, among other measures, the Consumer Product Safety Act of 1972 and the Magnuson-Moss Act of 1974. The latter empowered the Federal Trade Commission to set industry-wide rules barring unfair practices.[33] The postwar era's three most forceful environmental measures won enactment during Nixon's first term. Senator Henry Jackson's National Environmental Policy Act (NEPA) of 1969, the first, required the already mentioned "environmental impact statements." Senator Edmund Muskie's Clean Air Act of 1970 set ambitious standards and

(New York: St. Martin's Press, 1983), chap. 5 ("Domestic Policy: Restructuring Higher Education").

30. Conlan, *New Federalism*, chap. 4; A. James Reichley, *Conservatives in an Age of Change: The Nixon and Ford Administrations* (Washington, D.C.: Brookings Institution Press, 1981), pp. 154–64.

31. Derthick, *Policymaking for Social Security*, chap. 17, quotation at p. 346; Patterson, *America's Struggle against Poverty*, pp. 158, 165. On entitlements growth in general, see R. Kent Weaver, "Controlling Entitlements," chap. 11 in John E. Chubb and Paul E. Peterson, eds., *The New Direction in American Politics* (Washington, D.C.: Brookings Institution Press, 1985), pp. 311–18 ("A Decade of Expansion, 1965–74").

32. Vogel, "The 'New' Social Regulation," p. 157; Vogel, "The Power of Business in America: A Re-appraisal," *British Journal of Political Science* 13 (1983), 24. See also Richard A. Harris, "A Decade of Reform," chap. 1 in Harris and Sidney M. Milkis, eds., *Remaking American Politics* (Boulder, Colo.: Westview Press, 1989). Robert Higgs cites 1964 through 1976 as the time when "many major regulatory laws" were passed: "Under LBJ and Nixon the federal government's intrusion in the economy took another leap." *Crisis and Leviathan: Critical Episodes in the Growth of American Government* (New York: Oxford University Press, 1987), pp. 246–54, quotation at p. 246.

33. On consumer protection: Meier, *Regulation*, chap. 4.

deadlines for reduction of auto emissions. And Muskie's Water Pollution Control Act of 1972, besides being costly, set official national goals for cleaning up water.[34] Drives to protect health and safety in the workplace produced the Coal Mine Health and Safety Act of 1969 and the cross-industry Occupational Safety and Health Act (OSHA) of 1970. Both acts erected tough new standards.[35] Private pension plans came under comprehensive government regulation for the first time through the Employee Retirement Income Security Act (ERISA) of 1974.[36]

The impulse to plan extended beyond regulation of private industry. Statutory regulation of the affairs of state and local governments, such as through requirements for clean air and water and non-discrimination in public employment, set new records under Nixon and Ford (see table 4.2).[37] A case in point is the National Health Planning and Resources Development Act of 1974, which ushered those governments into unprecedented planning of the use of health resources.[38] Campaign finance received detailed and stringent federal

34. On the environment: ibid., chap. 6. See also David Vogel, *Fluctuating Fortunes: The Political Power of Business in America* (New York: Basic Books, 1989), chap. 4; John C. Whitaker, *Striking a Balance: Environment and Natural Resources Policy in the Nixon-Ford Years* (Washington, D.C.: American Enterprise Institute, 1976), chaps. 4, 5. "After decades of incrementalism and accommodation, why did Congress suddenly enact a series of relatively extreme federal environmental statutes in the early 1970s?" This question is posed in E. Donald Elliott, Bruce A. Ackerman, and John C. Millian, "Toward a Theory of Statutory Evolution: The Federalization of Environmental Law," *Journal of Law, Economics, and Organization* 1 (1985), 318.

35. On OSHA: "In late 1970, faced with the choice of vetoing or accepting a bill that included almost all of organized labor's demands, Nixon signed and took credit for it. American business was forced to accept a program that it had unconditionally rejected in 1968." Charles Noble, *Liberalism at Work: The Rise and Fall of OSHA* (Philadelphia: Temple University Press, 1986), p. 94. See also Meier, *Regulation*, chap. 8, and Levitan, Carlson, and Shapiro, *Protecting American Workers*, chap. 6. On coal mining: Michael S. Lewis-Beck and John R. Alford, "Can Government Regulate Safety? The Coal Mine Example," *American Political Science Review* 74 (1980), 745–56.

36. Levitan, Carlson, and Shapiro, *Protecting American Workers*, chap. 10.

37. Conlan, *New Federalism*, pp. 84–89. "The Nixon administration also presided over and contributed to the greatest expansion of federal regulation of state and local governments in American history" (p. 84).

38. Ibid., pp. 88–89; Odin W. Anderson, *Health Services in the United States: A Growth Enterprise since 1875* (Ann Arbor, Mich.: Health Administration Press, 1985), pp. 213–14.

regulation for the first time in the Federal Election Campaign Act of 1974. Commitments to long-term public-purpose planning of federal forests and rangelands became law through the National Forest Management Act (NFMA) of 1976 and the Federal Land Policy Management Act (FLPMA) of 1976.[39] Reaction to these two mandates figured in the West's Sagebrush Rebellion of the late 1970s, just as the era's many new constraints on private industry kindled a conservative countermobilization in the mid-1970s led by the Business Roundtable.[40] Confronted by the country's economic troubles in the early 1970s, Congress reached for planning, not market, remedies. Two instances are the Economic Stabilization Act of 1970, which authorized wage and price controls that Nixon later applied, and the Emergency Petroleum Allocation Act of 1973, which provided for allocation of oil and petroleum products by government formula.[41] The planning impulse appeared also in two major congressional moves to rationalize government processes in response to Nixon's aggressive presidency—the War Powers Act of 1973 and the Budget and Impoundment Act of 1974.[42]

39. Arrandale, *Battle for Natural Resources*, pp. 57–75.

40. On the Sagebrush Rebellion: ibid., pp. 50, 72–75; Hanna J. Cortner and Helen M. Ingram, "The Case of the Sagebrush Rebellion," chap. 7 in James L. Regens, Robert W. Rycroft, and Gregory A. Daneke, eds., *Energy and the Western United States: Politics and Development* (New York: Praeger, 1982), p. 116. On the Business Roundtable: Vogel, "Power of Business in America," pp. 34–35, 40.

41. On wage and price controls: Hugh Rockoff, *Drastic Measures: A History of Wage and Price Controls in the United States* (New York: Cambridge University Press, 1984), chap. 7. On oil allocation: Richard H. K. Vietor, *Energy Policy in America since 1945: A Study of Business-Government Relations* (New York: Cambridge University Press, 1984), chap. 10.

42. But, it may be objected, these two acts should not be allowed to augment a list of legislative accomplishments during a time of divided control. This amounts to padding. Were they not exactly a result of divided party control? Wouldn't they have been gratuitous otherwise? These questions require an empirical, not an abstract, answer. In fact, efforts to alter the power, capability, or political coloration of governmental institutions, through laws or constitutional amendments that reform structure, are normal events in the American system. They have occurred during both unified and divided times. Unified control did not ward off spirited conflict in 1937–38, for example, between Roosevelt and congressional majorities over court-packing and executive reorganization, or in 1953–54 between Eisenhower and a congressional majority over the Bricker amendment. The War Powers Act of 1973

Elsewhere on the legislative calendar, equity triumphed over economic-growth incentives in the "massive" Tax Reform Act of 1969, which Nixon did not originate but did sign. In the view of one policy expert, this was "the first clearly liberal tax bill since 1936— and the last."[43] The oil depletion allowance, which reformers had assailed for half a century, finally gave way (at least for large firms) in the Tax Reduction Act of 1975.[44] The Ninety-second Congress of 1971–72 enacted "a bumper crop of women's rights legislation—considerably more than the sum total of all relevant legislation that had been previously passed in the history of this country." Included were the ERA and provisions of the Equal Employment Opportunity Act of 1972.[45] Finally, the recasting of foreign aid in 1973 moved it away from economic development toward attending to "basic human needs" of the poorest populations abroad.[46]

Many of these enactments will be familiar to readers. But I for one, before combing through works in a variety of policy areas, had not been aware that liberal legislative victories continued in such volume right up through the mid-1970s. Most analysts would agree that Johnson's years easily outstripped Truman's, Kennedy's, or Carter's as postwar producers of liberal legislation. But Nixon's years easily did too, if taken alone—though the continuous record shown here suggests strongly that they should be coupled with Johnson's years rather

and the Budget and Impoundment Act of 1974 are arguably members of a larger set of enactments that would include, for example, the Tenure of Office Act of 1867 (UNI), the Seventeenth Amendment to elect senators directly (approved by Congress in 1912, DIV), the Executive Reorganization Act of 1939 (UNI), the Hatch Act of 1939 (UNI), the Legislative Reorganization Act of 1946 (UNI), and the Twenty-second Amendment to limit presidential terms (approved by Congress in 1947, DIV). These are an important kind of legislative initiative in the American system, and under what circumstances they occur is, again, an empirical question. On the 1973 and 1974 acts, see James L. Sundquist, *The Decline and Resurgence of Congress* (Washington, D.C.: Brookings Institution Press, 1981), chaps. 8, 9.

43. Witte, *Politics and Development of the Income Tax*, pp. 165–75, quotations at p. 166. See also Vogel, *Fluctuating Fortunes*, pp. 61–64.

44. Witte, *Politics and Development of the Income Tax*, pp. 182–87; Vietor, *Energy Policy in America*, pp. 224–29.

45. Jo Freeman, *The Politics of Women's Liberation: A Case Study of an Emerging Social Movement and Its Relation to the Policy Process* (New York: David McKay, 1975), chap. 6, quotation at p. 202.

46. Pastor, *Congress and Foreign Economic Policy*, pp. 257, 278–79.

than taken alone. The case for coupling will be considered again in chapter 6.

If single Congresses rather than the Johnson or Nixon presidencies are examined for legislative achievements, the Ninety-third Congress of 1973–74 seems to stand out. It produced the acts noted above addressing foreign aid, foreign trade, housing (block grants), agriculture (target prices), employment (CETA), mass transit, trade practices (Magnuson-Moss), private pensions (ERISA), health planning, campaign finance, war powers, and the budgetary process. For good measure, it voted a minimum wage hike, a charter for health management organizations (HMOs), Conrail's charter, and home rule for the District of Columbia (see table 4.1). That is a striking record, whether the test is sheer motion or ideological commonality (almost all these acts were liberal victories of one sort of another).[47] Since World War II, probably only the Congresses of 1965–66 under Johnson and 1981–82 under Reagan have produced more. And the Watergate investigations took place in 1973–74 also. That serves as a reminder that the mid–1960s through the mid-1970s supplied not only a liberal lawmaking surge but an accompanying series of anti-administration "exposure probes"—the Fulbright, Watergate, and Church-Pike investigations. As is shown by the extreme case of 1867–69, when Reconstruction laws won enactment while Andrew Johnson was being impeached, nothing prevents a Congress from legislating and investigating with great strenuousness at the same time. In fact, in 1973–74 as in 1867–69, one supply of ideological energy can help to fuel both activities.

None of the Nixon and Ford Congresses, however, seems to have acquired much of a reputation for legislative achievement. That is partly because none of them followed an appropriate script. Probably most of us, for evidence that vigorous lawmaking is taking place, tend to rely on the familiar narrative in which a presidential candidate presents a program, wins an election, claims a mandate, and then stages a well-publicized "hundred days" of passing laws. Reagan's conservative program, his election victory in 1980, and his resulting

47. In the cases of CETA and the housing act, both Nixon and the liberals can be said to have come out ahead. The president won decentralization of functions to state and local governments, and the liberals won CETA jobs and housing expenditures.

legislative drive in 1981 are a case in point.[48] Lyndon Johnson, the inheritor in 1963 of a liberal program that had been taking shape for nearly a decade, enjoyed in effect two separate "hundred day" stretches of highlighted lawmaking. His party's landslide victory in the 1964 election drew the media to his legislative agenda in 1965. But previously, President Kennedy's assassination in 1963 had allowed Johnson to set forth a script of "let us continue" that helped to structure his quite effective legislative campaign in 1964. Kennedy's major bills still needed to be passed.[49]

But no such familiar or engaging script fit the Nixon and Ford experience. Nixon entered office without much of a program, and the New Federalism he later proposed did not catch on as a commanding national agenda. There was never a "hundred days." In 1969 and later, statutes tended to pass in a jumble at the close of a Congress rather than according to someone's plan at the start of one.[50] Legislation moved along not all that visibly under a canopy of verbal shellfire about Vietnam, Nixon's and Agnew's "social issues," the "imperial presidency," and Watergate. When legislating did make headlines, often they were caused by sharp conflict between Nixon and congressional Democrats that ended by leaving government policy roughly where it had been in the first place. That happened, for example, in the area of elementary and secondary education.[51] Journalists, in effect, deprived of an opportunity for a carry-out-the-mandate script, tended to reach for a deadlock-between-institutions counter-script that probably under-reported real legislative motion.[52]

48. The "hundred days" here is metaphorical. Reagan's drive took longer.

49. Rowland Evans, Jr., and Robert Novak, *Lyndon B. Johnson: The Exercise of Power* (New York: New American Library, 1966), pp. 348–50. "The assassination had a profound impact on congressional politics. It abruptly changed the atmosphere on Capitol Hill during the latter stages of the Eighty-eighth Congress from one of intransigence and obstruction to a collective attitude of guilt, fatigue, and reluctant cooperation with the White House." Eugene Eidenberg and Roy D. Morey, *An Act of Congress: The Legislative Process and the Making of Education Policy* (New York: W. W. Norton, 1969), pp. 30–31.

50. As in 1990 under Bush.

51. Orfield, *Congressional Power*, chaps. 7, 8.

52. This may help to explain why, in chapter 3, Sweep Two's retrospective methodology added on a particularly large number of laws during the Nixon-Ford years. Sweep One's contemporary methodology had "missed" them, so to speak.

In general, it was hard for journalists or others to grasp what was going on in a process that followed a model, if any, of creative disorder. Policy specialists since then have had no difficulty tracking the Nixon and Ford era's major enactments in their fields, but no one has written a dramatic, comprehensive story about lawmaking during the Nixon and Ford years of the sort that James L. Sundquist told about Johnson's Great Society.[53] There does not seem to exist a suitable script.[54]

With scripts, the discussion has moved away from long "ideological surges" toward the second variant of holism introduced earlier— "ideological programs" set forth by presidents. These will now be taken up directly. Such programs are a basic mechanism of American politics, featuring as they do a route to legislative action, highly publicized presidential leadership, a claimed electoral connection, ideology as a way of presenting a general cross-issue stance to the mass public, and ideology also as a means of harnessing the energy and allegiance of political activists—Progressives, New Dealers, Reaganites, and the like. Not every president presents a program that is at once legislatively ambitious and ideologically invigorating. Since 1946, in addition to Johnson's Great Society, we have experienced probably three. These are Truman's Fair Deal, which had its chance for enactment in 1949–50 after Democratic recapture of Congress in 1948; Kennedy's New Frontier in 1961; and Reagan's program to roll back the public sector in 1981. By contrast, the programs presented by Eisenhower, Nixon, Ford, Carter, and Bush proved to be relatively unexciting to core party activists or unambitious or both.

The point in singling out the Truman, Kennedy, Johnson, and Reagan programs is to allow some comparative analysis. Ideological programs are sets of proposals, not achievements. Some succeed on Capitol Hill, some do not. It becomes an interesting question how

53. Sundquist, *Politics and Policy*. Reichley's *Conservatives in an Age of Change* is an authoritative treatment of legislative action during 1969–76, but just of action involving the Nixon-Ford agenda—not Congress's.

54. Whether table 4.1's laws had a place in a suitable script probably influenced whether contemporary observers thought they were of extraordinary, historic importance. That, though the evidence is soft, was the criterion for printing nineteen measures in capital letters in the table. Some laws that did not achieve capital-letter status—for example, the Clean Air Act of 1970— might have done so if presidents had provided an appropriate public framing for their enactment. One can imagine what Theodore Roosevelt would have done with the Clean Air Act.

their success or failure maps onto whether party control of government is unified or divided. In fact, between 1946 and 1988, unified control proved neither a necessary nor a sufficient condition for a president's success. Truman's Fair Deal largely failed. In the judgment of one analyst, Truman was "only slightly more successful in dealing with the Democratic Eighty-first and Eighty-second Congresses than he had been with the discredited Republican Eightieth."[55] Victories occurred on housing, Social Security, and a few other matters. But the administration's Brannan Plan for agriculture foundered on Capitol Hill, repeal of the Taft-Hartley Act did not come close, and plans for civil rights, national health insurance, and federal aid to education went nowhere. One can read the legislative history in table 4.1 from 1947 through, say, 1960 and not realize that the Fair Deal Congress of 1949–50 was supposed to stand out.[56]

Kennedy did little better in 1961–63. He too enjoyed some victories. But Democratic Congresses rejected his farm program, buried his education bill in committee, refused to move on Medicare, held over his heralded tax cut until after he was assassinated, and discouraged him from proposing any legislation at all on civil rights until after the Birmingham demonstrations in 1963. As in Truman's case, Kennedy's most notable Capitol Hill victories came in foreign affairs—the Trade Expansion Act of 1962 and the test-ban treaty in 1963.

Johnson's domestic program of course succeeded. But so did Reagan's, insofar as judgments can be pronounced on such matters. One goes as follows: "Very few Presidents can claim legislative triumphs that are truly turning points in domestic policy. In this century, Franklin D. Roosevelt and Lyndon B. Johnson can legitimately make that case.... Ronald Reagan could claim such a breakthrough in 1981."[57] Like Johnson, but unlike Truman or Kennedy, Reagan won the major

55. William Frank Zornow, *America at Mid-Century* (Cleveland: Howard Allen, 1959), pt. 1, *The Truman Administration*, p. 113.

56. Particularly in the case of national health insurance, one interpretation of Truman's role is that he was trying less to get a reform enacted immediately than to educate the public to accept it eventually. That may be, but it says something about what unified party control— as in 1949–50—can and cannot achieve.

57. Charles O. Jones, "Ronald Reagan and the U.S. Congress: Visible-Hand Politics," chap. 2 in Jones, ed., *The Reagan Legacy: Promise and Performance* (Chatham, N.J.: Chatham House, 1988), p. 37. For an analysis of the distinctive effects of Reagan's budgetary program, see Mark S. Kamlet, David C.

legislation he asked for. For Truman and Kennedy, unified party control proved insufficient; for Reagan, it proved unnecessary.[58]

Explanations of these and other patterns will be attempted in chapters 5 and 6, but one point is worth making here. These Truman, Kennedy, Johnson, and Reagan results did not owe just to some timeless arithmetic having to do with proportions of congressional seats

---

Mowery, and Tsai-Tsu Su, "Upsetting National Priorities? The Reagan Administration's Budgetary Strategy," *American Political Science Review* 82 (1988), 1293–1307.

58. Single important acts (the 267) and comprehensive presidential programs (such as the Great Society) have been discussed. Is there a class of undertakings in between? As judged by scope, perceived importance, and rank on either Congress's or the president's agenda? Lloyd N. Cutler evidently aims in between in claiming that "there has never been in modern days any successful domestic legislative program at a time of divided government" *except* Reagan's 1981 tax cut and the Tax Reform Act of 1986. "Some Reflections about Divided Government," *Presidential Studies Quarterly* 18 (1988), 490. Perhaps these two ambitious moves deserve to be called "programs." (For one thing, they are among the nineteen acts capitalized in table 4.1 because contemporary observers judged them to be of historic significance.) But are these two in fact the only members of their class? Probably not. Here are a dozen other acts, or small clusters of acts, that passed during divided control between 1946 and 1990 and that seem to occupy the same intermediate niche. (1) The Republicans' labor-management relations program in 1947 (Taft-Hartley amounted to that). (2) Eisenhower's space program in 1958 (NASA, NDEA, and DOD reorganization). (3) The bipartisan civil rights "program" of 1957 (the 1957 act). (4) Eisenhower's budget-balancing program of 1957–60. (5) The bipartisan environmental drive of around 1970 (NEPA, clean air, clean water). (6) The cross-party entitlements expansion program during Nixon's first term (food stamps, Social Security, unemployment insurance, finally SSI though not the Family Assistance Plan). (7) Nixon's New Federalism (revenue sharing, housing block grants, decentralized manpower training). (8) Nixon's energy program of 1973–74. (9) Congress's program in 1973–74, during Watergate, to rein in the presidency and reform elections (the War Powers Act, budget reform, campaign finance reform, freedom of information). (10) Gramm-Latta II in 1981 (Reagan's expenditure cuts). (11) Speaker Jim Wright's domestic program of 1987–88 (welfare reform, catastrophic health insurance, housing, homeless aid, Grove City civil rights). (12) Bush's 1990 program, as laundered by the Democrats, to reduce the budget deficit by a half-trillion dollars over five years. On Eisenhower's space program, see Walter A. McDougall, *The Heavens and the Earth: A Political History of the Space Age* (New York: Basic Books, 1985), chap. 7. On Eisenhower's budget-balancing drive, see Iwan W. Morgan, *Eisenhower Versus "the Spenders": The Eisenhower Administration, the Democrats, and the Budget, 1953–60* (London: Pinter, 1990), chaps. 5–7 and Conclusions. "Despite being the majority party in Congress

held by Republicans, loyalist Democrats, and southern Democratic "boll weevils." Southern defectors from Democratic ranks unquestionably impeded Truman and Kennedy and helped Reagan. American parties tend to be like that. But consider Reagan. His victories on Capitol Hill would have been quite unlikely without changes that took place in the American political and intellectual climate during the late 1970s. In general, a reaction seems to have set in against government planning and spending. This manifested itself in, among other things, a winning drive to deregulate several industries, the Sagebrush Rebellion, a surprising business-oriented revision of the tax code in 1978, and California's Proposition 13 tax revolt in 1978, not to mention Reagan's campaign and election itself in 1980. By 1981 Reagan had a receptive audience. It is still startling to read that his tax cut and Gramm-Latta II cleared the Senate by votes of 89–11 and 80–15. The boll weevils supplied key assistance in the House. But where were the weevils—and the arithmetic—back under Nixon when their conservative causes needed them?

Mention of the Fair Deal and New Frontier can introduce an inquiry that was promised earlier. What did *not* pass between 1946 and 1990? What proposals were "much talked about" as potential laws but, for whatever reasons, did not win enactment? This question could perhaps be investigated directly and rigorously, but the methodology here is indirect and less than rigorous. It is a byproduct of Sweeps One and Two conducted for chapter 3. To be noted here are proposals whose failure to win passage caused what seemed to be prominent comment in the journalistic and other materials collected for those two sweeps. The results may at least jog readers' memories about old lost causes. What ever became of, for example, universal military training, the proposed consumer protection agency, or repeal of the right-to-work clause (14b) of the Taft-Hartley Act?

In the Truman era, the Republican Eightieth Congress of 1947–48 (DIV) proved unreceptive to presidential proposals that addressed housing (which Senator Taft championed also), the minimum wage, social security, national health insurance, civil rights, federal aid to education, universal military training, and construction of TVA systems in other river valleys.[59] The Democratic Eighty-first Congress of

for most of the Eisenhower era, the Democrats had come off second best in the budgetary battles" (p. 180).

59. Harold F. Gosnell, *Truman's Crises: A Political Biography of Harry S Truman* (Westport, Conn.: Greenwood Press, 1980), chap. 26; Susan M. Hartmann,

1949–50 (UNI) acted on the first three of these, stalled on the other five, and rejected two new major Truman requests—the Brannan Plan for subsidizing agriculture and repeal of the Taft-Hartley Act.[60] Nothing changed on any of the above during the Democratic Eighty-second Congress (UNI).[61] Conservative proposals that failed during these years are hard to track, but three significant ones come to light. In a victory of sorts for unified control, a Mundt-Nixon initiative that failed in 1948 (DIV) did later come alive and triumph as the McCarran Internal Security Act of 1950 (UNI).[62] Truman vetoed a bill to deregulate natural gas in 1950 and one to turn over oil tidelands to the coastal states in 1952.[63] The Taft-Hartley Act, it should be noted, won enactment under conditions of divided control in 1947 after a similar bill had lost out under unified control in 1946.[64]

Rarely in American history has a party not controlling the Senate, House, or presidency taken over all three at once. That has occurred only in 1800, 1840, and 1952. The Republicans in 1953, one might have thought, would immediately enact a long list of ready-made proposals they had been advocating for years. In fact, only one reasonably significant act followed that model—the tidelands oil act

Truman and the Eightieth Congress (Columbia: University of Missouri Press, 1971), pp. 22–25, 71–74, 94–95, chap. 6, pp. 169–72; Zornow, *America at Mid-Century*, pt. 1, pp. 38–42.

60. Barton J. Bernstein, "Economic Policies," in Richard S. Kirkendall, ed., *The Truman Period as a Research Field* (Columbia: University of Missouri Press, 1967), pp. 111–21; Donovan, *Tumultuous Years: The Presidency of Harry S Truman, 1949–1953* (New York: W. W. Norton, 1982), chap. 11; Gosnell, *Truman's Crises*, chap. 34; Zornow, *America at Mid-Century*, pt. 1, pp. 113–17; *New Republic*, October 24, 1949, p. 7; *New York Times*, September 10, 1950, p. IV:12, September 24, 1950, p. I:94; *Washington Post*, October 20, 1949, pp. A1, A3.

61. Donovan, *Tumultuous Years*, pp. 365–69; Gosnell, *Truman's Crises*, chap. 37; Zornow, *America at Mid-Century*, pt. 1, pp. 121–27; *New York Times*, October 21, 1951, pp. I:1, 55, IV:2, July 6, 1952, p. IV:4; *Washington Post*, October 21, 1951, p. 1B, July 6, 1952, p. 6M.

62. Donovan, *Tumultuous Years*, pp. 295–96. On 1950, see also William W. Keller, *The Liberals and J. Edgar Hoover: Rise and Fall of a Domestic Intelligence State* (Princeton, N.J.: Princeton University Press, 1989), pp. 36–65.

63. On natural gas: Vietor, *Energy Policy in America*, pp. 76–82. On tidelands oil: Gary W. Reichard, *The Reaffirmation of Republicanism: Eisenhower and the Eighty-third Congress* (Knoxville: University of Tennessee Press, 1975), pp. 149–50.

64. Hartmann, *Truman and the Eightieth Congress*, pp. 5–6, 79–90; R. Alton

of 1953.[65] In general, Eisenhower enjoyed success with the Republican Eighty-third Congress of 1953–54 (UNI), though some items of middle-level priority failed to pass—his plans for revising the Taft-Hartley and McCarran-Walter acts and for Hawaiian statehood.[66] And he had to wait for a Democratic Congress in 1955 (DIV) to extract a satisfactory multi-year foreign-trade bill.[67] Hawaiian statehood came later in 1959 (DIV). On the congressional side, the Bricker amendment to curb presidential treaty-making powers failed in 1954 (UNI).[68] Not many thwarted Republican or conservative initiatives arise from the record of Eisenhower's last six years. To cite two, Eisenhower like Truman vetoed a producer-oriented natural gas bill in 1956 (DIV), and Senate Majority Leader Lyndon Johnson blocked, in 1958 (DIV), a family of measures aimed at curbing the Supreme Court's authority in the area of civil liberties.[69] In the late 1950s (DIV), a growing program of stalled liberal Democratic initiatives came to preoccupy Congress and the press. These called for action on housing, the minimum wage, area redevelopment, civil rights, medical care for the aged, and federal aid to elementary and secondary education.[70]

Enter Kennedy (UNI), who like Truman won enactments that he wanted on housing and the minimum wage (as well as area redevelopment), but could not crack the tougher nuts of civil rights, health insurance (for the aged, this time), and federal aid to education. Democratic Congresses also blocked or outwaited him on agriculture, aid to higher education, his Keynesian tax cut, a wilderness program,

Lee, *Truman and Taft-Hartley: A Question of Mandate* (Lexington: University Press of Kentucky, 1966), chaps. 2–4.

65. Reichard, *Reaffirmation of Republicanism*, pp. 148–53.

66. Ibid., pp. 85–87, 143–46; *New York Times*, August 4, 1953, pp. 1, 13, August 21, 1954, pp. 1, 8, 9.

67. Reichard, *Reaffirmation of Republicanism*, pp. 77–84; Raymond A. Bauer, Ithiel de Sola Pool, and Lewis Anthony Dexter, *American Business and Public Policy: The Politics of Foreign Trade* (New York: Atherton, 1963), chaps. 2–5.

68. Reichard, *Reaffirmation of Republicanism*, pp. 58–68; Duane Tananbaum, *The Bricker Amendment Controversy: A Test of Eisenhower's Presidential Leadership* (Ithaca, N.Y.: Cornell University Press, 1988), chap. 10 ("Showdown in the Senate").

69. On natural gas: Vietor, *Energy Policy in America*, pp. 84–89; Evans and Novak, *Lyndon B. Johnson*, pp. 153–54. On curbing the Court: ibid., pp. 164–67; Walter F. Murphy, *Congress and the Court: A Case Study in the American Political Process* (Chicago: University of Chicago Press, 1962), chaps. 6–9.

70. Evans and Novak, *Lyndon B. Johnson*, chap. 10; *New York Times*, September

creation of a department of housing, and expansion of unemployment insurance.[71] Major action on all these fronts but the last occurred under Johnson in 1964–68 (UNI), when the old liberal calendar more or less cleared. But Democratic Congresses blocked Johnson in 1966 on repeal of the right-to-work clause (14b) of Taft-Hartley, home rule for the District of Columbia, and expansion of unemployment insurance—and in 1968 on ratification of a nuclear non-proliferation treaty.[72] The last three items passed later under Nixon (DIV). Repeal of 14b has never succeeded.

Nixon's most prominent legislative initiative to suffer defeat was his costly Family Assistance Plan (FAP), a casualty of Senate opposition in 1972.[73] From the conservative side during Nixon's years, various measures to curb school busing for racial balance emerged and foundered.[74] An ambitious protectionist trade bill fostered by the House failed in 1969–70.[75] The Ford administration's drives to decontrol oil and natural gas markets made, respectively, disappointing and no progress.[76] After about 1972, a growing menu of unenacted liberal initiatives came to include comprehensive health insurance, a new consumer protection agency, federal no-fault auto insurance, gun

14, 1959, pp. 1, 24, July 3, 1960, pp. IV:5, 6, September 2, 1960, p. 10; *Washington Post*, September 16, 1959, p. A1, September 2, 1960, p. A14. The most illuminating source is Sundquist, *Politics and Policy*, chaps. 2–8.

71. *New York Times*, September 28, 1961, p. 32, October 14, 1962, pp. I:1, 65, IV:8, October 15, 1962, p. 23, December 22, 1963, pp. I:27, IV:2, January 5, 1964, p. IV:8; *Washington Post*, September 28, 1961, pp. A1, A2. See also Evans and Novak, *Lyndon B. Johnson*, pp. 361–65; Sundquist, *Politics and Policy*, pp. 180–95 (on elementary and secondary education), 254–65 (on civil rights), 308–17 (on Medicare); Theodore R. Marmor, *The Politics of Medicare* (Chicago: Aldine, 1973), chap. 3; Anderson, *Health Services in the United States*, pp. 163–69 (on Medicare); Hugh Douglas Price, "Race, Religion, and the Rules Committee: The Kennedy Aid-to-Education Bills," chap. 1 in Alan F. Westin, ed., *The Uses of Power: Seven Cases in American Politics* (New York: Harcourt, Brace and World, 1962).

72. Evans and Novak, *Lyndon B. Johnson*, pp. 499–500; *New York Times*, October 23, 1965, pp. 1, 28, October 25, 1965, p. 40, October 24, 1966, p. 35, October 15, 1968, pp. 1, 35, 46.

73. Reichley, *Conservatives in an Age of Change*, chap. 7; Daniel P. Moynihan, *The Politics of a Guaranteed Income: The Nixon Administration and the Family Assistance Plan* (New York: Random House, 1973), chaps. 6, 7.

74. Reichley, *Conservatives in an Age of Change*, chap. 9.

75. Pastor, *Congress and Foreign Economic Policy*, pp. 124–28.

76. Reichley, *Conservatives in an Age of Change*, pp. 365–73.

control, reform of the criminal code, organized labor's common situs picketing bill, and regulation of strip mining.[77]

Carter's Ninety-fifth Congress of 1977–78 (UNI), despite Democratic majorities of 62–38 in the Senate and 292–143 in the House, proved to be a cemetery for liberal aspirations.[78] Strip- mining reform passed, but plans for national health insurance and the consumer protection agency came to nothing.[79] Labor suffered decisive defeats on its basic agenda items of common situs picketing and fortifying the right to organize.[80] The Humphrey-Hawkins bill to guarantee full employment passed in caricature form. Carter got nowhere during his four years with initiatives on welfare reform, hospital cost containment, and election-day voter registration. Reform of campaign finance and the criminal code absorbed energy without result in the Ninety-sixth Congress of 1979–80 (UNI); a version of the latter won enactment later under Reagan in 1984 (DIV). Finally, Carter's SALT II treaty foundered in the Senate in 1980 (UNI)—the only such loss suffered by a president on a major U.S.-Soviet undertaking since World War II.[81]

In 1981–82 (DIV), Reagan had less success with his version of "new federalism"—devolution of powers to the states—than with his tax and spending proposals. Throughout the two Reagan terms (DIV), needed votes never materialized for the conservative side's plan for

77. *New York Times*, December 22, 1974, pp. I:1, 27, December 21, 1975, p. I:30, December 23, 1975, p. 22, October 3, 1976, pp. I:1, 20; *Washington Post*, December 23, 1973, p. A2, December 26, 1973, p. A18, December 21, 1974, pp. A1, A6. On common situs picketing: Reichley, *Conservatives in an Age of Change*, pp. 395–96.

78. See Vogel, "Power of Business in America," pp. 38–40; Vogel, *Fluctuating Fortunes*, chap. 7; and Thomas B. Edsall, "Congress Turns Rightward," *Dissent* 25 (Winter 1978), 12–18.

79. On the consumer protection agency: Haynes Johnson, *In the Absence of Power: Governing America* (New York: Viking, 1980), pp. 233–41.

80. Thomas Byrne Edsall, *The New Politics of Inequality* (New York: W. W. Norton, 1984), pp. 134–35, 149–50; Vogel, *Fluctuating Fortunes*, pp. 150–59.

81. The Soviet invasion of Afghanistan finally sank Salt II, but even before that Carter was having considerable trouble mobilizing the two-thirds of the Senate needed for ratification. See Dan Caldwell, "The Salt II Treaty Ratification Debate and Domestic Politics" (Paper presented at the 1990 Annual Meeting of the American Political Science Association). On 1977–80 in general: Jimmy Carter, *Keeping Faith: Memoirs of a President* (New York: Bantam Books, 1982), pp. 83–89, 224–25, 261–65; *New York Times*, December 18, 1977, pp. I:1, 38, IV:2, October 16, 1978, p. 6, October 17, 1978, p. 51,

tuition tax credits, or for constitutional amendments to ban abortion, authorize school prayer, require balanced budgets, and institute the line-item veto.[82] Cross-party protectionist initiatives foundered. A nuclear-freeze resolution advanced by the liberal side lost in the Senate in 1983. In Reagan's later years, as under Eisenhower and Nixon-Ford, liberals gained the spotlight for a number of initiatives that remained aspirations as of December 1988—on health insurance for the unemployed, campaign finance reform, paid parental leave, the minimum wage, and day care.[83]

Bush and the 101st Congress acted on the last two items, but stalled on a capital-gains tax cut, an anti-flag-burning amendment, expansion of capital punishment, campaign finance reform, parental leave, and a civil rights measure aimed at job discrimination (vetoed by the president).[84] Today, civil rights initiatives are more likely to lose out to presidential vetoes—though Reagan had one overridden in 1988 (DIV)—than to real or anticipated Capitol Hill opposition as happened under Truman and Kennedy (both UNI).

What can one say? Many initiatives rise to prominence. Many fail and are forgotten. Some lose at first but succeed later. Sometimes a loss is retrieved after a shift from divided to unified party control. Sometimes a shift in the other direction seems to help. A switch to a presidency like Johnson's evidently helps a great deal. But there is no easy formula for such retrievals. Most of all, perhaps, failures occur all the time—even in what would seem the most favorable political circumstances. The course is tough and not easily predictable.

November 6, 1978, p. 51, December 22, 1979, p. 38, December 17, 1980, p. A30; *Washington Post*, October 16, 1978, pp. A1, A8, December 21, 1979, p. A3, December 14, 1980, p. A2.

82. On the failure of a school prayer amendment in 1983–84: Matthew C. Moen, *The Christian Right and Congress* (Tuscaloosa: University of Alabama Press, 1989), chap. 8.

83. On 1981–88: *New York Times*, December 19, 1981, p. 14, December 25, 1982, pp. 1, 5, December 26, 1982, p. IV:4, November 20, 1983, pp. I:1, 38, October 14, 1984, pp. 1, 32, December 22, 1985, pp. I:1, 26, IV:1, October 19, 1986, pp. I:1, 30, December 27, 1987, p. IV:4, October 24, 1988, pp. A1, B7; *Washington Post*, December 17, 1981, p. A2, November 20, 1983, pp. A1, A6, December 23, 1987, p. A6, October 23, 1988, pp. A4, A5.

84. *New York Times*, November 19, 1989, p. IV:1, November 24, 1989, pp. A1, B22, October 29, 1990, pp. A1, A15; *Washington Post National Weekly Edition*, December 4–10, 1989, p. 13, November 5–11, 1990, pp. 8, 27; *Los Angeles Times*, October 28, 1990, pp. A1, A24.

5 ◆ EXPLAINING

THE PATTERNS, I

T he lawmaking non-pattern of chapter 4 proves to resemble the investigating one of chapter 2. Neither result allows a flat claim that unified as opposed to divided party control makes "no difference." The evidence cannot simply be added up into a verdict. But a judgment of at least "very little difference" seems safe in each case, even taking into account Watergate's probes and the Great Society's laws.

Why is this? One answer can be dismissed. It is not as if parties do not amount to anything in American national politics. They amount to a great deal. Although scarcely monoliths, they do advance different policies and ideologies, mobilize distinctive coalitions, and contend against each other regularly in Washington. A president ordinarily depends on his own party's House and Senate members. Party affiliation does well as a predictor of congressional roll-call voting. Conflict between the parties' core loyalists is probably as intense, if that could be measured, as in most European capitals. It rose to levels of bitterness under Truman and Nixon. So a finding that divided party control diminishes lawmaking and augments hostile investigating would hardly come as a surprise. But those effects do not occur, or at least they do not occur very prominently. What is it that evens things out, so to speak, across circumstances of unified and divided control?

If I were aware of one over-arching, integrated answer to this question, I would try to present it here. But I doubt that one is achievable. For one thing, there seem to exist, in principle and in practice, not one but three distinct kinds of *counter-pattern* to the conventionally hypothesized pattern regarding party control—that is, the one that associates divided control with less lawmaking and more investigating. Any of the three counter-patterns, taken to the limit, can entirely neutralize the conventional pattern. Yet each counter-pattern points toward its own variety of explanations of why the conventional hypothesis might fail. These explanations, turned upside down, amount to positive statements about why lawmaking and investigations might take place when they actually do.

The first counter-pattern is one of *alternative variation* over time. By this I mean alternative to a conventional unified-versus-divided-control pattern, but still showing temporal variation. To take a bizarre case, suppose we discovered that important lawmaking takes place during leap years, to the same extent each leap year, and never at any other time. In this scenario, lawmaking would probably come out even across times of unified as opposed to divided party control. And to explain why it does—and beyond that, why lawmaking takes place when it does—our minds no doubt would wander to theories involving leap years. We might zero in on presidential elections, which always occur then. In fact, plenty of "alternative variation" comes to light in the records of 1946 through 1990 (though it does not bear a leap-year versus non-leap-year profile). Lawmaking and investigating display obvious ups and downs that are unrelated to any pattern of unified versus divided control. These ups and downs invite distinctive exercises in generalizing or theorizing.

The second counter-pattern is one of *constancy*. Suppose we discovered that exactly equal amounts of important lawmaking always take place during all two-year inter-election periods. Nothing ever changes. That would eliminate differences between periods of unified as opposed to divided party control, and it would push us toward accounts of lawmaking that would accommodate the constancy. In fact, it is impossible to stare at the postwar lawmaking or investigative data very long without concluding that a tendency toward constancy is one important thing going on. Constancy is not easy to address; it lacks the convenient handles of variation. But it should not be by-passed for that reason; in the present context it calls for lines of speculation about why lawmaking or investigating might amount to just one item after another, year after year.

The third counter-pattern is one of *compensation*. The discussion so far has assumed that the effects of unified versus divided control go all one way. But a distinction is in order; in fact, the patterns arrived at in chapters 2 and 4 show the *net* effects of unified versus divided control. What if some particular effects push in, so to speak, the wrong direction? As an analogy, suppose we were investigating a theory that economic "good times," when contrasted with "bad times," cause an upsurge in human happiness. No doubt they do, on balance, for the expected reasons, but they may nevertheless cause increased gloominess among masochists, bankruptcy lawyers, economists who made false predictions, the envious who see more Cadillacs, and environmentalists who worry about boom-times pollution. These are compensating effects. They form their own pattern. Add up enough of them and the primary, "correct-direction" theory fails. Surprisingly, in the realm of unified versus divided party control there seems to exist at least one compensating effect.

These three counter-patterns inform the analysis in this chapter and the next, which are attempts to explain the "evened-out" non-patterns arrived at in chapters 2 and 4. The discussion is organized under six different rubrics: electoral incentives, presidential leadership, and broad congressional majorities in chapter 5; and external events, issue cleavages, and public moods in chapter 6. In general, though the distinction is not carried out strictly, the first three subjects have to do with politicians and governmental processes, the second three with external influences that impinge on government. The treatment throughout is speculative, and the set of topics does not aim to be exhaustive. Left out, for example, is a discussion of "norms" connected with both lawmaking (do it assiduously) and investigating (go after iniquity) that unquestionably animate many House and Senate members and no doubt help as much as anything to even out activity over times of unified and divided party control.[1] Norms push toward *constancy*. But I could not think of anything illuminating to say about them. The arguments chosen for development below were ones that seemed to promise some analytic leverage as well as some less than wholly obvious moves.

ELECTORAL INCENTIVES

Whatever else they aspire to do, politicians need to try to win elections. Are there ways in which ordinary electoral incentives help to "even out" lawmaking or investigating across times of unified as opposed to divided control? The answer seems to be yes, though the subject is complicated.

Let us start with the electoral drives of individual House and Senate members and the realm of lawmaking. Notwithstanding the parties,

1. These seem to have been Jimmy Stewart's two main impulses in the movie *Mr. Smith Goes to Washington*: Pass laws and denounce iniquity.

members of Congress normally have to build and tend their own personal electoral bases. To that end, they need to engage nonstop in self-promotional "advertising," "credit claiming," and "position taking." These are individualistic enterprises.[2] The implication is as follows: If members can believably claim credit for taking the steps to win passage of important legislation, no doubt they will work just as hard at those steps and aim for as much electoral profit in divided times as in unified times. Why wouldn't they?

Still, the case needs considerable qualification. Most members lack both the influence to move important bills and the visibility to register an impression that they did so. They can only "take positions" on issues or measures—a course that stops well short of actually packaging and driving through enactments. The electoral incentive thus fails to connect with any enactment incentive.[3] But some members do possess the necessary influence, will, eye for electoral gain, and visibility or the prospect of achieving it. Some senior committee or subcommittee chairmen qualify. One well-documented instance is Senator Warren Magnuson, chairman of the Senate Commerce Committee, who nearly lost an election in 1962 and afterwards sought "prominence as a national legislative leader" in order to stave off further trouble. A result was the Fair Packaging and Labeling Act of 1966.[4] Senator Walter F. George of Georgia, facing a difficult Democratic primary in 1956, made a surprising yet credible move to establish himself as author of that year's disability insurance act.[5] Senator Claiborne Pell, a subcommittee chairman running a sagging re-election campaign in 1972, helped to usher through that year's higher-education "Pell grants" as, for one thing, an achievement he could claim credit for.[6] The three acts discussed here all appear in table 4.1. House members aiming for the Senate, especially in large states, probably gain from well-publicized lawmaking maneuvers. One suspects

2. See the argument in David R. Mayhew, *Congress: The Electoral Connection* (New Haven and London: Yale University Press, 1974), pt. 1.

3. Ibid., pp. 61–73, 85–87, 97–102, 110–36.

4. David E. Price, *Who Makes the Laws? Creativity and Power in Senate Committees* (Cambridge, Mass.: Schenkman, 1972), pp. 25–37, quotation at p. 29.

5. Martha Derthick, *Policymaking for Social Security* (Washington, D.C.: Brookings Institution Press, 1979), pp. 305–07.

6. "He was up for re-election in 1972 and faced a stiff challenge. In fact, in the spring of 1972, during the conference [committee negotiations], he was rated a distinct underdog. Part of his re-election problem was his record of

that Phil Gramm's role in advancing Gramm-Latta II in 1981 helped along his winning campaign for a Texas Senate seat in 1984.

In general, House and Senate members run for re-election, and House members seek Senate seats, regardless of background circumstances of unified or divided party control. The above arguments therefore predict a systemic thrust toward lawmaking *constancy*. Another strand of logic goes one better to raise the possibility of *compensation*. It proceeds as follows. House and Senate members influential enough to maneuver laws through Congress—that is, particularly committee and subcommittee chairmen of the majority party—can gain somewhat more electoral credit for doing so if they are *not* members of the president's party. This is because committee chairmen who happen to belong to the president's party tend to work in the shadow of the White House; legislative proposals they handle tend to be identified as presidential agenda items; surrounding publicity tends to go to the president. If effective lone-wolf lawmaking is less likely to earn electoral points, as it may be in the circumstance of White House overshadowing, then it may happen less. It will come into its own when committee chairmen do *not* belong to the president's party—that is, when party control is divided. This is an argument for *compensation*, since it predicts divergent unified-versus-divided-control effects in the "wrong" direction. The case is intriguing, and it may have some value, though I do not see a solid evidential basis for it in the record of 1946 through 1990. It is best to suspend judgment. A safer conclusion is the earlier one that electoral incentives nudge the system toward lawmaking *constancy*.

But electoral drives to stay in place or rise to the Senate are not the only ones that send pulses surging on Capitol Hill. There is also the presidency. One feature that jumps from the record of 1946–90 is effective lawmaking by members of Congress aiming for the presidency—especially senators. In what amounts to a credentialing process, they try to show they can do more than just talk. By actually putting through bills, they compete to exhibit the vision, responsibility, and talent for wheeling and dealing that are thought to be needed in the White House. It is the old Henry Clay or Stephen Douglas role.

---

legislative accomplishment, which, at least to the public eye, looked rather scanty. Guiding the Education Amendments, with the 'Pell Grants' included, into law would be an important achievement bolstering his record." Lawrence E. Gladieux and Thomas R. Wolanin, *Congress and the Colleges: The National Politics of Higher Education* (Lexington, Mass.: D. C. Heath, 1976), p. 172.

It emerges again and again in the legislative history of the last four decades. And an interesting pattern comes to light. Presidential aspirants who win headline attention by securing passage of bills tend to be members of a party that controls Congress though not the White House.

Here both logic and evidence make a good case for a *compensation* effect. The logic is better than that for sub-presidential electoral incentives. When power is divided, not only can congressional influentials operate as legislators outside the White House shadow, they have an open shot at the White House. Their party, not holding that office, is likely on average to generate more Capitol Hill aspirants for it. This is because ambitious members of Congress are likelier to maneuver for the presidency if their own party lacks a presidential incumbent who can run again or an heir apparent like Nixon in 1960. In short, under conditions of divided party control, a larger number of members of Congress than otherwise will at once possess the means (control of legislative levers), command the publicity (less White House shadow for out-party legislators), and harbor the immediate ambition (an open shot at the White House) that make for ostentatious lawmaking in the service of presidential aims.

That is the logic. In general, the pattern of evidence from 1946–90 backs it up. Two especially well-documented cases of lawmaking correlated with presidential ambition involve Democratic Senators Edmund S. Muskie and Lyndon B. Johnson. Muskie, as chairman of a relevant Senate subcommittee in the late 1960s, one account goes, "sought to associate his name so intimately with environmental protection that he would effectively preempt efforts by rival aspirants [to the presidency] to claim credit for legislation on the issue." In 1970 he piloted through the Clean Air Act against a background of contestation with President Nixon over who could do more for the environment.[7] That initiative was an achievement Muskie could exhibit in 1971, according to another account, when he "seemed likely to be the Democratic presidential nominee in 1972 and had made the environment a centerpiece of his campaign."[8] The Johnson instance is

7. E. Donald Elliott, Bruce A. Ackerman, and John C. Millian, "Toward a Theory of Statutory Evolution: The Federalization of Environmental Law," *Journal of Law, Economics, and Organization* 1 (1985), 327–29, 333–38, quotation at p. 327. See also Charles O. Jones, *Clean Air: The Policies and Politics of Pollution Control* (Pittsburgh: University of Pittsburgh Press, 1975), chap. 7.

8. E. J. Dionne, "Greening of Democrats: An 80s Mix of Idealism and Shrewd

from 1957 during his time as Senate Majority Leader. It was "indispensable to Johnson's national political aspirations" to "get credit for the passage of" that year's ground-breaking civil rights act.[9] "For both his Texas and his national ambitions, he needed to pass through a Senate where it could be filibustered a civil rights bill which would be palatable to the South."[10] He managed to achieve exactly these aims. In general, Johnson reached for the White House by building a reputation as an effective, responsible assembler of coalitions that could enact laws.

Motives of politicians are seldom so directly addressed in print, but we can take note of who does what under what circumstances. Senator Taft assumed a lead role in passing the Taft-Hartley Act in 1947 just before his presidential run in 1948.[11] Republican Senator Arthur Vandenberg won acclaim as a possible presidential candidate in 1948, though he did not run, by helping the Truman administration engineer the Marshall Plan and aid to Greece and Turkey. Under Nixon and Ford, a number of Senate or House Democrats aiming for the presidency—Senators Henry Jackson and Birch Bayh and Representative Wilbur Mills as well as Muskie—put their brands on notable measures. Jackson promoted the National Environmental Policy Act of 1969 as well as the Jackson-Vanik amendment of 1974 that sought to lever increased Jewish emigration from the Soviet Union.[12] Bayh ushered through the constitutional amendments regarding women's rights (ERA) and the eighteen-year-old vote. Mills, from his formi-

Politics," *New York Times*, June 14, 1989, p. A23. Dionne cites Senator Al Gore of Tennessee as a source on this matter.

9. Rowland Evans, Jr., and Robert Novak, *Lyndon B. Johnson: The Exercise of Power* (New York: New American Library, 1966), p. 124, and more generally chap. 7.

10. Michael Barone, *Our Country: The Shaping of America from Roosevelt to Reagan* (New York: Free Press, 1990), p. 295, and more generally pp. 295–98.

11. See Robert W. Merry, "Robert A. Taft: A Study in Legislative Power Accumulation" (Paper presented at the 1990 Annual Meeting of the American Political Science Association), pp. 20–23.

12. On the Jackson-Vanik amendment, which was attached to the Trade Act of 1974 listed in table 4.1: Robert A. Pastor, *Congress and the Politics of U.S. Foreign Economic Policy, 1929–1976* (Berkeley: University of California Press, 1980), pp. 174–76. On the connection between Jackson's environmental initiative and his presidential ambitions, see Elliott, Ackerman, and Millian, "Toward a Theory of Statutory Evolution," pp. 327–28.

dable station as Ways and Means Chairman, advanced the 20 percent
Social Security hike of 1972 as the centerpiece of his surprising presidential bid that year.[13] Under Reagan, there were at least the roles
of Democratic Senators Al Gore in planning missiles systems and Bill
Bradley in paving the way for the Tax Reform Act of 1986.[14] Note
that many of the enactments mentioned here were exceptionally significant ones.

All the above instances are from times of divided party control.
This is not to say that none at all come to light from times of unified
control. Under Reagan, Republican Senate Majority Leaders Howard
Baker and Bob Dole no doubt helped along their presidential ambitions by showing they could package legislative results on such subjects as deficit reduction. Senator Edward M. Kennedy evidently
served his White House aims by promoting deregulation statutes under both Ford (DIV) and the vulnerable Carter (UNI).[15] But despite
some exceptions as well as soft evidence and small numbers, the general point seems to hold: Effective, high-publicity lawmaking by pres-

13. "The Congressman visualized himself as a possible presidential candidate.
As chairman of the Ways and Means Committee the best thing he could do
to further his ambition was to sponsor and push through a big increase in
social security benefits. This he did." Herbert Stein, *Presidential Economics: The
Making of Economic Policy from Roosevelt to Reagan and Beyond* (New York: Simon
and Schuster, 1985), p. 188. See also Derthick, *Policymaking for Social Security*,
pp. 339, 358–62.

14. On Bradley's role: Jeffrey H. Birnbaum and Alan S. Murray, *Showdown
at Gucci Gulch: Lawmakers, Lobbyists, and the Unlikely Triumph of Tax Reform* (New
York: Random House, 1987).

15. "Kennedy embraced deregulation in part because he lacked a significant
record of achievement in 1974 as subcommittee chairman. And because he
was a potential presidential candidate and a highly visible political personality,
he was in an excellent position to initiate reform. Kennedy's well-publicized
hearings on airline deregulation launched the issue and helped capture Ford's
attention. Kennedy's actions also prodded Carter to adopt trucking deregulation as an issue. The two were locked in a bitter rivalry during the 1980
primaries and both claimed credit during the campaign for the reform movement—Kennedy calling himself the 'father of deregulation.'" Gary Mucci-
aroni, "The Decline of Client Politics: Understanding Reform in the Tax and
Regulatory Arenas" (Paper presented at the 1990 Annual Meeting of the
American Political Science Association), p. 10. See also Martha Derthick and
Paul Quirk, *The Politics of Deregulation* (Washington, D.C.: Brookings Institution Press, 1985), pp. 40–41, 106–07, 238, 255.

idential aspirants during 1946–90 seems to have taken place decisively more commonly during times of divided control.

There is a case for one more *compensation* effect in the realm of lawmaking. It involves the two parties as such, rather than individual politicians. It has its own logic and requirements for evidence, though its instances can overlap those discussed above under the topic of presidential aspirants. The logic is that an out-party—that is, one not controlling the presidency—gains an option when it controls one or both houses of Congress that it does not enjoy when it is just a minority element in both houses. The option is a chance to claim credit. An out-party holding the House or Senate, since its support is both really needed and readily seen to be needed if laws are to pass, is in a position to compete with the president's party for electoral credit for passing laws that advance popular causes. Such competition can bring victories for laws that otherwise might not pass.

This is a slippery subject. Majorities of the two congressional parties join hands to vote for popular causes all the time. Saying so is like announcing that water runs downhill. The argument accordingly needs tight rules of evidence. Perhaps an enactment of a law should qualify as an instance if it meets the following tests. First, out-party participants in the enactment process assert freely that a "party position" is being forged—or else close observers such as journalists size up the transactions that way. More is in progress, in short, than just individual members registering their own positions. Second, close observers claim that the out-party, through its actions, is vying with the president's party for electoral favor. Third, close observers judge that the enactment effort might have failed if not for the out-party's competing bid for favor.

As for actual instances, works on at least two major enactments of recent times suggest that they met, more or less, these tests. One was the Tax Reform Act of 1986: "What actually drove tax reform forward was not Republican pressure in the face of Democratic resistance, but a process of interparty competition in which leaders of both groups first sought to win credit with the public for enacting reform and later competed to avoid blame for killing it.... In this instance, divided party control over the two chambers of Congress, and between the Democratic House and the Republican White House, helped advance the TRA."[16] The other was the Clean Air Act of 1970: The competition

16. Timothy J. Conlan, Margaret T. Wrightson, and David R. Beam, *Taxing*

between the Muskie and Nixon sides to enact a stiff measure is sometimes given a straightforward Democrats-versus-Republicans interpretation.[17]

These two items seem to meet the specifications, but it would be a daunting task to try to canvass the lawmaking record since 1946 for anything like a full or representative list of such instances. The needed evidence would be voluminous and the rules for using it are shaky. On balance, the argument for a *compensation* effect seems plausible, but it requires more work. Where, for example, are the instances from the last six years of Eisenhower's presidency? Also, in a disturbing turn, a textbook case of electorally based party competition driving a law through comes to light from 1954. The case exhibits all the essentials except one: That was a time of *unified* party control, under Eisenhower and a Republican Congress.

That statute, which is listed in table 4.1, was the Communist Control Act of 1954 outlawing the Communist party. According to a contemporary report, the Democratic minority "seized the initiative, possibly because this is an election year and they might score as the party taking direct, legal action against the Reds and their avowed or innocent helpers. The Republicans quickly joined the march."[18] It was clear that "the whole idea of outlawing the Communist party by legislation had its origin in partisan politics. Democratic Senators, nettled by the repeated Republican indictment of New Deal and Fair Deal administrations as 'twenty years of treason,' decided there was in the outlawing vehicle an opportunity to bring Republican chickens home to roost."[19] Senator Hubert Humphrey took the lead. The law passed

Choices: The Politics of Tax Reform (Washington, D.C.: Congressional Quarterly Press, 1990), p. 237. See also Conlan, "Competitive Government: Policy Escalation and Divided Party Control" (Paper presented at the 1990 Annual Meeting of the American Political Science Association), pp. 5–12; Catherine E. Rudder, "Accounting for Synoptic Change in U.S. Tax Policy Making" (Paper presented at the 1989 Annual Meeting of the American Political Science Association).

17. See Conlan, Wrightson, and Beam, *Taxing Choices*, pp. 237–38; Conlan, "Competitive Government," pp. 12–13; Jones, *Clean Air*, chap. 7, especially at pp. 183, 193, 209–210.

18. C. P. Trussell, "Senate, By 85 to 0, Votes to Outlaw the Communist Party," *New York Times*, August 13, 1954, p. 1.

19. C. P. Trussell, "Eisenhower Aides Try to Block Bill Outlawing Reds," *New York Times*, August 14, 1954, p. 1. The rest of the story: Alvin Shuster,

by 79–0 in the Senate and 265–2 in the House. There is nothing particularly surprising about this story, but note the context. The Democrats, acting as a party, could bring about passage of a law for electoral reasons even though they controlled no government institutions at all. The more often this can happen, the less compelling is the case for such competitive lawmaking as *compensation* effect; if it can take place under unified control too, the case recedes toward one for random occurrence or *constancy*.

All the incentive structures discussed above—those involving individual House or Senate members aiming to stay on Capitol Hill, the same bidding for the presidency, and the two parties juggling for electoral advantage—seem to foster at least lawmaking *constancy*. The most compelling, albeit not the only, case for *compensation* has to do with the presidential aspirants. The logic of it works well and the evidence lines up nicely. Like power contenders in the Roman Republic who headed for Gaul or Spain to win battles, would-be American presidents try to score points by showing they can actually do something—pass laws.

So much for lawmaking. How about electoral incentives as spurs to investigations? Here also a possible case for *constancy* arises. House and Senate members bent on re-election may profit from suitable headlines regardless of whose misbehavior they expose—their own party's or the other party's. The role of scourge of corruption probably resonates especially well regardless of who is being scourged. Democratic Senator John McClellan's image as a hard-nosed investigator, for example, grew from pursuit of a variety of targets ranging from labor racketeers in the 1950s through dubious transactions in the Agriculture Department under Kennedy. Still, electoral incentives obviously leave a great deal unexplained about the many exposure probes listed in table 2.1. Whatever animated Senator McCarthy during the McCarthy-Army hearings in 1953–54, re-election must have

"G.O.P. Chiefs Seek Red Curb to Meet President's Ideas," *New York Times*, August 15, 1954, pp. 1, 32; Trussell, "House Vote Backs Senate on Bill to Outlaw Reds; Issue of a Veto Is Posed," *New York Times*, August 18, 1954, pp. 1, 12; Trussell, "Congress Passes Softened Version of Communist Ban," *New York Times*, August 20, 1954, p. 1. See also William W. Keller, *The Liberals and J. Edgar Hoover: Rise and Fall of a Domestic Intelligence State* (Princeton, N.J.: Princeton University Press, 1989), pp. 65–67, and Richard M. Fried, *Nightmare in Red: The McCarthy Era in Perspective* (New York: Oxford University Press, 1990), pp. 171–72.

ranked low.[20] Senator Fulbright could have found a better way to please his Arkansas constituency than to attack Johnson's and Nixon's Vietnam policies. Senator Ervin's behavior in the 1973 Watergate inquiry may be assignable chiefly to "norms."

Inspected closely, moreover, the record of 1946–90 suggests that the particular election aim of winning the presidency helped to concentrate investigations during times of *divided* party control. Instead of working to "even things out," that aspiration evidently caused a pattern that itself needs evening out. Democratic presidential aspirants Estes Kefauver, Stuart Symington, and Frank Church all targeted administrations of the Republican party in, respectively, their probes of Dixon-Yates in 1955, air-power planning in 1956, and FBI and CIA covert operations in 1975. Senator Edward Kennedy played a key role in the 1972 probe of the Nixon administration's ITT dealings. While it is anyone's guess how high Nixon's own ambitions already reached during his first term in the House in 1948, we know that he went after Alger Hiss that year as a member of the Republican Eightieth Congress under Truman. These are dog-bites-man stories.

By contrast, according to the evidence of table 2.1, the only presidential aspirant who ran a headline-catching probe of his own party's administration was Senator Russell in 1951. That was the relatively friendly investigation regarding the Korean war. Howard Baker, a Republican member of Senator Ervin's Watergate committee, seems to have aided his presidential cause during that unit's televised hearings, but he too played a mediating rather than an assault role. Even if exposing misbehavior by one's own party's national administration can impress a local constituency—and that claim needs more evidence—it has not become a beaten track to winning a presidential nomination. Perhaps it just generates too much of an image of disloyalty or instability to pay off in coalition-building processes at the

20. There is a standard case that McCarthy took up anti-Communism in the first place at least partly because he needed a Senate re-election issue for 1952. See Robert Griffith, *The Politics of Fear: Joseph R. McCarthy and the Senate* (Lexington: University Press of Kentucky, 1970), p. 29; Richard Rovere, *Senator Joe McCarthy* (Cleveland: World, 1961), p. 120. But what drove him after that during the 1953–54 hearings is not at all clear. Watching McCarthy from the White House, Eisenhower did speculate that the senator was aiming for the presidency but also, on one occasion, confidently read him as driving for higher fees as an after-dinner speaker. See Stephen E. Ambrose, *Eisenhower*, vol. 2, *The President* (New York: Simon and Schuster, 1984), pp. 60, 82, 162.

national level.[21] One of the better-known political lessons of the 1950s was that Estes Kefauver won powerful party enemies by digging up damaging evidence about local Democratic bosses during his investigations of organized crime in 1950–51. The bosses remembered that during his presidential drives in 1952 and 1956.[22] Of course nominating processes have changed greatly since then. But this discussion is not proving very helpful. Much congressional investigating is not illuminated by reference to electoral incentives. And much that is— that by White House aspirants who unsurprisingly attack administrations of the other party—does not offer any clues why exposure probes take place as commonly under unified as under divided party control.

PRESIDENTIAL LEADERSHIP

In any study of the ups and downs of national lawmaking, presidential leadership cries out for attention.[23] Many, if well short of all, major enactments are presidential projects. Few would doubt that presidential leadership can help to pass laws, or that the extent to which it does so varies over time. Yet these are elusive claims that require discussion. Of concern here is how such variation, if it exists, might map onto patterns of unified versus divided party control.

To proceed with an argument, two analytic questions need to be addressed. First, as regards lawmaking, what in principle should we consider presidential leadership to be? Evidently it has three necessary components: an agenda, will, and skill. Presidents' agendas vary from ambitious to modest. (Some but not all ambitious ones are "ideological" in the sense used in chapter 4.) As for will, sometimes presidents throw themselves into their legislative programs: Johnson in 1964–65 is a case in point. Sometimes they lie back: Nixon's Family Assistance Plan was a strikingly ambitious proposal, but his actions after

21. It is not at all out of the question that a high-publicity probe of one's own party's administration might lead to higher office. Charles Evans Hughes, for example, began his career in New York politics exactly that way. Many a reformer has risen by attacking his own party's state or local machine.

22. See Charles L. Fontenay, *Estes Kefauver: A Biography* (Knoxville: University of Tennessee Press, 1980), pp. 174–83, 200, 209, 224; Joseph Bruce Gorman, *Kefauver: A Political Biography* (New York: Oxford University Press, 1971), pp. 78–85, 90–91, 113, 142–44, 155–56, 219–20.

23. Presidential leadership is no doubt partly shaped by electoral incentives, but little would be gained by considering it under that rubric.

introducing it do not suggest that he cared a great deal whether it passed.[24] Skill in this context is a familiar checklist of talents including the abilities to set priorities, package proposals, time moves, court, persuade, and bargain with members of Congress, and mobilize public opinion to bring it to bear on Capitol Hill.[25] Skill should probably be attributed to a full White House legislative team rather than to a president alone, but then presidents vary in their ability to pick effective teams. Diminish any of the above components—agenda, will, or skill—and the potential to cause enactment of laws diminishes. Moreover, during any one president's tenure, any of the three components can vary across policy areas or time. A president may choose, for example, to devote attention and staff talent to foreign-policy measures and skimp on domestic ones. To cite a time disparity, Franklin Roosevelt showed legendary legislative skill during the "hundred days" of 1933 yet clumsiness in launching his court-packing bill in

24. See Barbara Kellerman, *The Political Presidency: Practice of Leadership* (New York: Oxford University Press, 1984), pp. 146–55; Stephen E. Ambrose, *Nixon*, vol. 2, *The Triumph of a Politician, 1962–1972* (New York: Simon and Schuster, 1989), pp. 291–94, 366–67, 405–06.

25. Useful discussions of presidential skill appear in Charles O. Jones, "Presidential Negotiation with Congress," chap. 4 in Anthony King, ed., *Both Ends of the Avenue: The Presidency, the Executive Branch, and Congress in the 1980s* (Washington, D.C.: American Enterprise Institute, 1983); Reo M. Christenson, "Presidential Leadership of Congress," chap. 19 in Thomas E. Cronin, ed., *Rethinking the Presidency* (Boston: Little, Brown, 1982); and George C. Edwards III, *Presidential Influence in Congress* (San Francisco: W. H. Freeman, 1980), chaps. 5, 6. With television ever more pervasive, it is sometimes argued that the mix of skills needed by presidents in their lawmaking role has changed greatly since 1946—from insider bargaining to mobilization of the public. This seems at least overdrawn. It would be difficult to find a more impressive instance of inside bargaining than that provided by Reagan's legislative team at work on Capitol Hill in 1981. And here is a major instance of popular mobilization: "In short, the President clearly and deliberately was bringing to bear here the full range of weapons in his arsenal for stirring public opinion and focusing it upon a reluctant Congress." That refers to Theodore Roosevelt's ultimately successful campaign to pass the Hepburn Act in 1904–06. He made "swings around the circle" (that is, delivered speeches around the country) and manipulated the "emerging mass media" (then, mass-circulation newspapers) through press conferences, feeding stories to reporters, and the like. See Elmer E. Cornwell, Jr., *Presidential Leadership of Public Opinion* (Bloomington: Indiana University Press, 1965), pp. 13–26, quotations at pp. 14, 23, 25–26. On the general point, see Marc A. Bodnick, " 'Going Public' Reconsidered: Reagan's 1981 Tax and Budget Cuts, and Revisionist Theories of Presidential Power," *Congress and the Presidency* 17 (1990), 13–28.

1937.[26] Woodrow Wilson drew applause for his legislative maneuvering in 1913–14 and 1916 but fell victim to his own stubbornness in dealing with the Senate on the Versailles treaty in 1919.[27]

The second analytic question has to do with measurement. How in principle might we detect levels of agenda, will, or skill? The question is worth asking even if exact calibration is never likely to result. Skill poses a particularly interesting problem: Much evidence about it has to derive from actual presidential behavior in lawmaking enterprises, yet levels of skill cannot be inferred from levels of success. Too much else contributes to success—the current coalitional structure in Congress, for example, or crises that induce Congress to follow the White House lead. In any search for skill, such other factors need to be given their due. For Kennedy through Reagan, an impressive effort to do that appears in a 1984 work by Barbara Kellerman. Systematically tracking background circumstances that might also have worked toward success or failure, she examines evidence for the degree of skill each president showed in advancing his highest domestic legislative priority during his first year in office. The items in question are Kennedy's aid-to-education bill, Johnson's anti-poverty program, Nixon's Family Assistance Plan (here the problem of "will" intrudes), Ford's anti-recession tax cut, Carter's omnibus energy plan, and Reagan's 1981 expenditure cuts (Gramm-Latta II).[28]

Kellerman concludes that Johnson and Reagan decisively out-

26. On Roosevelt's legislative leadership in general: William E. Leuchtenburg, "Franklin D. Roosevelt: The First Modern President," chap. 1 in Fred I. Greenstein, ed., *Leadership in the Modern Presidency* (Cambridge: Harvard University Press, 1988), pp. 21–27. On the court-packing plan: Joseph Alsop and Turner Catledge, *The 168 Days* (Garden City, N.Y.: Doubleday, 1938); James MacGregor Burns, *Roosevelt: The Lion and the Fox* (New York: Harcourt, Brace, 1956), chap. 15.

27. On 1913–14 and 1916: John Milton Cooper, Jr., *Pivotal Decades: The United States, 1900–1920* (New York: W. W. Norton, 1990), pp. 195–202, 214–16. On the Versailles treaty: Alexander L. George and Juliette L. George, *Woodrow Wilson and Colonel House: A Personality Study* (New York: John Day, 1956), chaps. 14, 15.

28. The criteria for selection: "At some point during the president's first year in office they were declared by him to be his most important domestic policy goal; they constituted an issue on which he demonstrably staked his reputation; and they were the beneficiaries of the president's time and attention in the effort to secure early follower support." Kellerman, *Political Presidency,* quotation at p. 51, and chaps. 6–11.

stripped the rest in "political skill."[29] This is not a surprise: It accords with much analysis and casual observation by other writers and probably most people's memories. But Kellerman's use of evidence is particularly convincing. Johnson's handling of his anti-poverty plan exhibited astute timing, resourceful framing of a problem, a compelling "war on poverty" metaphor, energetic mobilization of public support, and the trademark one-on-one "Johnson treatment" of members of Congress.[30] Other analysts of Johnson's early presidential years have pointed to, for example, his clever stage-managing of a 1964 deal that yielded cotton, wheat, and food-stamps legislation—this is political science's favorite example of a cross-issue-area logroll—and his executive pre-packaging of the Elementary and Secondary Education Act of 1965.[31] That was done largely to ward off wrangling between Catholics and Protestants over parochial schools that had sent similar Truman and Kennedy bills to House defeats in 1949–50 and 1961.[32] Reagan's campaign for spending cuts in 1981 featured a simple, saleable message, good timing, one-on-one charm for members of Congress, an unsurpassed touch in mobilizing public opinion,

29. In this paragraph and the next, I probably do Kellerman's subtle analysis injustice in abstracting from it.

30. Kellerman, *Political Presidency*, pp. 116–24. See also Evans and Novak, *Lyndon B. Johnson*, pp. 428–34. Johnson's use of the military metaphor is emphasized in David Zarefsky, *President Johnson's War on Poverty: Rhetoric and History* (University: University of Alabama Press, 1986), chap. 2.

31. On agriculture and food stamps: Evans and Novak, *Lyndon B. Johnson*, pp. 380–81. On ESEA: Eugene Eidenberg and Roy D. Morey, *An Act of Congress: The Legislative Process and the Making of Education Policy* (New York: W. W. Norton, 1969), chap. 4; Philip Meranto, *The Politics of Federal Aid to Education in 1965: A Study in Political Innovation* (Syracuse, N.Y.: Syracuse University Press, 1967), pp. 104–09.

32. On the losses under Truman and Kennedy: Robert Bendiner, *Obstacle Course on Capitol Hill* (New York: McGraw-Hill, 1964), pp. 90–97, 180–89. Speaker Tip O'Neill's judgment on Johnson: "But it wasn't just a matter of gimmicks. Lyndon Johnson worked more closely with the Congress and followed the details of legislation more carefully than any other president I've seen. He left nothing to chance. The Kennedy people had been excellent when it came to the details of campaigning, but they didn't follow through legislatively. Johnson was the opposite. He wasn't scientific about campaigning, but when it came to dealing with Congress, he was the best I've ever seen." *Man of the House: The Life and Political Memoirs of Speaker Tip O'Neill* (New York: Random House, 1987), p. 186.

and tough horsetrading by White House agents to produce needed House votes through concessions on such matters as sugar prices.[33]

By contrast, according to Kellerman, Kennedy's aid-to-education effort exhibited overconfidence, lack of imaginative definition or dramatization of the issue, little actual work to build a coalition, little stroking of relevant congressional figures (notably James J. Delaney of New York), and mediocre performance by, taken as a whole, the Cabinet, White House staff, and legislative liaison team.[34] Nixon's campaign for his FAP featured poor timing, unsteady White House focus, "meager effort" by Nixon himself to win public support, little mobilization of relevant interest groups, and uninspired handling of key members of the Senate Finance Committee.[35] Ford, in pursuing his tax cut, sent inconsistent signals about what he wanted and "never gave his would-be followers the impression that they had much of anything to lose by lining up against him."[36] Finally, Carter brought to his energy initiative a well-known distaste for politics that manifested itself in an absence of early political groundwork on Capitol Hill, inept coalition building, and unlikely personal encounters with members of Congress.[37] He displayed "a failure to understand either intuitively or intellectually that the energy program would have to be

33. Kellerman, *Political Presidency*, pp. 244–53. See also Hedrick Smith, "The President as Coalition Builder: Reagan's First Year," chap. 20 in Cronin, ed., *Rethinking the Presidency*, and Mitchell Bard, "Interest Groups, the President, and Foreign Policy: How Reagan Snatched Victory from the Jaws of Defeat on AWACS," *Presidential Studies Quarterly* 18 (1988), 593–600. Tip O'Neill on Reagan's White House legislative team in 1981: "They knew where they were going and they knew how to get there. They put only one legislative ball in play at a time, and they kept their eye on it all the way through." "All in all, the Reagan team in 1981 was probably the best-run political operating unit I've ever seen." *Man of the House*, pp. 341–46, quotations at pp. 342, 345.

34. Kellerman, *Political Presidency*, pp. 79–88. In general, according to Speaker O'Neill, Kennedy's liaison people were "unusually adept at doing political favors for individual congressmen. Unfortunately, they weren't nearly as effective at their job, which was to help get the president's legislation through Congress. Other than the Manpower bill, there wasn't much Kennedy legislation that actually passed during his shortened term in office. Eventually, most of his legislation did go through, but it took the political skills of Lyndon Johnson to make it happen." *Man of the House*, p. 175.

35. Kellerman, *Political Presidency*, pp. 146–55, quotation at p. 149.

36. Ibid., pp. 179–84, quotation at p. 184.

37. Ibid., pp. 209–19.

approved by a great many different people—in and out of government—whose wants, needs, and wishes would finally have to be taken into account."[38]

If the analysis were carried further back, it seems a good bet that neither Truman nor Eisenhower would earn a skill rating as high as Johnson's or Reagan's on a comparable domestic initiative. (Foreign affairs would be another story: The Truman team's performance on the Marshall Plan and aid to Greece and Turkey evidently qualifies as extraordinary.[39]) More recently, there is Bush's less than gripping performance on deficit reduction—"Read my lips" through "Read my hips."

All the above judgments are at least plausible, which is enough for purposes here. To be sure, skill is not the only consideration. As argued earlier, there is also will, which in practice is hard to disentangle from skill. And the presidential agendas that will and skill can apply to differ in volume and importance. But few would deny that Johnson and Reagan, at least in their early years, ranked unusually high also in will and agenda ambition. It is thus plausible that presidential leadership intruded into the national legislative arena in uniquely large doses in 1964–65 and 1981. Such doses—at least on prize early domestic programs—have probably been smaller under other postwar presidents. So much for a not easily pinned-down independent variable. As it happens, this estimated variation in postwar presidential leadership doses has corresponded—at least in key particulars—to variation in actual legislative output: The Johnson and Reagan years scored high and other periods lagged. Hence the case for presidents as causal agents.

Hence also a credible source of *alternative variation*. Presidential leadership can evidently contribute powerfully to lawmaking, but as was argued in chapter 4, nothing guarantees that it will do so during times of unified party control (as under Truman and Kennedy) or bars it from doing so during times of divided control (as under Rea-

38. Ibid., p. 214. Tip O'Neill on Carter: "When I tried to explain how important it was for the president to work closely with Congress, he didn't seem to understand." "When it came to helping out my district, I actually received more cooperation from Reagan's staff than from Carter's." *Man of the House*, pp. 302, 308, and more generally chap. 3. See also Jones, "Presidential Negotiation with Congress," pp. 118–23, 125.

39. See, for example, Joseph M. Jones, *The Fifteen Weeks (February 21–June 5, 1947)* (New York: Viking, 1955).

TABLE 5.1
Numbers of Important Laws Passed in First and Second Halves of
Presidential Terms

	Presidency	First half	Second half
1945–48	Roosevelt-Truman		10
1949–52	Truman	12	6
1953–56	Eisenhower	9	6
1957–60	Eisenhower	11	5
1961–64	Kennedy-Johnson	15	13
1965–68	Johnson	22	16
1969–72	Nixon	22	16
1973–76	Nixon-Ford	22	14
1977–80	Carter	12	10
1981–84	Reagan	9	7
1985–88	Reagan	9	12
1989–92	Bush	9	
	Total	152	115
	Mean	13.8	10.1

gan). It performs on its own schedule. Throughout the twentieth
century, American political scientists have done their best to identify
presidential leadership with party control through arguments about
"deadlock," "stalemate," and "party government." But regardless of
its theoretical merits, that effort runs into an empirical problem. At
least since the 1930s, the real world has refused to follow the script.

Before leaving presidential leadership, another pattern is worth
mentioning. It is not earthshaking, but it is interesting. As table 5.1
shows, using the 267 important postwar laws from table 4.1, more
such laws ordinarily pass during the first two years of a presidential
term than during the second two. Reagan's second term is the only
exception. Presidential leadership is no doubt one reason for the
pattern, since presidents ordinarily make their chief programmatic
pitches just after winning an election. Possibly another reason is that
both Capitol Hill and the White House tend to switch their attention
from policymaking to politics as another presidential election approaches.[40] At any rate, the biennial ups and downs shown in table

40. Here is a more particular pattern that evidently holds without exception
during the twentieth century: Enactment of a sizable White House domestic

5.1 present another instance of *alternative variation*. The reversed relation during Reagan's second term—more laws in 1987–88 than in
1985–86—suggests still another source of *alternative variation*:
Congressional leadership can vary in dosage too. The 1987–88 record
seems to have owed mainly to Speaker Wright's leadership.[41]

BROAD MAJORITIES

This section also addresses just lawmaking (not investigations). It dem-
onstrates and explores the significance of the fact that notable American laws tend to pass by broad majorities, regardless of conditions of
party control. "Broad" will have two meanings. First, laws tend to pass
by two-thirds majorities—that is, by two-to-one margins. Second, they
tend to pass by bipartisan majorities—that is, with the support of
majorities of both parties.

The discussion will hinge on a collection of data—the House and
Senate roll-call votes on final passage by which the 267 laws listed in
table 4.1 were enacted.[42] In many cases, earlier roll calls on amendments to these measures had closer outcomes than did the votes on
final passage. Political scientists and rating groups like Americans for
Democratic Action (ADA) tend to dwell on such close amendments,

---

agenda never happens beyond any president's sixth year in office. The seventh
and eighth years (and beyond) are always fallow. The instances are Theodore
Roosevelt (UNI in 1907–09), Wilson (DIV in 1919–21), Franklin Roosevelt
(UNI in 1939–45), Truman (UNI in 1951–52), Eisenhower (DIV in 1959–60),
and Reagan (DIV in 1987–88). By the seventh year, a president no doubt runs
out of programs, will, or skill, or else Congress settles into an attitude of
boredom, hostility, or simply unforthcomingness toward a president now
perceived as a lame duck.

41. See Susan F. Rasky, "Congress Regains Its Voice on Policy in 1987–88
Sessions," *New York Times*, October 24, 1988, p. A1; Helen Dewar and Tom
Kenworthy, "Activist Congress Exits with Gains, Problems," *Washington Post*,
October 23, 1988, pp. A4, A5; "Jim Wright, Unlikely Sparkplug," *New York
Times* (editorial), October 22, 1988, p. 26; Richard E. Cohen, "False Parallel,"
National Journal, October 15, 1988, p. 2629; Fred Barnes, "The Wright Stuff,"
New Republic, May 15, 1989, pp. 13–16.

42. This means, for either house, the roll-call vote on a measure's "final
passage" as that term is conventionally defined (with a voice vote counting as
a unanimous yes), unless the house in question recorded a later roll call on
a conference report, a move to accept the other house's version of the measure, or a veto override. In that event, the last of the later roll calls was used.
(Voice votes from such later rounds were never used.)

partly from a belief that politics is in some deep sense "really" about conflict. That view does not have to be accepted. There is nothing wrong with seeing legislative politics as, for example, a problem-solving enterprise in which close decisions on options often precede a "really" consensual result.[43] But in any case, the concern here is with laws and their enactment, not with conflict. Votes on final passage are the ones that pose an up-or-down choice between passing a bill or doing nothing and that actually produce laws.[44] Victorious amendments are incorporated in the final measures; others are left behind. Members' yes or no votes on final passage seem to be particularly easy to understand back home, and political missteps can be costly.[45]

Let us begin with displays of data, then discuss the implications later. Table 5.2 shows how many of the 267 laws won the support of at least two-thirds of voting members (regardless of party) in both the House and Senate, how many won it in just one house, and how many won it in neither house.[46] The results are sorted according to unified and divided party control. A difference emerges: 84 percent of the

43. A good example: In analyzing German politics in 1990, consider how misleading it would be to overlook the consensual thrust toward reunification and dwell instead on roll-call conflict among the parties over the terms and pace of reunification.

44. In the great majority of the 267 cases of concern here, "doing nothing" meant preserving the status quo. But a negative vote had a different meaning in some cases, such as foreign trade extensions, where government authority was about to run out unless a new act passed.

45. Freshman Republican Fred Eckert lost his re-election bid in a Rochester, N.Y., House district in 1986. One likely reason is that he "was the sole legislator from New York opposed to bills that passed with huge majorities." He "had outraged various constituencies with [among other things] votes against legislation to impose sanctions on South Africa and against the reauthorization of the Superfund." Linda L. Fowler and Robert D. McClure, *Political Ambition: Who Decides to Run for Congress?*(New Haven and London: Yale University Press, 1989), p. 214.

46. Any coding is awkward for the eight treaty ratifications. In this and succeeding tables, they are treated as if the real Senate result in fact occurred in both houses. In the few cases where measures listed in table 4.1 passed as parts of other instruments—such as bills to raise the debt ceiling—the final passage votes used here are those for the parent instruments. This causes particular embarrassment in the case of the 1990 child care package, which passed as part of that year's deficit-reduction act and hence shared that measure's close final-passage vote (228–200 in the House and 54–45 in the Senate).

TABLE 5.2
Important Laws Passed by Two-thirds Majorities

	During divided control			During unified control		
	⅔ in both houses	⅔ in one house	⅔ in neither house	⅔ in both houses	⅔ in one house	⅔ in neither house
1947–48	10					
1949–50				9	3	
1951–52				5	1	
1953–54				6	2	1
1955–56	5	1				
1957–58	10	1				
1959–60	5					
1961–62				7	7	1
1963–64				9	1	3
1965–66				14	5	3
1967–68				12	4	
1969–70	20	1	1			
1971–72	15	1				
1973–74	20	1	1			
1975–76	11	1	2			
1977–78				9	2	1
1979–80				7	2	1
1981–82	5	3	1			
1983–84	6	1				
1985–86	6	2	1			
1987–88	10	2				
1989–90	5	2	2			
Total	128	16	8	78	27	10
Percent	84	11	5	68	23	9

In this and succeeding tables, the effect is to double-count the close deficit-reduction results. This is probably misleading, since child care in its final compromise version seems to have drawn broad support. But there is no way to avoid making an arbitrary coding decision somehow.

TABLE 5.3
Important Laws Passed with the Support of Majorities of Both Democrats
and Republicans

	During divided control			During unified control		
	D + R in both houses	D + R in one house	D + R in neither house	D + R in both houses	D + R in one house	D + R in neither house
1947–48	6	3	1			
1949–50				8	3	1
1951–52				4	2	
1953–54				6	3	
1955–56	6					
1957–58	11					
1959–60	5					
1961–62				7	6	2
1963–64				7	3	3
1965–66				13	5	4
1967–68				15	1	
1969–70	19	3				
1971–72	16					
1973–74	18	3	1			
1975–76	11		3			
1977–78				7	2	3
1979–80				6	3	1
1981–82	6	3				
1983–84	6	1				
1985–86	6	2	1			
1987–88	7	3	2			
1989–90	6	1	2			
Total	123	19	10	73	28	14
Percent	81	13	7	63	24	12

laws, for example, passed by two-thirds in both houses when party
control was divided, but only 68 percent did when it was unified. That
difference is in the direction we would expect: Under divided control,
in effect, wider assent is needed to permit action. But the disparity
between 84 percent and 68 percent is not enormous. It is more striking
that a large majority of laws drew two-thirds support in both houses,

TABLE 5.4

A Selection of Important Laws Passed by Both Two-thirds and Bipartisan
Majorities in Both Houses

During divided control		During unified control	
1948	Marshall Plan		
1948	Hope-Aiken Act	1949	NATO treaty[a]
		1949	Agricultural Act
		1950	Social Security plan
		1950	Internal Security Act
		1950	Defense Production Act
1956	Disability Insurance	1952	McCarran-Walter Act
1956	Federal Highway Act	1953	Tidelands oil act
1957	Civil Rights Act		
1958	NDEA (education)		
1959	Landrum-Griffin Act	1962	Trade Expansion Act
		1963	Test ban treaty[a]
		1964	Civil Rights Act
1969	NEPA (environment)	1964	Kennedy tax cut
1969	Coal mine safety act	1964	Wilderness Act
1970	Clean Air Act	1965	Voting Rights Act
1970	OSHA (job safety)	1965	Immigration reform
1970	Food stamps expansion	1965	Higher Education Act
1970	Organized crime act	1966	Traffic Safety Act
1972	Water quality act		
1972	Revenue sharing		
1972	Social Security up 20%		
1972	ABM treaty[a]		
1972	SSI (income floor)		
1972	Consumer product act		
1973	CETA (public jobs)		
1974	Trade act		
1974	ERISA (pensions)		
1974	Campaign finance act		
1974	Congressional budget act		
1974	Health planning act		
1974	Housing Act		
1976	Tax reform	1977	Strip mining act
1976	NFMA (forests)	1978	Tax revision
		1978	Airline deregulation
		1980	Banking deregulation
1981	Reagan tax cut	1980	Toxic wastes Superfund
1983	Social Security plan		
1984	Criminal code revision		
1986	Tax Reform Act		
1986	South Africa sanctions		
1988	INF treaty[a]		
1990	Clean Air Act		

[a]Senate only.

and nearly all did in at least one house, regardless of how the government was organized. Table 5.3 performs a similar operation for party majorities. How many laws were backed by majorities of both Democrats and Republicans in both houses? Considerably over half, it turns out. Such bipartisan victories appeared somewhat more often under conditions of divided control, which is again what we would expect. But in general, regardless of context, the bulk of the laws drew bipartisan support.

In all, 186 of the 267 laws won broad majority support by both criteria: They passed by two-thirds majorities in both houses *and* they won the backing of Democratic and Republican majorities in both houses. To put some flesh on this statistic, table 5.4 presents a selection of some of the better-known acts among the 186. They range from such diverse instruments as the Marshall Plan, Social Security consolidation, and the McCarran Internal Security Act under Truman through the 1981 tax cut, the 1986 Tax Reform Act, and South Africa sanctions under Reagan. Some of the 186 measures just achieved the two-thirds mark. The Civil Rights Act of 1964, for example, passed by 289–126 in the House and 73–27 in the Senate. But other major innovations passed almost unanimously—for example, the National Environmental Policy Act of 1969 by 372–15 and a voice vote, food stamps expansion in 1970 by 391–2 and 71–6, Senator Muskie's Clean Air Act of 1970 by 374–1 and 73–0, and airline deregulation in 1978 by 363–8 and 83–9. By dwelling on conflict, one can overlook results such as these and lose track of what the government is doing.

At the other end of the scale, what enactments fell short of winning broad majority support in both houses? Table 5.5 presents two lists, one for each of the two defining criteria. Eighteen laws drew two-thirds support in neither house but still passed. They are a mixed lot, although housing or other urban measures appear six times. More interesting are the twenty-four measures that drew bipartisan support in neither house but still passed. That is, one party put them through—it was always the same party in both houses, not surprisingly. The Republican side won in these cases only twice—on the Twenty-second Amendment to limit presidential terms in 1947 and the Gramm-Rudman-Hollings Act in 1985. Nine of the twenty-four were partisan New Frontier or Great Society items. But eight, including the controversial deficit-reduction act of 1990, were measures voted by Democratic congressional majorities and signed by Nixon, Ford, Reagan, or Bush, or in one case (the Grove City civil rights act)

TABLE 5.5

Important Laws Not Passed by Two-thirds or Bipartisan Majorities

Not passed by a two-thirds majority in either house		Not passed by a bipartisan majority in either house	
Under divided control			
		1947	22nd Amendment
1970	Agricultural Act		
1973	Foreign Assistance Act	1973	Foreign Assistance Act
1975	Energy Act	1975	Energy Act
		1975	Tax cut
1975	New York City bailout	1975	New York City bailout
1982	Deficit reduction		
1985	Gramm-Rudman Act	1985	Gramm-Rudman Act
		1987	Deficit reduction
		1988	Grove City civil rights act
1990	Deficit reduction	1990	Deficit reduction
1990	Child care (part of deficit reduction)	1990	Child care (part of deficit reduction)
Under unified control			
		1950	Point Four program
1954	St. Lawrence Seaway		
1961	Housing Act	1961	Housing Act
		1961	Area Redevelopment Act
1964	Anti-poverty act	1964	Anti-poverty act
1964	Mass Transit Act	1964	Mass Transit Act
1964	Cotton-wheat program	1964	Cotton-wheat program
1965	HUD established	1965	HUD established
1965	Housing Act	1965	Housing Act
		1965	Appalachian Act
1966	Demonstration cities	1966	Demonstration cities
		1977	Minimum wage hike
1978	Energy package	1978	Energy package
		1978	Panama Canal treaties
1979	Chrysler bailout	1979	Chrysler bailout

enacted over Reagan's veto.[47] There is a 14–10 bias toward times of unified party control.

Specialists may have noticed that a roll call not exhibiting Democratic and Republican majorities on the same side is, with a trivial

47. On the deficit-reduction measure, Democrats voted 181–74 and 35–20; Republicans voted 47–126 and 19–25.

qualification, a "party vote."[48] That, in the tradition of political science, is a vote on which a majority of one party opposes a majority of the other party. On the roll calls to pass the 267 laws enacted between 1946 and 1990, "party votes" occurred in both houses only 8 percent of the time, and in one or both houses only 26 percent of the time. If one employs another customary but more demanding test of "party voting" that requires at least 90 percent of Democrats to oppose at least 90 percent of Republicans, *none* of the 267 laws met it in either house. None whatever. These are all meager results at best.[49]

What parties or blocs emerged on the losing side, when any did, in the 267 final-passage votes? It is instructive to canvass for appearances of the familiar "conservative coalition"—that is, votes on which a majority of Republicans voted on the same side as a majority of southern

48. The qualification has to do with ties. The set of roll calls that do not exhibit majorities of the two parties on the same side is not quite identical to the set on which majorities of the two parties take opposing sides. Of the twenty-four non-bipartisan instances in table 5.5, three featured results in which the party that lost in one house cast a tie vote in the other house. The tie votes contribute to instances of non-bipartisanship but not of party voting.

49. For time series of House and Senate "party voting" between 1949 and 1988, see Samuel C. Patterson and Gregory A. Caldeira, "Party Voting in the United States Congress," *British Journal of Political Science* 18 (1988), 116, and John R. Crawford, "Party Unity Scores Slip in 1988, But Overall Pattern Is Upward," *Congressional Quarterly Weekly*, November 19, 1988, p. 3335. For each year, these series give the proportions of all roll calls that were "party votes"—that is, a Democratic majority opposed a Republican majority. During these four decades, there is no evident relation between variation in this statistic and in the volume of notable lawmaking, or in whether a legislative program (a president's or, for example, Jim Wright's) was being successfully passed, or for that matter in whether party control of the government was divided or unified. Nor does the statistic seem to rise and fall with intensity of conflict in Washington. That would be no bargain to measure, but one might expect peaks under Truman and Nixon. In the House, the "party voting" series peaks under late Truman, has spikes in 1957, 1959, and 1964, plummets between 1964 and 1970, bottoms out under Nixon, and peaks again under late Reagan. The Senate series peaks under late Truman, has a spike in 1961, registers rather low under Nixon, and otherwise bounces around. You would never know from either series that anything special took place legislatively in 1965 or 1981. However interesting the "party voting" statistic may be in itself, its ups and downs do not seem to correspond to those of anything of importance that goes on in government.

TABLE 5.6
Important Laws on Which the "Conservative Coalition" Appeared or
Southern Democrats Were Isolated

Majorities of Republicans and southern Democrats opposed majorities of northern Democrats in both houses	Majorities of Republicans and northern Democrats opposed majorities of southern Democrats in both houses
1947 Portal-to-Portal Act	
1947 Taft-Hartley Act	
1952 McCarran-Walter Act	
	1954 St. Lawrence Seaway
	1957 Civil Rights Act
	1958 Alaska statehood
	1959 Hawaii statehood
	1960 Civil Rights Act
	1963 Higher Education Act
	1964 Civil Rights Act
	1965 Voting Rights Act
	1965 Immigration reform
1965 HUD established	
1965 Housing Act	
	1968 Open Housing Act
	1970 VRA extension
1970 Agricultural Act	
1981 Agriculture Act	
1985 Gramm-Rudman Act	

Democrats against a majority of northern Democrats.[50] The coalition surfaced in both houses on passage of just eight laws, or 3 percent of the time. (See the first column in table 5.6.) In two 1965 instances the northern Democrats won notwithstanding the alignment pattern; in the other six they emerged as the distinctive losers, notably on the Taft-Hartley Act. The coalition emerged in at least one house on thirty laws—or 11 percent of the time—but on only fifteen of these did the conservative side win. One instance was the House vote on Reagan's 1981 tax cut.[51] Even conceding the exceptionally important

50. Southern Democrats are those from any of the eleven ex-Confederate states or Kentucky or Oklahoma. All other Democrats are considered to be northerners.

51. On Gramm-Latta II in 1981, majorities of both northern and southern Democrats voted no in the House. Majorities of both voted yes in the Senate.

Taft-Hartley Act and the tax cut, these are rather paltry results for the much-discussed cross-party alliance. Successful as that combine often was as a blocking coalition under Roosevelt, Truman, and Kennedy, one might have thought it would figure as an *enacting* coalition when Republican presidents faced Democratic Congresses. Rarely has it done so. Eisenhower, Nixon, and Reagan just did not join hands all that often with congressional Republicans and southern Democrats against northern Democrats—at least not in actually passing important laws.

Table 5.6 also lists eleven laws on which majorities of southern Democrats uniquely voted no and lost. In both houses, that is, majorities of Republicans and northern Democrats formed winning coalitions against them. These results document a once basic cleavage. All eleven measures passed between 1954 and 1970 when tension between the sections ran high over civil rights. All but one—authorization of the St. Lawrence Seaway—raised racial questions, at least indirectly. Southern segregationists worried, for example, that statehood for Alaska or Hawaii would usher in more senators who favored civil rights.

Table 5.7 shows how often majorities of Democrats and Republicans in the House and Senate, as well as presidents, did *not* emerge as components of enacting coalitions. That is, it shows how often each of them voted against passage of a law and lost. House Republicans lost most often—on forty-seven laws or 18 percent of the time.[52] Senate Republicans voted no 10 percent of the time; Senate and House Democrats did so 3.4 percent and 2.6 percent of the time. Presidents vetoed bills and suffered overrides 4.2 percent of the time; otherwise they signed on.[53] This is not a picture of relentless zero-sum conflict between the parties. As a sideline in table 5.7, note that when a president faced a Congress controlled by the other party, it was the president's congressional party that tended to end up on the losing side— when either congressional party did—in coalition-building.[54] Again, a spirited cross-party "conservative coalition" passing laws under Ei-

52. The denominator for either party in the House is 259—that is, 267 minus the eight treaties.

53. The denominator for the presidents is 264—that is, 267 minus the three constitutional amendments.

54. Table 5.7 exhibits, more or less, a flow of entries from its top left-hand corner down diagonally to its bottom right-hand corner. It was organized so as to do that. The flow goes from the "party control" conditions under which

TABLE 5.7
Numbers of Times Majorities of Each Congressional Party Voted on the
Losing Side, or Presidents Had Vetoes Overridden, in the Passage of
267 Laws

Party control	Years	Democrats lost			Republicans lost		
		Senate party	House party	Pres veto beaten	Senate party	House party	Pres veto beaten
R Pres R Cong	1953–54	2	1				
D Pres R Cong	1947–48	3	2	2			
R Pres	1981–82	1	2				
R Senate	1983–84					1	
D House	1985–86	1	1			1	1
R Pres D Cong	1955–56						
	1957–58						
	1959–60						
	1969–70	1			1	1	
	1971–72						1
	1973–74	1			1	3	2
	1975–76				2	3	
	1987–88				3	4	3
	1989–90		1		2	2	
D Pres D Cong	1949–50			1	1	4	
	1951–52			1		2	
	1961–62				4	5	
	1963–64				3	6	
	1965–66				5	7	
	1967–68					1	
	1977–78				3	4	
	1979–80				2	3	
	Total	9	7	4	27	47	7

senhower, Nixon, and Reagan would have generated a quite different result.

What are we to make of Congress's thrust toward broad majorities? Again, it is understandable that two-thirds or bipartisan majorities

congressional Democrats proved most likely to end up excluded losers, to those under which congressional Republicans proved most likely to suffer that fate.

might occur somewhat more often under divided than under unified party control (see tables 5.2 and 5.3). Obviously, under divided conditions one party cannot pass laws by itself; more participants are needed if anything is to be done at all. The more intriguing question is: Why are broad majorities the norm regardless? What is it about the legislative process that produces this near *constancy*? In the cases of twenty-two of the enactments, the answer is straightforward: The eight treaties, three constitutional amendments, and eleven veto overrides needed two-thirds majorities to win.

More generally, two explanations come to mind. First, the Washington community seems to have a powerful tendency to work itself into a mindset of problem-solving.[55] That is, presidents, members of Congress, and other relevant actors often come to believe—sometimes quickly and surprisingly—that a "problem" exists in some area and that it can and must be "solved."[56] Agreement materializes on ends, more or less, and attention is given to means. A drive toward action builds from a pervasive view that something has to be done. Shifts into a problem-solving mode can result from external precipitating events (see chapter 6), but ordinarily the provocations are much less clearly grounded or time-specific than that. Defining states of affairs as remediable "problems" is a high political art. Witness Ralph Nader and the suddenly conspicuous problem of traffic deaths in the mid-1960s.[57]

Commonplace as it may seem, problem-solving is of course not the only collective mindset or mode of action that a legislature might resort to. It is not the one, for example, that today's state legislatures apply to a divisive issue like abortion, or that the British Parliament applied in nationalizing the steel industry after World War II—an

55. On this subject, see John W. Kingdon, *Agendas, Alternatives, and Public Policies* (Boston: Little, Brown, 1984), chap. 5.

56. Public opinion can enter in also: "As a result of some dramatic series of events . . . or for other reasons, the public suddenly becomes both aware of and alarmed about the evils of a particular problem. This alarmed discovery is invariably accompanied by euphoric enthusiasm about society's ability to 'solve this problem' or 'do something effective' within a relatively short time. The combination of alarm and confidence results in part from the strong public pressure in America for political leaders to claim that every problem can be 'solved.' " Anthony Downs, "Up and Down with Ecology: The 'Issue-Attention Cycle,' " *Public Interest* 28 (Summer 1972), 38–50, quotation at p. 39.

57. Price, *Who Makes the Laws?* pp. 49–61.

ideological move cheered on by Labourites but resisted by Tories. Nor is problem-solving unremarkable as a theoretical matter. Political scientists tend to anchor their models of lawmaking in social or economic determinisms borrowed from sociology or in strategy games borrowed from economics. Either way, constellations of fixed interests or preferences enter into legislative processes that take the shape of bloc warfare or choose-up-sides arithmetic. Divided party control, given such assumptions about conflict, can easily predict "deadlock." Problem-solving, by contrast, has elements familiar to psychology (how does a mindset arise?) and to anthropology (what explains the habits of a group in a setting?). Among explicitly political writings, a basis for it has to be searched for in, say, John Dewey rather than in pluralism, Marxism, interest-group liberalism, or public choice.

In the American lawmaking record since 1946, a strong flavor of problem-solving comes through from times of both divided and unified party control. Examples during the former might include the Hope-Aiken Agricultural Act of 1948 (a consensual solution regarding postwar commodity supports), the Clean Air Act of 1970 (spurred by, among other things, sudden alarm about air pollution), campaign finance reform in 1974, regulation of private pensions (ERISA) in 1974, narcotics control measures in 1986 and 1988, welfare reform in 1988, and the Clean Air Act of 1990. Times of unified control featured, for example, the McCarran Internal Security Act of 1950 (nearly everyone but Truman supported it during that year of McCarthyism), the Communist Control Act of 1954, the higher education acts of 1963 and 1965 (the parties came to agree that college costs needed addressing), the Traffic Safety Act of 1966, the Crime Control Act of 1968, and creation of the toxic wastes Superfund in 1980.

The second possible explanation of broad majorities has to do with the logic of aggregating support to pass a bill. Doing that is not easy in a system that features an executive and two legislative houses, a sprawling committee system, and legislators not disposed to lock-step party-line voting. Promoters of bills ordinarily need to enlist allies, appease executive agencies and interest groups, accept amendments, sometimes compromise principles, make deals, woo neutrals, and navigate a host of committees in the two separate houses. There are many veto-points or at least stall-points. A Senate filibuster or presidential veto can threaten. In this complicated setting, it seldom makes sense to aim for a 51 percent majority. What does make sense is to try to cut down the size and intensity of a bill's opposition—whichever side of the aisle that might come from. The intensity can matter as much as the size. Not surprisingly, many bills that make it through to final passage enjoy wide appeal, or at least assent.

Unified party control might seem a magic solution to these aggregative problems, but although it helps, it is not that. The process stays largely the same. Under both divided and unified control during the last four decades, it is easy to find many instances of strenuous, imaginative coalition building that seems to have been entirely necessary but that ended in broad majority victories. It was necessary because the bills could have been derailed. Despite the one-sided or bipartisan results, there does not seem to have been much slack. Well-crafted strategies worked. From times of divided control one thinks of, for example, the Marshall Plan in 1948, extension of reciprocal trade authority in 1955, the Civil Rights Act of 1957, extension of the Voting Rights Act in 1970, revenue sharing in 1972, the Comprehensive Employment and Training Act (CETA) of 1973, the Housing and Community Development Act of 1974, the Job Training Partnership Act (JTPA) of 1982, the refinancing of Social Security in 1983, immigration reform in 1986 (one-sided and bipartisan in one house), and the Tax Reform Act of 1986.[58]

There are equally good instances from times of unified control. Creation of the National Science Foundation required several years of entrepreneurial maneuvers that came to nothing in 1948 and 1949 because of House Rules Committee blockades. In 1950, once the plan's advocates bypassed Rules by resort to the twenty-one-day rule, passage took place easily by 247–126 in the House and unanimously (by voice

58. On the Marshall Plan: H. Bradford Westerfield, *Foreign Policy and Party Politics: Pearl Harbor to Korea* (New Haven: Yale University Press, 1955), chap. 13. On reciprocal trade: Raymond A. Bauer, Ithiel de Sola Pool, and Lewis Anthony Dexter, *American Business and Public Policy: The Politics of Foreign Trade* (New York: Atherton, 1963), chaps. 2–5. On civil rights in 1957: Evans and Novak, *Lyndon B. Johnson*, chap. 7 ("The Miracle of '57"). On voting rights extension in 1970: Abigail M. Thernstrom, *Whose Votes Count? Affirmative Action and Minority Voting Rights* (Cambridge: Harvard University Press, 1987), chap. 2. On revenue sharing: A. James Reichley, *Conservatives in an Age of Change* (Washington, D.C.: Brookings Institution Press, 1981), chap. 8. On CETA: Grace A. Franklin and Randall B. Ripley, *CETA: Politics and Policy, 1973–1982* (Knoxville: University of Tennessee Press, 1984), pp. 12–17. On housing: R. Allen Hays, *The Federal Government and Urban Housing: Ideology and Change in Public Housing* (Albany: State University of New York Press,

vote) in the Senate.[59] Authorization of the St. Lawrence Seaway, a losing cause for three decades, lost again in 1953 when the House Public Works Committee stalled. But in 1954 Eisenhower took an interest, "intense White House activity" turned around some senators, the House Republican leadership ceased opposition, House Rules went along by 7–5 after two months of obstruction, and the bill cleared both houses by three-to-two margins that enrolled majorities of both parties. Despite the healthy margins, there is no sign of wasted effort.[60] A bill creating the national wilderness system passed the Senate in 1961, but Democratic Congressman Wayne Aspinall of Colorado, chairman of the House Interior Committee and a spokesman for producer interests, held out until his terms were met. Once that finally happened, one full Congress later, passage came about almost unanimously in 1964.[61]

Also in unified circumstances, shepherding through the Civil Rights Acts of 1964 and 1965 required elaborate bipartisan coordination as well as enough stamina to outlast long Senate filibusters ended by cloture votes of 71–29 and 70–30. Republican Senator Everett Dirksen played a major role. Notwithstanding the one-sided outcomes, there was no slack.[62] Johnson's 1968 tax surcharge passed after ten months of conflict between the president and Wilbur Mills, chairman of the House Ways and Means Committee, who held out for accompanying expenditure cuts. Aided by Republican Senator John J. Williams, a compromise took shape that drew majority support from both parties

1985), pp. 145–46. On JTPA: Richard F. Fenno, Jr., *The Making of a Senator: Dan Quayle* (Washington, D.C.: Congressional Quarterly Press, 1989), chaps. 2, 3. On Social Security in 1983: Paul Light, *Artful Work: The Politics of Social Security Reform* (New York: Random House, 1985). On immigration reform in 1986: Michael C. LeMay, *From Open Door to Dutch Door: An Analysis of U.S. Immigration Policy since 1820* (New York: Praeger, 1987), chap. 6. On the Tax Reform Act of 1986: Birnbaum and Murray, *Showdown at Gucci Gulch.*

59. Nelson W. Polsby, *Political Innovation in America: The Politics of Policy Initiation* (New Haven and London: Yale University Press, 1984), pp. 44–55.

60. Gary W. Reichard, *The Reaffirmation of Republicanism: Eisenhower and the Eighty-third Congress* (Knoxville: University of Tennessee Press, 1975), pp. 164–74, quotation at p. 169.

61. Sundquist, *Politics and Policy,* pp. 358–61.

62. Ibid., pp. 259–75.

and cleared Senate and House by votes of 64–16 and 268–150.[63] That was a typical Wilbur Mills result. As reported by Richard F. Fenno, Jr., Mills's committee followed a norm in the 1950s and 1960s that virtually guaranteed super-majority floor victories or else no action at all in the areas of foreign trade, taxes, and Social Security: "In return for its extraordinary independence, the Committee promises to make decisions that are acceptable to the great majority of House members."[64] As a final instance, trucking deregulation, advanced by Senate reformers under Carter, had to navigate the pro-industry House Surface Transportation Subcommittee in 1980. That unit's chairman, Democrat James J. Howard of New Jersey, though not prepared to go to the wall for the industry, insisted on a process of negotiation among all concerned parties that appeased the truckers and defused what remained of Capitol Hill conflict.[65] Passage took place by 70–20 in the Senate and 367–13 in the House. Again, a normal aggregative process helped push victory well beyond the 51 percent mark.

It will be apparent that broad majorities do not explain anything by themselves. Instead, they provide an occasion for explanations, of which two have been offered here. Broad majorities, the argument goes, are promoted by a Capitol Hill mindset of problem-solving and a logic of aggregation. Both tendencies arguably contribute to law-making *constancy* by operating during times of divided as well as un-ified party control. Problem-solving no doubt makes a special contribution during times of divided control: It facilitates cooperation across party lines, which is particularly needed then. The aggregative logic does its most interesting work during times of unified control: It impedes runaway action by narrow party majorities. Broad coali-

63. Lawrence C. Pierce, *The Politics of Fiscal Policy Formation* (Pacific Palisades, Calif.: Goodyear Publishing, 1971), pp. 146–72.

64. Richard F. Fenno, Jr., *Congressmen in Committees* (Boston: Little, Brown, 1973), p. 55, and more generally pp. 51–57, 114–18. "Close observers testify to [Mills's] passion for 'vast majorities.' 'He is happiest when all twenty-five [Ways and Means Committee] members agree and the House is unanimous.' 'He wants at least twenty votes.' If his aim is consensus, his technique is compromise. 'He is a consensus seeker. He never pushes things to votes, we reach a compromise.' 'He leads by compromising' " (p. 115). See also John F. Manley, "Wilbur D. Mills: A Study in Congressional Influence," *American Political Science Review* 63 (1969), 448–49.

65. Derthick and Quirk, *Politics of Deregulation*, pp. 100–101, 113–16, 172–74.

tion-building turns out to be needed at those times anyway, despite the availability of the misnamed party whip.[66] To suppose that an American party winning Congress and the presidency thereby wins the leeway of a British parliamentary party is to be deluded by the election returns.

66. R. Douglas Arnold offers a somewhat different, though also *constancy-serving*, argument about congressional aggregative processes and large majorities: "How large a coalition do leaders seek to build? Do they aim for a minimum winning coalition, or do they seek to build a grand coalition that includes all legislators? All else equal, leaders prefer large coalitions because they provide the best insurance for the future. Each proposal must survive a long series of majoritarian tests—in committees and subcommittees, in House and Senate, and in authorization, appropriations, and budget bills. Large majorities help to insure that a bill clears these hurdles with ease. Moreover, large majorities are often required to overcome filibusters, presidential vetoes, and other obstructions that determined minorities may erect. Finally, once programs are passed and implemented, they need annual appropriations and occasional reauthorizations. Again, oversized majorities protect programs in the long run against defections, the retirement or defeat of habitual supporters, or changes in the mood of Congress." *The Logic of Congressional Action* (New Haven and London: Yale University Press, 1990), pp. 117–18.

6 ◆ EXPLAINING

THE PATTERNS, II

Politicians and processes seem to account for much of the "evening out" of differences across unified and divided control. But that is not the whole story. For more illumination, one needs to shift the emphasis away from inside-the-Beltway modes of aspiration and action and to focus on influences from the outside world. That is the task of chapter 6. All the arguments in it will address investigating as well as lawmaking.

EXTERNAL EVENTS

Some laws, as noted earlier, are obviously triggered by events.[1] If "events" occurred randomly and entirely outside the control of political actors, and if an "event" were a necessary, sufficient, and immediate cause of a law, there would be little point in writing this work. Real politics, of course, has much more play in it than that. Still, one can point to perhaps a fifth of the 267 laws listed in table 4.1 and say at least the following: Yes, because of a time-specific triggering cause more or less external to American national politics, it is quite understandable that a law passed during the one- or two-year period when it did rather than earlier or later. Here are some plausible examples: aid to Greece and Turkey in 1947, the Marshall Plan in 1948, the NATO treaty in 1949, the Defense Production Act and two Korean war tax increases in 1950–51, the creation of NASA in 1958 (just after the Soviets orbited Sputnik), drug regulation in 1962 (just after the thalidomide tragedy), the Gun Control Act of 1968 (after the assassinations of the Rev. Martin Luther King, Jr., and Senator Robert Kennedy), the coal mine safety act of 1969 (following a West Virginia mining disaster that left seventy-eight dead), the anti-recession tax

1. See the discussion in John W. Kingdon, *Agendas, Alternatives, and Public Policies* (Boston: Little, Brown, 1984), chap. 5.

cut of 1971, the creation of Conrail in 1973 (just after the northeastern railroads went bankrupt), various energy acts in 1973–75 during the energy crisis, the New York City bailout of 1975, the Chrysler bailout of 1979, the anti-recession jobs measure of 1983, and the savings-and-loan bailout of 1989.

Similar in being "forced," though they were triggered by previous government decisions rather than by external events, are the several renewals of the 1965 Voting Rights Act and of basic agricultural and foreign-trade law. In such cases, executive authority runs out after a specified number of years, and some new move has to be made.[2] External "events" occur more or less randomly. Renewals of authority tend to occur regularly. One obvious effect either way is a thrust toward lawmaking *constancy* across Congresses—and no doubt also across periods of unified and divided party control. That needs to be said in this analysis, although it is more of a background point than a pathbreaking discovery. And it is worth emphasizing that a large

2. This somewhat overstates the regularity and the problem. In the foreign trade area, seven of the eight acts listed in table 4.1—those of 1951, 1955, 1958, 1962, 1979, 1984, and 1988—were enacted at least partly because executive authority was running out. But one multi-year extension—that of 1949 (UNI) for two years—did not make it into table 4.1's net. Also, Truman in 1948 (DIV) and Eisenhower in 1953 (UNI) and 1954 (UNI) managed to win only one-year extensions of trade authority. Johnson in 1968 (UNI) and Nixon in 1969 (DIV) asked for extensions and got nothing; authority simply ran out. As a result, the important trade act of 1974 (listed in table 4.1) was evidently enacted without the stimulus of lapsing authority. In the agriculture area, twelve of the fifteen measures listed in table 4.1 were enacted as general government authority was running out or as current commodity supports were about to revert to fallback levels established by earlier statutes. Those were the measures of 1948, 1949, 1954 (flexible prices), 1956, 1958, 1965, 1970, 1973, 1977, 1981, 1985, and 1990. The other three do not seem to have had that stimulus, though in two cases the statutory background is murky. All three of the VRA extensions made table 4.1 by stipulation, but in fact government authority over voting rights was significantly expanded each time. Foreign trade, agriculture, and VRA authority aside, no policy area featured re-authorization acts that passed more or or less regularly through-out, say, a twenty-year period during 1946–90 and that table 4.1's metho-dologies more or less routinely picked up. Many foreign aid authorization bills passed during these decades, but only a few landmark ones appear in table 4.1. A dozen or more other acts listed in the table—such as the food stamps expansion of 1970—happen to have been enacted as government authority was lapsing. But they were significant initiatives in their own right; that is why they appear in the table.

majority of important laws do not seem to attach to particular times in any such determinate way.

The "event" of investigative politics is executive misbehavior, and that fact quickly poses two analytic problems. First, in contrast to perceptions of Sputnik or assassinations, members of Congress often do not agree whether misbehavior has occurred. That is what is at issue. Consider the controversies associated with the Hiss probe, the McCarthy-Army hearings, Senator Fulbright's Vietnam hearings, and the Iran-Contra inquiry. Second, instead of reacting to "events" that independently came to light, investigative committees often reveal, shape, or even fantasize "events" themselves. They themselves ferreted out the major alleged misbehavior in, for example, the Hiss probe, the RFC investigation of 1951, Dixon-Yates in 1955, the regulatory agencies probe of 1958, and the EPA probe of 1983. They seem to have largely fantasized it in the loyalty probes staged after 1948.[3]

These considerations make an event-triggered model of investigations problematic, although obviously extra-congressional events or at least revelations often do lead to probes. Truman's firing of MacArthur provoked the Korean war hearings. Media revelations brought on, for example, the Bert Lance inquiry.[4] It is a relevant question here whether some underlying level of "real" executive misbehavior, perhaps more or less randomly distributed, tends to provoke investigations also more or less randomly across Congresses. If so, that would help to nudge the incidence of probes toward *constancy* or else *alternative variation*—and toward equality across times of unified and divided party control. Perhaps corruption, at least, tends to occur randomly—or at least not according to any pattern related to party control—and thus helps to produce such an equalizing effect. But who knows? Self-motivated action by House and Senate members generates much of the information that ever comes our way about any such underlying reality. Without Nixon and HUAC, there might

3. See, for example, the conclusions reached by Earl Latham in *The Communist Controversy in Washington: From the New Deal to McCarthy* (Cambridge: Harvard University Press, 1966), chaps. 10, 11.

4. See Haynes Johnson, *In the Absence of Power: Governing America* (New York: Viking, 1980), pp. 208–13, and Richard E. Neustadt, *Presidential Power: The Politics of Leadership from FDR to Carter* (New York: John Wiley and Sons, 1980), pp. 225–27.

never have been a Hiss case.[5] At any time during Reagan's second term, some congressional committee could have delved into the ample corruption at HUD, but none did.[6] It evidently took Congressman Tom Lantos's entrepreneurial ability to get a HUD inquiry going, later in 1989.[7]

ISSUE CLEAVAGES

It is in order to introduce a standard pluralist argument about public opinion and issue cleavages. Obviously, an issue can divide the public along a line different from that of Democratic versus Republican party identification. Just as obviously, such an issue cleavage can win reflection in a non-party-line roll-call vote on Capitol Hill; one or both congressional parties may divide internally because they have home constituencies tilting both ways. Finally, it does not take advanced mathematics to show that such issue reflection can help along lawmaking under divided party control or impede it under unified control. It is all a matter of where the cleavages cut.

That having been stated, a caveat needs to be entered also. The existence of a public opinion cleavage cannot be inferred with anything like certainty from a division expressed in a roll-call vote. For one thing, as members of Congress go about solving problems and building coalitions, public opinion may figure as a raw material rather than as an array of judgments about a finished product. For another, on most roll-call questions public opinion probably does not, in any meaningful sense, exist. The specifics are too arcane. It would be an immense, not to say frustrating, task to try to match available opinion data with roll-call divisions on this study's 267 laws. That task will not be undertaken here. In the absence of it, the best course may be to reach for some particularly plausible cases—to argue that the distributions and effects posited above can occur without making claims about how often in fact they do occur. Such a case, let us say, is one

5. See Allen Weinstein, *Perjury: The Hiss-Chambers Case* (New York: Alfred A. Knopf, 1978), chap. 1.

6. Clifford D. May, "With Hindsight, Lawmakers Admit They Ignored Warnings on H.U.D.," *New York Times*, July 3, 1989, p. 9. "Members of the Congressional committees that oversee the Department of Housing and Urban Development acknowledge that they were repeatedly warned about mismanagement and fraud in the department but did little to stop them."

7. See Susan F. Rasky, "Lawmaker Finds Niche in Investigating H.U.D.," *New York Times*, July 6, 1989, p. B5.

that features: (a) intense and enduring views held by two substantial opposing sides within an opinion population at least as large as a nationwide political elite of several million people, and (b) a resulting roll-call cleavage that behaves as posited in times of unified or divided party control or both.

Civil rights between the mid-1950s and the early 1970s provides one plausible case. Few opinion cleavages have ever achieved such prominence. Among voters and their representatives, an aroused North confronted a resistant white South. In Congress, as table 5.6 shows, a roll-call cleavage of most southern Democrats versus most Republicans and most northern Democrats appeared on six civil-rights enactments during those years. (Note that nearly all Republican House and Senate members were still northerners back then.) The acts of 1957, 1960, and 1970 passed during divided control; those of 1964, 1965, and 1968 passed during unified control.[8] Obviously, the sectional cleavage differed from and dominated the party cleavage.

Another good example is basic labor-management relations. Since World War II, the Democrats have repeatedly failed to overhaul labor law to the unions' taste even when they have held the presidency and large congressional majorities. Sometimes anti-labor Senate filibusters intruded, but a deeper cause seems to be a longstanding North-South opinion cleavage within the Democratic party. Unions have not been popular with southern electorates. Accordingly, scores of congressional Democrats from the South have ordinarily voted with the Republicans on labor-management issues. Since the Republicans normally put up a solid front, the union side keeps losing.[9]

8. The Equal Employment Opportunity Act of 1972 came one Senate vote away from adding a seventh instance to the list. On final passage, Republicans voted 119–55 in the House and 30–4 in the Senate. Northern Democrats voted 154–4 and 26–0. Southern Democrats voted 30–51 and 6–6. By 1972, black enfranchisement was starting to tell in the southern Democratic delegations.

9. Thomas Byrne Edsall ascribes the Democrats' Capitol Hill failure in 1977–78, under Carter, to a mid-1970s party shift away from its traditional working-class orientation toward middle-class "procedural reform," and also to increased financing of Democratic House and Senate incumbents by business PACs. See *The New Politics of Inequality* (New York: W. W. Norton, 1984), pp. 31–66, 134–35, 149–50. But these are "local" explanations. Union-backed efforts to reform labor-management law fared no better in 1949–50 under Truman or in 1965–66 under Johnson. The large Democratic congressional majorities during those times were not held back by business-PAC support or

Civil rights and labor-management relations provide especially plausible cases. But many other issue areas could be argued for. One of the striking features of congressional politics, after all, is its unceasing production of new roll-call alignments issue by issue. No doubt these often have bases in public opinion. For purposes here, the summary effect of all Capitol Hill representation of non-party-line opinion cleavages is probably a thrust toward lawmaking *constancy*.

The argument for issue cleavages also works quite well for some high-publicity investigations—particularly in the area of national-security policy. Here are the ingredients. First, the Constitution, by inviting congressional oversight of the executive branch, invites also a highly charged kind of policy warfare in which a Capitol Hill opposition can oppose current executive policies by identifying them with, or simply casting them as, misbehavior. It can be a brilliant strategy. Second, the same characteristic that makes the national security area difficult to control by statute—the area calls for unusual discretionary authority for the executive—confers on it a great deal of behavior targetable in probes. And in fact, probes have rivaled laws as a way to exercise congressional influence. Third, if one canvasses for instances of intense, polarized American opinion since World War II, some of the cleavages over national-security policy will probably make any short-list. Fourth, to an appreciable degree those cleavages have crosscut party lines. Fifth, though a law cannot be passed without a floor majority, a policy can be promoted through investigative action without one. Normally the only requirement is a committee majority— as in the case of the Senate Foreign Relations Committee in the late 1960s. The media willing, views held by only a minority of House or Senate members can gain considerable force.

All this adds up to a potent recipe. The two major clusters of national-security probes took place in, again, 1948 through 1954 and 1966 through 1975. In the first period, the case for a more aggressive anti-Communist foreign policy—for unleashing Chiang Kai-shek, MacArthur, and more—traveled on such misbehavior stories as the

---

by any commitment to middle-class "procedural reform." On the unsuccessful move to repeal the Taft-Hartley Act in 1949, see R. Alton Lee, *Truman and Taft-Hartley: A Question of Mandate* (Lexington: University Press of Kentucky, 1966), chap. 7. A naive empiricist knowing only the legislative record of 1946 through 1990, which featured the Landrum-Griffin Act of 1959 (DIV) as well as the Taft-Hartley of 1947 (DIV), might understandably leap to a conclusion that divided party control is a necessary condition for major legislation in the area of labor-management relations.

"betrayal" at Yalta, Truman's "no-win" policy in Korea, and "who lost China?" In the second period, the anti-Indochina war cause fed on Johnson's Tonkin Bay "deception," the "credibility gap," "abuses of power," and the "secret Cambodian bombing." Opinion cleavages that divided the ruling party figured in some of these eras' most prominent probes that took place during times of unified control. It was Mc-Carran versus Truman in 1951–52 on China policy, McCarthy versus Eisenhower in 1953–54 on the country's alleged internal-security problems, and Fulbright versus Johnson in 1966–68 on Indochina. That is an impressive array of intra-party antagonisms.[10]

In general, the logic of the argument here is that crosscutting opinion cleavages should be expected to contribute to *constancy* of investigative activity across times of unified and divided party control. And in fact, it seems clear that the contribution to "evening out" across those times is quite important: Consider especially the Army-McCarthy and Fulbright investigations. But the record of 1946 through 1990 suggests beyond that a case for *alternative variation*, given the time locations of the two clusters of national-security probes. That suggestion can serve as a lead-in to the next topic.

PUBLIC MOODS

None of the arguments so far has addressed the tendency of high-publicity investigations and lawmaking to concentrate in waves that last several years and exhibit both a high volume of activity and a coherent ideological thrust.[11] The chief case in point is the "ideological surge" of the mid-1960s through the mid-1970s. This presents an

10. In all three cases, it is probably more accurate to say that the senators were reflecting sectors of opinion within their national parties rather than, in any simple sense, their home constituencies.

11. Also worth considering are one-shot changes in background conditions that might have caused changes in legislative or investigative activity during the forty-four years. Morris Fiorina has theorized, for example, referring to the 1960s and 1970s, that "the growth of an activist federal government has stimulated a change in the mix of congressional activities. Specifically, a lesser proportion of congressional effort is going into programmatic activities and a greater proportion into pork-barrel and casework activities." And: "I seriously doubt that congressmen resist their gradual transformation from national legislators to errand boy-ombudsmen." *Congress: Keystone of the Washington Establishment* (New Haven and London: Yale University Press, 1977), pp. 46, 47. But it seems very doubtful that such a substitution ever took place. For one thing, the first statistical jump in the electoral advantage

obvious pattern of *alternative variation*, but what, as a general proposition, was happening and why? For explanatory leverage—more
such surges would help—it may be useful to consult two prominent
cyclical interpretations of American politics that reach back at least
to the beginning of the twentieth century. In both views, certain segments of political history are depicted or coded as waves of intense,
ideologically driven activity. In both cases, such waves figure as phases
in cycles and are argued to constitute the country's paramount form
of political action.

"Electoral realignment" theory, the first of these accounts, features
quick major changes in voter alignments as causes of the country's
important departures in policymaking.[12] The connecting mechanisms
are political parties. In the theory's most familiar scenario, parties
freshly empowered by new voter coalitions preside over surges of
decisive national lawmaking.[13] They did that, for example, under
Lincoln and under Franklin Roosevelt. Unfortunately, electoral realignments offer no help whatever for the decades after World War
II since, according to the canonical listing of them, none has occurred
since the 1930s. Beyond that, the theory does little to illuminate the
last hundred years. During that time, such realignments, which took
place only in the mid-1890s and early 1930s, proved to be neither a
sufficient nor a necessary condition for exceptional surges of national

---

of House incumbency, which is often tied to rising casework opportunities,
took place in the mid-1960s—at the *beginning* of one of the longest and most
energetic bursts of lawmaking in American history. Casework, lawmaking,
and House incumbency advantage evidently soared all at once. As a causal
connection, if one exists, it seems at least as likely that better casework and
higher resulting electoral margins freed up members to concentrate on lawmaking. For another thing, it probably romanticizes Senate and House members of previous eras to see them as "national" legislators more so than are
today's. The oldtimers did not need any lessons in, for example, pork-
barreling. A better bet for a one-shot change in the mid-1960s is that fast-
accelerating staff support on Capitol Hill aided the legislative take-off. But
at best, that can only partly account for the ideological dynamism of that take-
off.

12. See, for example, Walter Dean Burnham, "Party Systems and the Political
Process," chap. 10 in William Nisbet Chambers and Burnham, eds., *The Amer-
ican Party Systems: Stages of Political Development* (New York: Oxford University
Press, 1967), pp. 287–304.

13. For an undiluted assertion that realignments relate one-to-one to important surges of lawmaking, see David W. Brady, *Critical Elections and Congressional Policy Making* (Stanford, Calif.: Stanford University Press, 1988).

lawmaking. The realignment of the 1930s did of course help to generate the New Deal and its legislative record. But that of the 1890s, which worked to stave off William Jennings Bryan's threat to the status quo, was followed by what one historian has termed "policy inertia."[14] Not much memorable legislating occurred under President McKinley.[15] As for not being a necessary condition, the lawmaking surges of the Progressive era and of the 1960s through the 1970s came and went without the assistance of electoral realignments. If we had to depend on realignments either to foster or to explain such surges, it seems fair to conclude, we might as well fold our tents.

Much more promising is Arthur Schlesinger, Jr., and his scheme of American thirty-year cycles in which pursuit of "public purpose" has alternated with pursuit of "private interest." During a "public purpose" phase, much of the general population throws itself into political activity to help achieve ambitious reform goals through gov-

14. Richard L. McCormick, "Walter Dean Burnham and 'The System of 1896,'" *Social Science History* 10 (1986), 245. "The scholarly findings on policy change after the 1890s realignment have been inconclusive in the extreme" (p. 256).

15. Probably no one unpropelled by "realignment theory" would suppose that a burst of innovative lawmaking took place under McKinley in 1897–1901. The notable measures of those years were evidently the Dingley Tariff Act of 1897, raising duties to new heights, and the Gold Standard Act of 1900, confirming that standard. But it was a Republican tradition to raise the tariff to new heights, and a commitment to the gold standard was hardly innovative. It continued Grover Cleveland's policy of 1893–97. "The existing gold standard must be maintained," exhorted the 1896 Republican platform, and it was. For any one Congress, a good bet for the most substantial lawmaking record between Reconstruction and the Progressive era is that of 1889–91, under Benjamin Harrison. A Republican "Billion Dollar Congress," called that for its extravagance, passed the Sherman Antitrust Act, the Sherman Silver Purchase Act, the McKinley Tariff Act (an earlier increase of duties), the Naval Act of 1890 (inaugurating the modern navy), and the Dependent Pension Act of 1890 (greatly expanding the Civil War pension system). Recent scholarship has highlighted the pension measure: "In effect, an open-ended old-age pension system was established for over three-quarters of a million former soldiers (along with a liberalized survivors' pension for widows and dependents)." "The post–Civil War pension system at its fullest development in the 1890s and early 1900s was an extraordinary public social welfare effort." Theda Skocpol and John Ikenberry, "The Political Formation of the American Welfare State in Historical and Comparative Perspective," in Richard F. Tomasson, ed., *Comparative Social Research: The Welfare State, 1883–1983*, vol. 6 (London: JAI Press, 1983), p. 97.

ernment action. Schlesinger's three twentieth-century exhibits of "public purpose" are the Progressive era, the New Deal era, and the Kennedy-Johnson-Nixon era of the 1960s and 1970s.[16] Samuel P. Huntington, in a dovetailing though not identical cyclical model, points also to the Progressive era and the period of 1960 through 1975—though not the New Deal—as what he calls periods of "creedal passion." In 1960 through 1975, the American public opted for "moralism and protest, outrage and exposure, ideals and reform."[17]

For purposes here, the attractiveness of these two authors lies less in their theories of whether or why politics travels in cycles—those can be taken or left—than in their morphologies of public engagement. That is, both of them isolate and investigate long continuous periods of such engagement—of "public purpose" or "creedal passion." Such periods share a status with electoral realignments in that they can be mobilized to try to explain other phenomena—notably Capitol Hill lawmaking "surges," to use the terminology of this work. In fact, the three periods of public engagement map rather nicely onto the twentieth century's major lawmaking surges. In tracking engagement in the 1960s and 1970s, neither Schlesinger nor Huntington has any difficulty combining Nixon's years with the earlier Democratic ones to form one continuous era. And as intense, lengthy lawmaking enterprises, the Progressive and New Deal eras do indeed seem to be the appropriate counterparts of the 1960s and 1970s.[18]

16. Arthur M. Schlesinger, Jr., "The Cycles of American Politics," chap. 2 in Schlesinger, *The Cycles of American History* (Boston: Houghton Mifflin, 1986), pp. 31–34.

17. Samuel P. Huntington, *American Politics: The Promise of Disharmony* (Cambridge: Harvard University Press, 1981), chaps. 5, 7, quotation at p. 196. A useful discussion of Schlesinger's and Huntington's ideas about cycles appears in David Resnick and Norman C. Thomas, "Cycling through American Politics," *Polity* 23 (1990), pp. 8–10, 19–20.

18. Current writers have been grouping these periods into a threesome of policy-making eras: "Within a state structure so discouraging of unified, persistent class politics as US federal democracy has always been, it is perhaps not surprising that social policy breakthroughs have clustered in widely separated 'big bangs' of reform: during the Progressive Era of about 1906 to 1920; during the New Deal of the mid-1930s; and between the mid-1960s and the mid-1970s, during and right after the 'Great Society' period." Theda Skocpol, "A Society without a 'State'? Political Organization, Social Conflict, and Welfare Provision in the United States," *Journal of Public Policy* 7 (1987), 364–65. "Major reform periods in the Progressive Era and the New Deal not only preceded, but in many respects foreshadowed, the policy reforms of the

But the three-way analogy, if it is to suggest general propositions that can illuminate recent times, needs a passable concrete examination of the earlier eras. The strategy here will be to start with some arrays of factual material taken from standard secondary sources. As exercises in lawmaking, what did the Progressive and New Deal eras amount to? Though it will receive less attention, how about legislative investigating? Also, how did lawmaking and investigating correspond to patterns of unified as opposed to divided party control? For the Progressive era, lawmaking will be surveyed briefly at the state level—a site of more dynamism then than in later times—as well as at the national level. Once the factual material is presented, the discussion will circle back to Schlesinger and Huntington and the possible causes of legislative and investigative "surges."

At the state level, the Progressive era's lawmaking appears to have proceeded at high pitch from roughly 1905 through 1914.[19] Ideas for laws spread quickly from state to state; busy legislating was always in evidence somewhere. In general, the reform agenda shifted over the decade from political and economic regulation—direct primary laws, railroad commissions, corrupt practices acts, regulation of lobbying and the like—to social measures such as workmen's compensation, child labor codes, widows' pensions, and maximum-hour laws for women. Arresting legislative performances took place under an impressive variety of party circumstances. In some instances "party government" ushered in reform: That is, a governor and a legislature of the same party carried through an ambitious program in a competitive two-party state. New York's Republicans followed that pattern under Charles Evans Hughes in 1907, New York Democrats did so

1970s. An understanding of these two antecedent efforts at reform is instructive inasmuch as they also embodied a close linkage between reform of substance and reform of process in public policy. Indeed, it is precisely this linkage of policy substance and process that accounts for the significance of all three episodes in American history." Elsewhere the author refers to "the period from the late 1960s through the 1970s." Richard A. Harris, "A Decade of Reform," chap. 1 in Harris and Sidney M. Milkis, eds., *Remaking American Politics* (Boulder, Colo.: Westview Press, 1989), pp. 5, 9.

19. Some good general sources are: Richard L. McCormick, "The Discovery That Business Corrupts Politics: A Reappraisal of the Origins of Progressivism," *American Historical Review* 86 (1981), 266–68; George E. Mowry, *The Era of Theodore Roosevelt, 1900–1912* (New York: Harper and Brothers, 1958), pp. 71–84; and David Sarasohn, *The Party of Reform: Democrats in the Progressive Era* (Jackson: University Press of Mississippi, 1989), pp. 112–18.

in enacting a labor program in 1913, and Ohio Democrats did so under Governor James M. Cox in 1913–14.[20]

Wisconsin's Robert La Follette stage-managed a historic program through a legislature of his own party in 1903 and 1905, as did California's Hiram Johnson in 1911, but in both cases that fact is a part-truth: Their followers were progressive Republicans but their conservative oppositions were largely Republican too. La Follette relied on swing support from a three-member Democratic senate minority in 1903.[21] To cite a southern example, Governor Hoke Smith carried a reform program in Georgia in 1907–09, but that state's context was of course one-party Democratic.[22] North Dakota's chief burst of reform occurred in 1911 under Democratic Governor John Burke and a nominally Republican legislature, though in fact a cross-party coalition of Democrats and progressive Republicans dominated both houses.[23] Minnesota's Democratic Governor John A. Johnson ushered sizable programs through cooperative Republican legislatures in 1905 and 1907.[24] In Massachusetts in 1911–14, a notable set of measures including the country's first minimum wage law owed to Democratic

20. On New York in 1907: Robert F. Wesser, *Charles Evans Hughes: Politics and Reform in New York, 1905–1910* (Ithaca, N.Y.: Cornell University Press, 1967), chap. 7 and pp. 309–10, 328–30. On New York in 1913: J. Joseph Huthmacher, *Senator Robert F. Wagner and the Rise of Urban Liberalism* (New York: Atheneum, 1971), p. 7 and chap. 3; David M. Ellis et al., *A Short History of New York State* (Ithaca, N.Y.: Cornell University Press, 1967), pp. 389–90; Thomas M. Henderson, *Tammany Hall and the New Immigrants: The Progressive Years* (New York: Arno Press, 1976), pp. 123–24. On Ohio in 1913–14: James E. Cebula, *James M. Cox: Journalist and Politician* (New York: Garland Press, 1985), chaps. 4–6; Hoyt L. Warner, *Progressivism in Ohio, 1897–1917* (Columbus: Ohio State University Press, 1964), chap. 14.

21. On Wisconsin: Robert S. Maxwell, *La Follette and the Rise of the Progressives in Wisconsin* (New York: Russell and Russell, 1956), pp. 48–55, 73–82. La Follette's 1903 success came before much was going on in other states. On California: George E. Mowry, *The California Progressives* (Chicago: Quadrangle, 1963), pp. 135–40; Spencer C. Olin, Jr., *California's Prodigal Sons: Hiram Johnson and the Progressives, 1911–1917* (Berkeley: University of California Press, 1968), chaps. 2, 3.

22. Dewey W. Grantham, *Southern Progressivism: The Reconciliation of Progress and Tradition* (Knoxville: University of Tennessee Press, 1983), pp. 51–54.

23. Elwyn B. Robinson, *History of North Dakota* (Lincoln: University of Nebraska Press, 1966), pp. 264–68; Charles N. Glaab, "The Failure of North Dakota Progressivism," *Mid-America* 39 (1957), 199–206.

24. Winifred G. Helmes, *John A. Johnson, the People's Governor: A Political*

Governor Eugene Noble Foss and a formally Republican legislature's "progressive elements in both parties."[25] Finally, Woodrow Wilson, a year away from the White House, won "great national acclaim" by advancing an ambitious program through "the greatest reform legislature in the history of [New Jersey]" in 1911. But half that body was a Republican senate, and it evidently gave Wilson less difficulty than did the Democratic assembly.[26] There is no telling whether the examples cited here are exactly representative, but they comprise a good share of the era's best-known programmatic success stories, and their geographic spread and variety of party formats speak for themselves.[27]

At the national level, the era's reform lawmaking began with two dramatic achievements in 1906, sputtered for awhile, then more or less stabilized at a high-productivity pace that continued through 1916.[28] The opening achievements were major items of Theodore Roosevelt's Square Deal that the Republican Congress of 1905–07 (UNI) enacted: the Hepburn Act authorizing regulation of railroad rates, and two consumer measures ordinarily lumped together—the

Biography (Minneapolis: University of Minnesota Press, 1949), pp. 169–77, 209–13.

25. Richard B. Sherman, "Foss of Massachusetts: Demagogue or Progressive?" *Mid-America* 43 (1961), 86–90, quotation at p. 88; Richard M. Abrams, *Conservatism in a Progressive Era: Massachusetts Politics, 1900–1912* (Cambridge: Harvard University Press, 1964), pp. 257–60.

26. Arthur S. Link, *Wilson: The Road to the White House* (Princeton, N.J.: Princeton University Press, 1947), pp. 244–75, quotations at pp. 277, 267.

27. At least six of the cited governors came to figure as White House possibilities: Hughes, Cox, La Follette, Johnson of California, Johnson of Minnesota, and Wilson.

28. Except for the campaign finance measures, the list of statutes discussed here was drawn from standard general sources on the Progressive era: Mowry, *Era of Theodore Roosevelt*, chaps. 7, 11–14; Sarasohn, *Party of Reform*, chaps. 1, 3, 4, 6; John Milton Cooper, Jr., *Pivotal Decades: The United States, 1900–1920* (New York: W. W. Norton, 1990), pp. 46–48, 90–102, 109–21, 145–57, 162, 195–202, 212–19, 291, 298, 307–08; Lewis L. Gould, *Reform and Regulation: American Politics, 1900–1916* (New York: John Wiley and Sons, 1978), pp. 32–33, 51–73, 90–96, 105–06, 149–58, 168–75; Paolo E. Coletta, *The Presidency of William Howard Taft* (Lawrence: University Press of Kansas, 1973), chaps. 3, 5–7, 13; Arthur S. Link, *Woodrow Wilson and the Progressive Era, 1910–1917* (New York: Harper and Brothers, 1954), chaps. 2, 3, 9; Howard W. Allen, "Geography and Politics: Voting on Reform Issues in the United States Senate, 1911–1916," *Journal of Southern History* 27 (1961), 218.

Pure Food and Drug Act and Meat Inspection Act.[29] In promoting these bills, Roosevelt is said to have pioneered the modern presidential role of "chief legislator" by energetically marshaling public opinion so as to pressure Congress. That was not a nineteenth-century role. The campaign for the Hepburn Act required eighteen months as well as Democratic help. The result, according to one analyst: "It would not be unreasonable to suggest that the Hepburn Act gave birth to the modern administrative state."[30]

After two fallow years closing out the Roosevelt presidency (UNI), reform lawmaking came alive again under William Howard Taft in 1909.[31] Goaded by Democrats and Republican insurgents, the Republican Congress of 1909–11 (UNI) passed the Mann-Elkins Act—another major effort at railroad regulation; created a postal savings system—an idea that had brewed for some four decades; and approved the Sixteenth Amendment authorizing a federal income tax.[32] After the 1910 election gave Democrats control of the House, the Congress of 1911–13 (DIV) approved the Seventeenth Amendment

29. On the Hepburn Act: Mowry, *Era of Theodore Roosevelt*, pp. 197–206; Elmer E. Cornwell, Jr., *Presidential Leadership of Public Opinion* (Bloomington: Indiana University Press, 1965), pp. 24–26; John Morton Blum, *The Republican Roosevelt* (Cambridge: Harvard University Press, 1977), pp. 87–105; Stephen Skowronek, *Building a New American State: The Expansion of National Administrative Capacities, 1877–1920* (New York: Cambridge University Press, 1982), pp. 255–59; Jeffrey K. Tulis, *The Rhetorical Presidency* (Princeton, N.J.: Princeton University Press, 1987), chap. 4. On the drug and meat inspection acts: Mowry, *Era of Theodore Roosevelt*, pp. 207–08; Cooper, *Pivotal Decades*, pp. 97–99; Robert M. Crumden, *Ministers of Reform: The Progressives' Achievement in American Civilization* (New York: Basic Books, 1982), chap. 6.

30. Tulis, *Rhetorical Presidency*, p. 101.

31. Roosevelt was still promoting a considerable program in 1907–08, but his proposals "hit a stone wall on Capitol Hill." See Cooper, *Pivotal Decades*, pp. 109–21, quotation at p. 113.

32. On Taft's first Congress in general: Mowry, *Era of Theodore Roosevelt*, chap. 12; Cooper, *Pivotal Decades*, pp. 145–57; Gould, *Reform and Regulation*, pp. 90–96; Coletta, *Presidency of Taft*, chaps. 3, 5, and pp. 121–29. On the Mann-Elkins Act: Skowronek, *Building a New American State*, pp. 261–67; Kenneth W. Hechler, *Insurgency: Personalities and Politics of the Taft Era* (New York: Columbia University Press, 1940), chap. 8. On postal savings: Jean R. Schroedel, "Public Conflict and Private Cooperation: Executive-Congressional Relations Reappraised" (Ph.D. diss., MIT, 1989), pp. 86–104; Hechler, *Insurgency*, pp. 158–62. On the Sixteenth Amendment: Jerold Waltman, "Origins of the Federal Income Tax," *Mid-America* 62 (1980), 154–56; David

to require direct election of U.S. Senators,[33] voted an eight-hour day for workers on federal government contracts, and created a federal Children's Bureau and the Department of Labor.[34] In addition, Congress enacted the third and most ambitious of a 1907, 1910, and 1911 sequence of campaign-finance reforms that banned corporate contributions in federal elections, required disclosure of receipts and

E. Kyvig, "Can the Constitution Be Amended? The Battle over the Income Tax, 1895–1913," *Prologue* 20 (1988), 191–95; Hechler, *Insurgency*, chap. 6.

33. This work deals with national legislative enactments. But note that the Seventeenth Amendment is an instance also of something else: "democratizing" moves, whether through such enactments or otherwise, that have occurred during the twentieth century's three activist eras. In the Progressive era these included also the deflating of "Czar" Cannon's House speakership in 1910, and at the state level, the introduction of direct primaries (including presidential primaries in many states) and provisions for initiative, referendum, and recall. In the 1960s and 1970s such moves included the anti-organization reform of presidential nominating processes after 1968, the anti-oligarchy reforms of U.S. House procedures in the 1970s ending in the purge of three committee chairmen in January 1975, the Voting Rights Act of 1965, the vote for eighteen-year-olds, and perhaps the quasi-corporatist experiment with "maximum feasible participation" in the anti-poverty program of the mid-1960s. Such a list for the New Deal era might include the 1937 abandonment of Lochner-Court constraints on economic legislation (albeit not directly by way of Roosevelt's court-packing plan), the 1936 shift from two-thirds to majority rule in Democratic nominating conventions, and the quasi-corporatist resort to farmers' referenda to decide on crop controls and NLRB-staged elections to decide on unionization of bargaining units. One point is particularly relevant here. "Democratizing" reforms directly affecting Congress do not seem to have played a significant role as causes or conditions of the three eras' legislative surges. The Seventeenth Amendment kicked in too late to have much effect on Progressive lawmaking. The weakening of the House speakership lost its immediate relevance after the 1910 election, when pro-reform Democrats took over the House; under them an untrimmed speakership would most likely not have been an impediment to policymaking. And resort to a time warp would be needed to assign the House reforms of the 1970s much credit for the legislative surge of 1963 through 1975–76. In general, the causes of lawmaking surges seem to be deeper or more elemental than changes in congressional structure can reach. At least in the short term, such changes seem to be—like the surges—something to be explained rather than something that explains.

34. On Taft's second Congress: Mowry, *Era of Theodore Roosevelt*, pp. 262–64; Sarasohn, *Party of Reform*, chap. 4; Coletta, *Presidency of Taft*, pp. 132–40 and chaps. 7, 13. On the Department of Labor: Lawrence H. Chamberlain, *President, Congress, and Legislation* (New York: Columbia University Press,

expenditures by congressional candidates, and ultimately placed a ceiling on spending by congressional candidates.[35] In its political dynamics, the sequence had much in common with that on the same subject in 1971, 1972, and 1974 (see table 4.1).[36]

Once elected president, Woodrow Wilson proved as adept at operating under unified party control in Washington as he had under divided control in Trenton. His opening New Freedom legislative drive, like the earlier one in New Jersey, consisted of a few well-chosen, well-publicized, and successful strokes. The Democratic Congress of 1913–15 (UNI) followed his lead in enacting the Underwood tariff act, which lowered rates and also initiated a progressive income tax, the Federal Reserve Act, the Clayton Antitrust Act, and a measure creating the Federal Trade Commission. From outside Wilson's agenda came the La Follette Seamen's Act addressing conditions of maritime employment.[37] In the subsequent Congress of 1915–17, also Democratic (UNI), "a burst of new progressive legislation" in the 1916 session included the Federal Farm Loan Act, workmen's compensation for federal employees, a ban on interstate sale of goods produced by child labor (this was later struck down by the Supreme Court), the Adamson Act mandating an eight-hour day for railroad workers, and the Revenue Act of 1916—which "transformed the experimental income tax into the primary instrument of federal taxation."[38] Lagging

1946), pp. 143–45. On the creation of the Children's Bureau: Theda Skocpol, "Protecting Soldiers and Mothers: The Politics of Social Provision in the United States, 1870s–1920s" (MS, 1989), chap. 8. On the eight-hour law, a high-priority AFL item: Elizabeth Brandeis, *Labor Legislation*, vol. 4 in John R. Commons and Associates, *History of Labor in the United States, 1896–1932* (New York: Macmillan, 1935), p. 546.

35. James K. Pollock, Jr., *Party Campaign Funds* (New York: Alfred A. Knopf, 1926), pp. 180–84; Louise Overacker, *Money in Elections* (New York: Macmillan, 1932), pp. 234–38; Robert E. Mutch, *Campaigns, Congress, and Courts: The Making of Federal Campaign Finance Law* (New York: Praeger, 1988), pp. 1–16.

36. Although the earlier enactments, when compared with the later ones, lacked enforcement teeth.

37. On the Congress of 1913–15: Link, *Woodrow Wilson and the Progressive Era*, chaps. 2, 3; Gould, *Reform and Regulation*, pp. 149–58; Cooper, *Pivotal Decades*, pp. 195–202.

38. On the 1916 session: Link, *Woodrow Wilson and the Progressive Era*, chap. 9; Gould, *Reform and Regulation*, pp. 168–75; Cooper, *Pivotal Decades*, pp. 212–29; Sarasohn, *Party of Reform*, pp. 183–89, quotation at p. 183. On the Rev-

after the 1916 legislative drive—the era's last such campaign—were congressional endorsement of the Prohibition amendment in December 1917 (UNI) and the women's suffrage amendment in May 1919 (DIV).[39]

That was the era's lawmaking record, or at least a plausible rendition of its highlights. No effort will be made here to capsulize the period's legislative investigating, of which there was a great deal.[40] The targets were alleged dubious behavior in government, business, or a nexus of the two. At the national level, the Pujo "Money Trust Investigation," which began in the summer of 1912 and lasted eight months, is said to have been "the first Congressional investigation conducted in the 'grand manner' of modern times."[41]

The New Deal era, considered as a span of lawmaking aimed at either recovery or reform, is a story of four consecutive Congresses. The two during Franklin Roosevelt's first term unquestionably stand out. Major enactments of the Congress of 1933–34 (UNI), which opened with the celebrated "hundred days," have already been presented at the beginning of chapter 3.[42] The Congress of 1935–36 (UNI) compiled a comparable record.[43] Of Roosevelt's "second

enue Act: W. Elliot Brownlee, "Wilson and Financing the Modern State: The Revenue Act of 1916," *Proceedings of the American Philosophical Society* 129 (1985), 173–210, quotation at p. 173. "The boldness of the progressive shift is without equal in the history of American taxation" (p. 173). On the child labor measure: Chamberlain, *President, Congress, and Legislation*, pp. 145–52. On the Federal Farm Loan Act: ibid., pp. 269–75. On the Adamson Act: Robert Higgs, *Crisis and Leviathan: Critical Episodes in the Growth of American Government* (New York: Oxford University Press, 1987), pp. 116–21.

39. See Cooper, *Pivotal Decades*, pp. 307–08.

40. See, for example, McCormick, "The Discovery That Business Corrupts Politics," pp. 259–64.

41. Telford Taylor, *Grand Inquest: The Story of Congressional Investigations* (New York: Simon and Schuster, 1955), pp. 62–65, quotation at pp. 62–63; Sarasohn, *Party of Reform*, pp. 109–10, 165.

42. See William E. Leuchtenburg, *Franklin D. Roosevelt and the New Deal, 1932–1940* (New York: Harper and Row, 1963), chap. 3 and pp. 85–86, 90–91, 135, 203–05; Arthur M. Schlesinger, Jr., *The Coming of the New Deal* (Boston: Houghton Mifflin, 1958), chaps. 2, 3, 6, 15–17, 19, 20, 26, 28; Albert U. Romasco, *The Politics of Recovery: Roosevelt's New Deal* (New York: Oxford University Press, 1983), chap. 3.

43. The sources on 1935–36: Leuchtenburg, *Franklin D. Roosevelt and the New Deal*, pp. 124–33, chap. 7, pp. 171–73; Schlesinger, *Coming of the New Deal*, chaps. 18, 24; Arthur M. Schlesinger, Jr., *The Politics of Upheaval* (Boston:

hundred days" from June through August of 1935, one analyst writes that "no other session of Congress had ever adopted so much legislation of permanent importance."[44] Headed by the Social Security Act and the Wagner Labor-Relations Act, those measures included also the Public Utilities Holding Company Act (a move to break up large utility empires), the Wealth Tax Act of 1935 (a modest move to tax high incomes), the Banking Act of 1935 (an important centralization of monetary authority), and the Guffey-Snyder Coal Act (to regulate the coal industry). Earlier in 1935 had come the Emergency Relief Appropriation Act, which allocated $4.8 billion and served as a charter for Harry Hopkins's Works Progress Administration (WPA). Enactments during the 1936 session included the Soil Conservation and Domestic Allotment Act, authorization of the Rural Electrification Administration (REA) as an independent agency, and a $2 billion veterans' bonus bill passed over Roosevelt's veto.

The Congress of 1937–38 (UNI) ended up greatly disappointing New Dealers, considering its huge Democratic majorities. Many initiatives foundered even though Republicans had fallen to record lows of seventeen Senators and eighty-nine House members.[45] But at least five notable acts contributed to a respectable last phase of the era's legislative surge.[46] These were the Wagner-Steagall Housing Act of 1937 (a commitment to low-income public housing), the Farm Tenancy Act of 1937 (a shaky commitment to sharecroppers and tenant

Houghton Mifflin, 1960), pp. 261–70, chaps. 16–18, pp. 381–84; James T. Patterson, *Congressional Conservatism and the New Deal: The Growth of the Conservative Coalition in Congress, 1933–1939* (Lexington: University Press of Kentucky, 1967), chap. 2 and pp. 77–80. On the Wealth Tax Act of 1935: Mark H. Leff, *The Limits of Symbolic Reform: The New Deal and Taxation, 1933–1939* (New York: Cambridge University Press, 1984), pp. 119–68.

44. Leuchtenburg, *Franklin D. Roosevelt and the New Deal*, p. 162.

45. Among the losses was the House's close, emotion-charged defeat of Roosevelt's Executive Reorganization bill (growing out of the Brownlow Committee report) in April 1938. See Richard Polenberg, *Reorganizing Roosevelt's Government: The Controversy over Executive Reorganization, 1936–1939* (Cambridge: Harvard University Press, 1966), chap. 8.

46. The sources for 1937–38: Leuchtenburg, *Franklin D. Roosevelt and the New Deal*, pp. 135–42 and chaps. 10, 11; Patterson, *Congressional Conservatism*, pp. 11, 159, 233–46; James MacGregor Burns, *Roosevelt: The Lion and the Fox* (New York: Harcourt, Brace, 1956), chaps. 15–17; Barry D. Karl, *The Uneasy State: The United States from 1915 to 1945* (Chicago: University of Chicago Press, 1983), pp. 167–69.

farmers), the Fair Labor Standards Act of 1938 (the first federal minimum-wage law), the Agricultural Adjustment Act of 1938, and an expensive anti-recession pump-priming measure in 1938.[47]

The other Congress contributing to the era's surge was the first of the four—that of 1931–33 when a Republican Senate and a Democratic House faced Herbert Hoover (DIV).[48] From the standpoint of reform or recovery, as conceived at the time, the enactments of 1931–33 almost certainly rank with those of 1937–38.[49] Hoover sought and won his Reconstruction Finance Corporation (RFC), a recovery instrument.[50] The Glass-Steagall Act of 1932 authorized a more expansionary monetary policy.[51] The Emergency Relief and Construction Act of 1932, "providing local relief and extensive public works and including money for slum clearance and low-cost housing, represented a new course in American public policy."[52] The Revenue Act

47. New Deal liberals kept promoting domestic reforms after 1938, but they enjoyed little success on Capitol Hill. For accounts of that sparse legislative record, see John W. Jeffries, "The 'New' New Deal: FDR and American Liberalism, 1937–1945," *Political Science Quarterly* 105 (1990), 397–418; Edwin Amenta and Theda Skocpol, "Redefining the New Deal: World War II and the Development of Social Provision in the United States," chap. 2 in Margaret Weir, Ann Shola Orloff, and Theda Skocpol, eds., *The Politics of Social Policy in the United States* (Princeton, N.J.: Princeton University Press, 1988).

48. This was the last Congress to hold a final session during the first months of a post-election year. The Lame Duck amendment to the Constitution took effect in January 1935.

49. The general sources for 1931–33: David Burner, *Herbert Hoover: A Public Life* (New York: Alfred A. Knopf, 1979), pp. 270–82; Harris G. Warren, *Herbert Hoover and the Great Depression* (New York: Oxford University Press, 1959), chaps. 9–13; Jordan A. Schwarz, *The Interregnum of Despair: Hoover, Congress, and the Depression* (Urbana: University of Illinois Press, 1970), pp. 78–98 and chaps. 5, 6, 8; Martin L. Fausold, *The Presidency of Herbert C. Hoover* (Lawrence: University Press of Kansas, 1985), chap. 8.

50. See James Stuart Olson, *Herbert Hoover and the Reconstruction Finance Corporation, 1931–1933* (Ames: Iowa State University Press, 1977), chap. 4, pp. 89–90, chap. 10.

51. Schwarz, *Interregnum of Despair*, pp. 93–98; William J. Barber, *From New Era to New Deal: Herbert Hoover, the Economists, and American Economic Policy, 1921–1933* (New York: Cambridge University Press, 1985), pp. 139–40, 155.

52. Burner, *Herbert Hoover*, p. 276. "Under the authority of the Emergency Relief and Construction Act of 1932, the RFC assumed the responsibility for maintaining the quality of life in the United States until the economy revived. The federal government would never be able to abandon these commitments.

of 1932, a thrust toward corporate, estate, and high-bracket income taxes born of a Capitol Hill Democratic-cum-progressive Republican revolt against the leaderships of both parties, proved to be "the most progressive tax law of the decade.... The new rates were left essentially unchanged throughout the New Deal and for a generation after."[53] Also from the reform side, the Norris-La Guardia Act of 1932 curbing labor injunctions and outlawing yellow-dog contracts was "the first of the great labor laws of the thirties."[54] It was "the statute which made free collective bargaining a serious possibility."[55]

Later American presidents would only expand on that foundation." Olson, *Herbert Hoover and the RFC*, chap. 6, quotation at p. 118. The judgment of a labor historian: "In the development of both federal relief and federal public works July 21, 1932, was a historic day." (The relief bill was signed by Hoover that day.) Irving Bernstein, *The Lean Years: A History of the American Worker, 1920–1933* (Boston: Houghton Mifflin, 1960), chap. 14, quotation at p. 470. See also Schwarz, *Interregnum of Despair*, chap. 6, and Barber, *From New Era to New Deal*, pp. 178–80.

53. Burner, *Herbert Hoover*, p. 282. See also Schwarz, *Interregnum of Despair*, chap. 5; Leff, *Limits of Symbolic Reform*, pp. 20–30, 48–54; and Roy G. Blakey and Gladys C. Blakey, *The Federal Income Tax* (New York: Longmans, Green, 1940), chap. 12. "The 1932 act accounted for most of the progressive shift in effective income tax rates that occurred during [the 1930s]." John F. Witte, *The Politics and Development of the Federal Income Tax* (Madison: University of Wisconsin Press, 1985), p. 108. As a large tax increase, the Revenue Act of 1932 also had decisive deflationary effects, as did later the Social Security payroll tax starting in 1937. See E. Cary Brown, "Fiscal Policy in the 'Thirties: A Reappraisal," *American Economic Review* 46 (1956), 868–69. Countercyclical fiscal policy did not gain a firm hold in Washington until 1938. Good candidates for the decade's most effective measures in increasing the economy's aggregate demand are the veterans' bonus bills passed over Roosevelt's veto in 1936 and Hoover's in early 1931 (UNI). See ibid., pp. 863–69; Susan Previant Lee and Peter Passell, *A New Economic View of American History* (New York: W. W. Norton, 1979), pp. 384–87; and Barber, *From New Era to New Deal*, pp. 108–10.

54. Bernstein, *Lean Years*, chap. 11, quotation at p. 391.

55. Hywell Evans, *Governmental Regulation of Industrial Relations* (Ithaca, N.Y.: New York State School of Industrial Relations at Cornell University, 1961), pp. 7–9, quotation at p. 8. "In my opinion, the Norris-La Guardia Act was the most significant measure ever adopted in the field of United States labor relations" (p. 7). Another judgment: "The [union] right to use concerted activities unimpeded by federal law was won in 1932 when Congress enacted the Norris-La Guardia Act, the first of the four statutory cornerstones of the current national labor policy." (That is, as of 1960, along with the Wagner, Taft-Hartley, and Landrum-Griffin Acts.) Archibald Cox, *Law and the National*

The overall effect is symmetrical: extraordinary records in 1933–34 and 1935–36 bracketed by solid ones in 1931–33 and 1937–38. These four Congresses also staged a series of high-publicity investigations alleging misbehavior in the business world.[56] The Pecora hearings of 1933, sponsored by a lame-duck Republican Senate during an early stretch of choice revelations, put the spotlight on Wall Street: "No investigation before or since matches the Stock Exchange Investigation for sustained and sensational publicity, for the economic significance of the disclosures, or for prompt results by way of important and far-reaching regulatory legislation."[57]

Starting in 1934, Republican Senator Gerald P. Nye of North Dakota chaired a probe of the munitions industry—the "merchants of death"—as alleged promoters of World War I.[58] In 1935, Democratic Senator Hugo Black of Alabama investigated utilities lobbyists.[59] And beginning in late 1936, a committee run by Progressive Senator Robert M. La Follette, Jr., exposed anti-union practices in the steel, auto, and coal-mining industries. That considerably assisted CIO organizing efforts during the key first half of 1937.[60] There is a case, in short, for

Labor Policy (Los Angeles: Institute of Industrial Relations, University of California, 1960), pp. 4–8, quotation at p. 4. See also Chamberlain, President, Congress, and Legislation, pp. 159–65; and Warren, Herbert Hoover and the Great Depression, pp. 191–92. The Norris-La Guardia Act passed by 362–14 in the House and 75–5 in the Senate.

56. For general statements on such investigations during the New Deal era, see Taylor, Grand Inquest, pp. 65–69, and Jerold S. Auerbach, Labor and Liberty: The La Follette Committee and the New Deal (Indianapolis, Ind.: Bobbs-Merrill, 1966), pp. 2–3, 69–70.

57. Taylor, Grand Inquest, pp. 65–67, quotation at p. 65. "The immediate fruits of the Stock Exchange Investigation were the Securities Act of 1933, the Securities and Exchange Act of 1934, and the Public Utility Holding Company Act of 1935" (p. 67). See also Leuchtenburg, Franklin D. Roosevelt and the New Deal, pp. 19–22, 58–60; Arthur M. Schlesinger, Jr., The Crisis of the Old Order, 1919–1933 (Boston: Houghton Mifflin, 1957), pp. 457–59, 478–79; and Charles A. Beard and Mary R. Beard, America in Midpassage (New York: Macmillan, 1939), pp. 158–91.

58. Leuchtenburg, Franklin D. Roosevelt and the New Deal, pp. 217–18; John E. Wiltz, In Search of Peace: The Senate Munitions Inquiry, 1934–36 (Baton Rouge: Louisiana State University Press, 1963).

59. Leuchtenberg, Franklin D. Roosevelt and the New Deal, p. 156; Schlesinger, Politics of Upheaval, pp. 318–23.

60. Auerbach, Labor and Liberty.

a New Deal–era investigative "surge" matching the legislative one—although the targets were business firms rather than, as in chapter 2 of this work, the executive branch.[61]

That ends the factual arrays. Particularly as regards lawmaking, how did the Progressive and New Deal eras resemble the 1960s and 1970s? A number of interesting commonalities come to light. First, in all three cases, if the evidence can be credited, we really do see continuous high-energy activity during quite clearly bounded eras.

Three different "surges" did occur. Although legislative content shifted during each era—the opening moves of the surges hardly forecast the labor legislation after 1910, the basics of the "Second New Deal," or regulatory reform under Nixon—that was because the eras' reform agendas kept evolving. The dates of the surges are roughly 1905 through 1914 for Progressivism at the state level, 1906 through 1916 for it at the national level, 1932 through 1938 for the New Deal era, and 1963 through 1975–76 for the surge of recent times. To be sure, a 1907–08 hole appears in the national Progressive record, but that is a tolerable flaw; no such hole appears at the state level.[62]

Second, the attention-catching programs of Theodore Roosevelt, Woodrow Wilson, Franklin D. Roosevelt, and Lyndon B. Johnson—the Square Deal, New Freedom, New Deal, and Great Society—figure as something like important "moments" in these legislative surges. But they are not the be-all or end-all of the surges. We are continually misled by dynastic presidential scholarship that, for example, has history begin on March 4, 1913, with Wilson or on March 4, 1933, with Franklin Roosevelt.

Third, the three-way analogy undermines any idea that the "conservative coalition" of Republicans and southern Democrats during recent decades has been abnormal or bizarre. A no-less-determined

61. The "immense success, both psychological and legislative, of the Pecora hearings" set the mold: "From 1933 to 1938 Congress, working in close collaboration with the White House and the executive departments, continued to pour out regulatory statutes and to authorize the investigations which were the arsenal of the New Deal program." Taylor, *Grand Inquest*, p. 67. An inquiry into monopoly by Democratic Senator Joseph O'Mahoney's Temporary National Economic Committee, begun in 1938, can be said to have closed out the era's probes. But this was more of a study-group affair than an exposé. See Leuchtenburg, *Franklin D. Roosevelt and the New Deal*, pp. 257–59.

62. Again, for what it is worth, no twentieth-century president has had much luck pressing a domestic legislative program after his sixth year. Theodore Roosevelt in 1907–08 is an instance of that lack of luck.

coalition of Democrats and progressive Republicans played a similar muddling role during roughly 1909 through 1936, though ordinarily as enacters rather than blockers. The earlier alliance won significant legislative victories under Taft, Wilson, and Hoover—for example on progressive taxation.[63] Its Republican or ex-Republican element continued to spur enactments or investigations under Franklin Roosevelt; note the threesome of the Democrat Black, the Republican Nye, and the Progressive La Follette as aggressive investigators.[64] Lasting cross-party coalitions seem to be entirely normal twentieth-century politics.[65] Fourth, also undermined is the sometimes expressed view that "entrepreneurial" legislating by lone-wolf House or Senate members is a recent development—that Senator Hubert Humphrey and his postwar peers forged a new role. The role is traditional, as Lawrence H. Chamberlain demonstrated in 1946.[66] Probably no one in recent times has excelled George Norris, Robert F. Wagner, or the Robert M. La Follettes, Sr. and Jr., at the entrepreneurial role. Their influence pervades the record from Taft through Franklin Roosevelt. In labor-management relations, for example, the first major enactment of the 1930s owed largely to Norris and the second largely to Wagner.[67] Like cross-party coalitions, lone-wolf lawmaking is normal twentieth-century politics.

Finally, it will be evident that "surges" have extended across times of divided as well as unified party control. That happened at least to

63. On the often victorious cross-party pressure for progressive tax rates, see Witte, *Politics and Development of the Income Tax*, pp. 74–87, 96–98.

64. On the Senate's non-Democratic progressive component from the 1920s through 1936, see Erik Olssen, "The Progressive Group in Congress, 1922–29," *Historian* 42 (1980), 244–63; Ronald L. Feinman, *Twilight of Progressivism: The Western Republican Senators and the New Deal* (Baltimore: Johns Hopkins University Press, 1981), chaps. 1–6; and Ronald A. Mulder, *The Insurgent Progressives in the United States Senate and the New Deal, 1933–39* (New York: Garland Press, 1979), chaps. 1–3.

65. As are ephemeral ones. Sylvia Snowiss has shown that, surprisingly, the passage of much of Roosevelt's 1933 program in the form he wanted it required Republican votes on Senate roll calls. See "Presidential Leadership of Congress: An Analysis of Roosevelt's First Hundred Days," *Publius* 1 (1971), 59–87.

66. Chamberlain, *President, Congress, and Legislation.*

67. On Norris's role in passing the Norris-La Guardia Act: Bernstein, *Lean Years*, chap. 11. On Wagner's role in passing the Wagner Act: Schlesinger, *Coming of the New Deal*, pp. 400–406.

some degree in the Progressive and New Deal eras as well as more obviously in the 1960s and 1970s.[68] The New Deal lawmaking and investigative surges began under Hoover (DIV). In the Progressive era at the state level, legislative programs won enactment against all kinds of party backgrounds, unified and divided. The Progressive-oriented Congress of 1911–13 under Taft (DIV) had much in common with those of 1969–74 under Nixon (DIV): Political movements crested, party and factional controversy raged, a "stalemate" script came into play, but what seems like quite a respectable legislative record resulted anyway.[69] Also as with Nixon's years, one becomes uneasy with secondary sources that dwell on presidents and their programs. Historians who do that have accorded the Congress of 1911–13 little attention; it would probably require something like this work's Sweep Two retrospective methodology to do it justice. Along this line, the Norris-La Guardia Act of 1932 (DIV) has produced an interesting disparity. Specialist labor historians see it as path-breaking, but historians who emphasize presidential programs have given it scarcely more than footnote status.[70] It does not fit into a presidential story. The records of past divided-control Congresses do shine through, but with more sensitive methodology they would probably come into focus better.

To return to Schlesinger and Huntington, the argument derivable from their writings is that the causes of legislative or investigative surges can be found in extended expressions of "public purpose" or "creedal passion." To put it another way, they can be located in a certain kind of "public mood" that favors change via government

68. Note that, at the national level, there was not much time of divided control for surges to extend across during the earlier eras. In the half-century between 1896 and 1946, party control was divided for only six years.

69. "American politics had reached a particularly trying moment when Taft became president. The simmering discontents of the previous decade boiled over into full-blown political turmoil. At the same time the insurgencies and reform movements of the time spewed forth a welter of exciting, unsettling ideas and doctrines." Cooper, *Pivotal Decades*, p. 123. This was 1909, but the turmoil seems to have continued undiminished through 1911–13. Nixon would have recognized it.

70. See, for example, Schlesinger, *Crisis of the Old Order*, pp. 238–39, and Schwarz, *Interregnum of Despair*, p. 175. In general, the Schwarz work is exceptionally useful.

action.[71] (Some "moods" have that aim; others, as in the private-oriented 1920s, discourage government action.) A "mood" seems to be one of those phenomena that drive political scientists to despair by being at once important and elusive. But perhaps something useful can be said. In principle, a "public mood" probably has the following features. First, much of at least the politically aware public, inside and outside Washington, shares a certain outlook about what can and should be done right now on a wide range of political issues. Second, a large number of people who possess that outlook bring considerable intensity to it; they are not lukewarm. Third, to the extent that the outlook calls for it, an appreciable number of people go on to engage in, to use a term that is probably as serviceable as any, citizen action. They actually do things: They may form organizations, persuade others, go to meetings, give money, write letters, join protests, approach members of Congress, in general make themselves heard and felt. Fourth, the outlook in question is in some sense dominant: Non-sharers of it have a hard time wholly resisting its intellectual or political appeal or mustering intensity or action against it. Fifth, a "public mood" has a beginning and an end. The outlook, the intensity, and the citizen action emerge or balloon at some detectable juncture, and then several years later, at another juncture, they deflate or disappear.

The case for "public moods" as causal forces needs more development than can be undertaken here. But it may be illuminating to examine briefly what can be seen as a citizen-action component of the alleged Progressive, New Deal, and 1960s–1970s moods, as well as the junctures that evidently began and ended those moods.

An anti-government mood may not call for much citizen action, but a mood favoring change through government action requires—or at least seems to be associated with—a great deal. Levers need to be moved. Nothing emerges more readily from twentieth-century history than the association between pro-government moods and the form of citizen action we ordinarily call "political movements." The Progressive era largely derived from, depending on how one looks at it, one long-lived overall movement or else a family of more specialized efforts such as a women's movement that maneuvered the creation

71. The term is half-borrowed from John W. Kingdon, who presents an excellent discussion of "national moods" in *Agendas*, pp. 153–57.

of the Children's Bureau in 1912.[72] Era and movement are virtually synonymous; little more needs to be said.

During the New Deal era, movements evidently did not play much of a role during the legislative campaign of 1933, but they did, at least indirectly, during the "second hundred days" of 1935. The Social Security Act seems to have owed significantly to the drive of the million-member Townsend movement for old-age pensions, though the new law did not follow that movement's plan. "We have to have" Social Security, Roosevelt was quoted as saying: "The Congress can't stand the pressure of the Townsend Plan unless we have a real old-age insurance system."[73] The Wealth Tax Act of 1935 is often seen as a Roosevelt move to "steal the thunder" of Huey Long's Share Our Wealth movement.[74] Senator Wagner's National Labor Relations Act of 1935 was in large part a reaction to union organizing drives that kindled nationwide strikes in 1934 amounting to "social upheavals."[75] "Labor's mobilization was crucial. It is unlikely that the NLRA would have been passed without the labor upsurge of 1934–35."[76] In general, the Congress of 1935–36 met against a background of national move-

72. On the Children's Bureau: Skocpol, "Protecting Soldiers and Mothers," chap. 8.

73. See Abraham Holtzman, *The Townsend Movement: A Political Study* (New York: Bookman Associates, 1963), pp. 18, 25, 87–90, quotation at p. 88. "The Townsend Movement must be credited with having crystallized tremendous popular sentiment in favor of old-age security. And the threat posed by the plan weakened conservative opposition to the more moderate proposals encompassed in the Social Security Act" (p. 87). See also Alan Brinkley, *Voices of Protest: Huey Long, Father Coughlin, and the Great Depression* (New York: Vintage Books, 1983), pp. 224, 247; Jill S. Quadagno, "Welfare Capitalism and the Social Security Act of 1935," *American Sociological Review* 49 (1984), 638–40, 645; Skocpol and Ikenberry, "Political Formation of the American Welfare State," pp. 121–26; Leuchtenburg, *Franklin D. Roosevelt and the New Deal*, p. 131; and Schlesinger, *Politics of Upheaval*, pp. 40–41.

74. See Patterson, *Congressional Conservatism*, p. 59; Schlesinger, *Politics of Upheaval*, chap. 4, pp. 242–52, 325–34; and Brinkley, *Voices of Protest*, pp. 246–47.

75. On the 1934 strikes: Irving Bernstein, *Turbulent Years: A History of the American Worker, 1933–1941* (Boston: Houghton Mifflin, 1970), chap. 6, quotation at p. 217.

76. David Plotke, "The Wagner Act, Again: Politics and Labor, 1935–37," in *Studies in American Political Development*, vol. 3 (New Haven and London: Yale University Press, 1989), pp. 115–17, quotation at p. 117. See also Michael Goldfield, "Worker Insurgency, Radical Organization, and New Deal Labor

ment activity that featured the Townsendites, Huey Long, and burgeoning labor unions as well as Father Charles E. Coughlin's National Union for Social Justice and energetic mobilizing efforts among workers and others by the Communist party.[77] Note that two of the laws discussed above, the Social Security Act and the Wagner Act, stand out among all New Deal measures as arguably the most significant.

The 1960s and 1970s rivaled the Progressive era as a continuous tumult of causes. Among the centers of activity were interlocking civil rights, consumer, antiwar, labor, student, women's liberation, environmental, and "public interest" movements. As Jo Freeman has documented for the women's movement, there was a contagion effect: One movement could grow out of others.[78] Key legislation resulted. As suggested earlier, the Civil Rights Acts of 1964 and 1965 were triggered by the civil rights movement's demonstrations, along with violent white reactions to them, in Birmingham and Selma.[79] As in the passage of the Wagner Act thirty years before, both support of a growing cause and a need to restore public order rose to high places on the federal government's agenda. The consumer movement, which arose in the mid-1960s, stimulated a sizable number of enactments over a period of a decade, starting with the Traffic Safety Act and the Fair Packaging and Labeling Act of 1966. The consumer lobby was a Washington-centered enterprise, but it drew strong media and public support.[80] The environmental movement mushroomed in the year 1969 to a point where a reported million people observed Earth

---

Legislation," *American Political Science Review* 83 (1989), 1268–78. "Without the 1934 or some similar [labor] upsurge, it is unlikely there would have been an NLRA" (p. 1278).

77. On Coughlin: Schlesinger, *Politics of Upheaval*, chap. 2 and pp. 242–52, 553–61. On the Communist party: ibid., chaps. 11, 12; Harvey Klehr, *The Heyday of American Communism: The Depression Decade* (New York: Basic Books, 1984), chaps. 13–19.

78. Jo Freeman, *The Politics of Women's Liberation: A Case Study of an Emerging Social Movement and Its Relation to the Policy Process* (New York: David McKay, 1975), pp. 56–62.

79. See Harvard Sitkoff, *The Struggle for Black Equality, 1954–1980* (New York: Hill and Wang, 1981), chaps. 5, 6.

80. See Mark V. Nadel, *The Politics of Consumer Protection* (Indianapolis, Ind.: Bobbs-Merrill, 1971), pp. 31–35 and chap. 5; Michael Pertschuk, *Revolt against Regulation: The Rise and Pause of the Consumer Movement* (Berkeley: University of California Press, 1982); and David Vogel, *Fluctuating Fortunes: The Political Power of Business in America* (New York: Basic Books, 1989), chap. 3.

Day in April 1970. That was the setting for the National Environmental Policy Act (NEPA) of 1969, the Clean Air Act of 1970, and the
Water Pollution Control Act of 1972.[81] The women's liberation movement "took off" in 1970, preparing the way for a "bumper crop" of
women's rights victories in the Congress of 1971–72 including the
ERA.[82] As a final example, the public interest group Common Cause,
backed by a mass constituency, was instrumental in engineering the
Federal Election Campaign Act of 1974.[83]

In short, at least in the instance of moods calling for change through
government policy-making, interlocking political movements evidently play a major role by crystallizing favorable attitudes into citizen
action, which in turn can bring results. As stimulators of legislation,
movements are in some ways the peers or rivals of political parties.
Not constrained by election schedules, party lines, or problems of
divided party control, they can be more versatile than parties. Once
going at full tilt, they are capable of permeating and animating the
two parties—usually one more than the other, but to a substantial
degree both.

As for the beginnings and ends of "public moods," it is interesting
to see whether writers about the eras under discussion here have
noticed any such turning points, and if so what they have said. With
that as the guideline, it would be hard to find a better case for a
"mood" interpretation than the start of the Progressive era. The critical juncture was evidently 1905, or a bit more broadly 1904 through
1906. Richard L. McCormick writes: "The middle years of the first

81. See John C. Whitaker, *Striking a Balance: Environment and Natural Resources
Policy in the Nixon-Ford Years* (Washington, D.C.: American Enterprise Institute, 1976), chap. 1. On the Clean Air Act: "Curiously, in retrospect, there
was little debate within the [Nixon] administration about the wisdom of sign-
ing the bill. Besides, given the nearly hysterical support for the environmental
movement, a veto would have been futile: Congress would have promptly
overridden it" (p. 93). On the water quality act: "On November 2, 1971, over
administration protests, the Senate passed the bill with a vote of 86 to 0. The
political climate created by the environmental revolution was such that if the
President had sent out airplanes to fetch the missing fourteen senators,
the vote could well have been 100 to 0 against his position" (p. 82). See also
Vogel, *Fluctuating Fortunes*, chap. 4.

82. Freeman, *Politics of Women's Liberation*, pp. 148–50, 202–05, 209–21, quotations at pp. 148, 202.

83. Andrew S. McFarland, *Common Cause: Lobbying in the Public Interest*
(Chatham, N.J.: Chatham House, 1984), chap. 7.

decade of the twentieth century unmistakably mark a turning-point—
that point when the direction shifted, when the weight of opinion
changed."[84] According to another author, "a new political mood" pre-
vailed in 1905.[85] According to another: "Change was in the air by
1906"; by that time a "complex intellectual movement" had "captured
a good part of the educated elite."[86] Journalistic muckraking, the new
technique of exposing business and political corruption pioneered by
Lincoln Steffens, Upton Sinclair, Ida Tarbell, and others, had begun
slightly earlier in 1902. Muckraking can be seen as either a precipitating cause of the Progressive mood or—since it was itself an expression of a new consciousness—an early manifestation of that mood.
Either way it contributed to political events, of which one, following
Sinclair's *The Jungle*, was the enactment of the Pure Food and Drug
Act of 1906.[87] A "mood" interpretation also fits the end of the Progressive era, if one takes that to be 1918 at the close of World War
I. "Progressivism had been founded on a mood," Richard Hofstadter
has written, "and with the reaction that followed the war that mood
was dissipated."[88] According to David Burner: "Progressivism faltered
after 1918 because the mood upon which it had succeeded was largely
destroyed after the war."[89]

Perhaps because the Great Depression so obviously provided an
impetus, the start of the New Deal era is not customarily identified
with a "mood change." But some ingredients are plain enough. There
was a rising sense of emergency. The Pecora hearings of 1933, along
with other events and no doubt simple experience, delegitimized the

84. McCormick, "The Discovery That Business Corrupts Politics," pp. 247–
49, 259–70, quotation at p. 268.

85. Gould, *Reform and Regulation*, p. 59.

86. Mowry, *Era of Theodore Roosevelt*, chap. 4 and pp. 206–11, quotation at
p. 209. See also Cooper, *Pivotal Decades*, pp. 80–89, and Harold Underwood
Faulkner, *The Quest for Social Justice, 1898–1914* (New York: Macmillan, 1931),
pp. 110–14.

87. On the 1906 act: Crumden, *Ministers of Reform*, chap. 6. On muckraking:
Cooper, *Pivotal Decades*, pp. 83–89.

88. Richard Hofstadter, *The Age of Reform: From Bryan to F.D.R.* (New York:
Vintage Books, 1955), p. 282. "Moods are intangible, and yet the change in
America hung on mood as much as anything else."

89. David Burner, "1919: Prelude to Normalcy," in John Braeman, Robert
H. Bremner, and David Brody, eds., *Change and Continuity in Twentieth-Century
America: The 1920's* (Columbus: Ohio State University Press, 1968), p. 5.

business community: "By the time Roosevelt took office, the country had been whipped to a fury at the performance of bankers and businessmen."[90]

And an enthusiasm for government action, evidently popularly based, grew in Congress during 1932 and found its White House spokesman when Roosevelt took office in March 1933.[91] It is a plausible reading, in short, that an action-oriented reform and recovery "mood" set in in 1932–33. The New Deal's abrupt loss of public and congressional support in late 1937 and 1938 is sometimes identified with a "mood change." The precipitous business recession of that time, according to one account, "helped produce a national mood hostile to experimentation of any kind."[92] A "rather widespread disenchantment with reform" took hold.[93] "The country no longer quickened to the promise of the New Deal, and had wearied of assaults on business."[94]

As with the New Deal, the start of the activist era of the 1960s and 1970s is not ordinarily discussed in terms of "mood." Huntington identifies its beginning with a movement event—the anti-segregation sit-ins at North Carolina lunch counters in 1960.[95] Schlesinger reaches for President Kennedy's leadership.[96] There is one interesting analogy to the Progressive era. In a role that recalls muckraking, a series of widely read books helped to generate a new critical consciousness. John Kenneth Galbraith's *Affluent Society* (1958) dwelt on the shab-

90. Leuchtenburg, *Franklin D. Roosevelt and the New Deal*, p. 22.

91. On the handling of the relief issue in Congress in 1932, see Schwarz, *Interregnum of Despair*, chap. 6.

92. Polenberg, *Reorganizing Roosevelt's Government*, pp. 148–51, quotation at p. 151.

93. Richard Polenberg, "The Decline of the New Deal, 1937–1940," in John Braeman, Robert H. Bremner, and David Brody, eds., *The New Deal: The National Level* (Columbus: Ohio State University Press, 1975), quotation at p. 255.

94. Leuchtenburg, *Franklin D. Roosevelt and the New Deal*, p. 274. Schlesinger extends his New Deal era of "public purpose" to include all of Roosevelt's later years as well as Truman's Fair Deal. That seems to be a generous act by a good Democrat. Little in the record of 1939 through 1952 supports it. See Schlesinger, "Cycles of American Politics," pp. 32–34.

95. Huntington, *American Politics: The Promise of Disharmony*, p. 168.

96. Schlesinger, "Cycles of American Politics," pp. 32–33.

biness of the American public sector.[97] Michael Harrington's *Other America* (1962) served as a "catalyst" of the anti-poverty crusade; it inspired the Anti-Poverty Act of 1964 rather as Sinclair's *The Jungle* had done the Pure Food and Drug Act of 1906.[98] Rachel Carson's *Silent Spring* (1962), an exposé of damage to the environment, started "a continual stream of revelations in the mass media about the alleged deleterious effects of various products and production processes on the health and safety of consumers, employees and the public."[99] Betty Friedan's *Feminine Mystique* (1963) provided an important early text of the women's movement.[100] Jessica Mitford's *American Way of Death* (1963) exposed the practices of the funeral industry.[101] Ralph Nader's *Unsafe at Any Speed* (1965) targeted the auto industry for neglect of safety.[102] The cumulative influence of these and other writings was evidently considerable. All of them helped to stimulate a demand for government spending or regulation.

For the close of this most recent activist era, "mood change" has figured as the dominant explanation. The time of decisive change was evidently 1977–78 despite the Democrats' Capitol Hill majorities then of 292–143 and 62–38.[103] Again, those were the years when high-publicity probes of the national security establishment ceased, Carter's

97. John Kenneth Galbraith, *The Affluent Society* (Boston: Houghton Mifflin, 1958). President Kennedy took an interest in the work. See Sundquist, *Politics and Policy*, p. 113.

98. Michael Harrington, *The Other America: Poverty in the United States* (New York: Macmillan, 1962). See Michael Barone, *Our Country: The Shaping of America from Roosevelt to Reagan* (New York: Free Press, 1990), quotation at p. 371, and James L. Sundquist, *Politics and Policy: The Eisenhower, Kennedy, and Johnson Years* (Washington, D.C.: Brookings Institution Press, 1968), pp. 113–14.

99. Rachel Carson, *Silent Spring* (Boston: Houghton Mifflin, 1962). The quotation is from David Vogel, "The Power of Business in America: A Reappraisal," *British Journal of Political Science* 13 (1983), p. 22. See also Whitaker, *Striking a Balance*, pp. 7, 24, and Sundquist, *Politics and Policy*, p. 371.

100. Betty Friedan, *The Feminine Mystique* (New York: W. W. Norton, 1963). See Freeman, *Politics of Women's Liberation*, p. 53.

101. Jessica Mitford, *The American Way of Death* (New York: Simon and Schuster, 1963).

102. Ralph Nader, *Unsafe at Any Speed: The Designed-In Dangers of the American Automobile* (New York: Grossman, 1965).

103. Huntington places the boundary a bit earlier: on January 29, 1976, when the House voted not to release a report of the Pike intelligence oversight

domestic program foundered, the consumer protection agency failed
to pass, the labor movement lost its Capitol Hill campaigns, deregulation took hold, and a business-oriented tax measure passed that
Senator Edward M. Kennedy called "the worst tax legislation approved by Congress since the days of Calvin Coolidge and Andrew
Mellon."[104] There is a resemblance to 1937–38 when the New Deal
ran aground.

Why did these things happen? Answers at the time included an
"apparent climatic change," an "antigovernment mood," a "current
rightward trend," a "national conservative mood," and "the country
is indeed moving to the right."[105] There was "a reaction against the
civil rights, Vietnam war and other protests of the past and even more
against such current excesses as the use of children for pornography
and the aggressive assertion of homosexualism."[106] "The House is not
just conservative," a Cabinet-level official was quoted as saying in 1977,
"It's mean conservative."[107] Congress in 1977–78 "reflected the in-
creasingly conservative mood of the American electorate."[108] There
was "increased Congressional skepticism over the ability of the Government to improve many national situations."[109] "By 1977," accord-

committee until the White House cleared it. *American Politics: The Promise of
Disharmony*, p. 168. "Indignation exhausted itself" (p. 215).

104. "Kennedy, Liberal Groups Pressure Carter to Veto $18.7 Billion Tax-
Reduction Bill," *Wall Street Journal*, October 19, 1978, p. 10. The measure is
said to have "radically reversed two decades of changes making the federal
income tax more progressive." John E. Jackson and David C. King, "Public
Goods, Private Interests, and Representation," *American Political Science Review*
83 (1989), 1143. See also Robert Kuttner, *Revolt of the Haves: Tax Rebellions
and Hard Times* (New York: Simon and Schuster, 1980), chap. 14 ("The Light
Taxes of the Rich").

105. The quotations are respectively from Alan L. Otten, "Tilting Right?"
Wall Street Journal, July 7, 1977, p. 12; "Washington Wire," *Wall Street Journal*,
September 9, 1977, p. 1; "Thunder on the Right?" *Dissent* 26 (Winter 1979), 13;
Peter Connolly, "Conservative Drift in Congress," *Dissent* 26 (Winter 1979),
14–17, quotation at p. 15; and Ben J. Wattenberg, "The Second Shoe Falls—
and Maybe a Third," *Public Opinion* 1 (November–December 1978), 2.

106. Otten, "Tilting Right?" p. 12.

107. Ibid.

108. B. Drummond Ayres, Jr., untitled wrap-up story, *New York Times*, News
Service Supplement, October 17, 1978, p. 51.

109. Martin Tolchin, "Leaders Call Record of Congress Moderate," *New York
Times*, December 18, 1977, p. I:1. The most penetrating contemporary ac-

ing to a later analyst looking back at that time, "the faith that government could solve all problems was vanishing."[110] Another retrospective account goes: "Suddenly [around 1978] people were bored with air bags, enraged by child-proof aspirin bottles, making jokes about the government as National Nanny."[111] In progress was a "sea change in the public's attitude toward regulation."[112]

At the level of opinion intensity and citizen action, reports appeared about a flagging left. "We can't get members excited about anything any more unless we threaten a dues increase," a Washington labor attorney mused in 1977; "They worry about how their lawn looks, but legislation seems too distant. Social issues? They could care less."[113] "Liberal activists," according to another account, "have grown complacent and lethargic. They seem to have forgotten how to build strong public pressure for their own causes."[114] And the grassroots seemed to have gotten harder to mobilize: "Something has to come from the field on this; right now nothing is coming in," a lobbyist for the consumer protection agency observed during that cause's dying days.[115] What did come in during 1977–78 was less helpful: "Every day's mail seems mainly to be composed of bitter letters decrying lesbian plots to extend the ratification deadline for ERA, strident calls for a balanced budget coupled with threats of defeat, denunciations of the 'giveaway' of the 'American Canal in Panama' at the behest of New York bankers,' and tirades on government-as-parasite."[116] Republican Congressman John B. Anderson said he had switched sides on the consumer agency because of what constituents told him when he visited his district: "They are fed up with agencies, with more

counts of the "mood" of 1977–78 are Otten, "Tilting Right?" and Connolly, "Conservative Drift in Congress."

110. Barone, *Our Country*, p. 562.

111. Michael Kinsley, "Regulation Revisited," *Washington Post*, February 27, 1986, p. A23.

112. Susan J. Tolchin and Martin Tolchin, *Dismantling America: The Rush to Deregulate* (Boston: Houghton Mifflin, 1983), p. 147.

113. Quoted in James C. Hyatt, "Labor Striking Out on Capitol Hill," *Wall Street Journal*, June 2, 1977, p. 12.

114. Otten, "Tilting Right?" p. 12.

115. Barry M. Hager and James R. Wagner, "Consumer Agency Bill Stalled in Congress," *Congressional Quarterly Weekly*, June 11, 1977, p. 1147.

116. Connolly, "Conservative Drift in Congress," p. 15.

interrogatories, with more forms; there's a very, very strong feeling in my district against it."[117]

Capstoning it all, California voters seemed to send a message in June 1978 by ratifying Proposition 13, the state's massive rollback of property taxes. It certainly was accepted as a message. "As much as any other event, it seemed to signal an abrupt end to the era that had begun in 1933."[118] House members saw in the result "a popular revolt against inflation, taxes, and governmental expenditures, and they scrambled to make their voting records correspond with the new mood. Within days Congress was cutting everything in sight."[119] When Howard Jarvis, co-sponsor of the initiative, visited Capitol Hill soon afterward, "Democrats as well as Republicans, liberals and conservatives alike, seized at the chance to be seen with the high priest of the tax protest movement."[120] As of July 1978, according to Senator Muskie, "The mood of Washington these days can be summed up in two words—Proposition 13."[121] Opposition to taxes had kicked into place alongside opposition to regulation. The stage was set for Reagan.

That is the case for "mood changes" as brackets around the three twentieth-century activist eras. Note that in the cases of the New Deal and the 1960s and 1970s—though not the Progressive era— analysts have applied "mood change" interpretations more explicitly at the ends than at the beginnings. Other developments dominate accounts of the beginnings, though it seems a fair inference that "moods" changed then too. The same disparity between beginning and end would probably emerge in a discussion of the Civil War and Reconstruction era—the most obvious nineteenth-century counterpart of the three eras under discussion here. Reconstruction ended in the mid-1870s with what seems to have been a classic end-of-activism "mood change": "And since, as many whites reasoned, the former panaceas had failed, perhaps the achievement of equality between the races was indeed hopeless. Once that assumption had gained suprem-

117. Hager and Wagner "Consumer Agency Bill," p. 1148.

118. Kuttner, *Revolt of the Haves*, p. 17.

119. R. Douglas Arnold, *The Logic of Congressional Action* (New Haven and London: Yale University Press, 1990), p. 174.

120. Albert R. Hunt, "Capitol Hill Offers Tax-Protest Leader a Warm Embrace," *Wall Street Journal*, June 20, 1978, p. 19.

121. Quoted in Christopher R. Conte, "Proposition 13 Fallout: Congress Weighs the Message," *Congressional Quarterly Weekly*, July 8, 1978, p. 1724. See also Kingdon, *Agendas*, pp. 102–03.

acy, retreat gathered momentum and from 1874–1876 it turned into a rout."[122]

What causes "mood changes" to occur? In the category of general as opposed to ad hoc causes, leadership, war, a cyclical impulse, and changes in economic conditions are sometimes proposed. Inspirational leaders such as Kennedy and both Roosevelts have helped to get "moods" under way, although like muckraking, such leadership can be regarded as either a cause or an early manifestation of a "mood."[123] War seems to have extinguished the Progressive mood. Perhaps Schlesinger's idea of cycles has merit: Large numbers of people may indeed enlist in altruistic public activism until they get their fill of it, then take to self-seeking private activity until they get their fill of that.[124] In the realm of economic conditions, the Great Depression ushered in the New Deal era and the acute recession of 1937–38 helped to usher it out; the oil crisis, growing inflation, and budget problems are said to have spurred the "conservative mood" of the late 1970s.[125] Sometimes it is argued that a background economic condition—rather than, strictly speaking, a change in conditions—underpinned the activist mood of the 1960s and 1970s: A prosperous economy with budgetary slack was needed to back up that era's ambitious government enterprises. But the New Deal demolishes any general claim about such a relation. Obviously, an activist mood and ambitious government enterprises can thrive during a depression too.

Elections do not map onto "mood changes" in any consistent way. Some seem to figure as expressions or announcements of mood shifts. The Democratic landslide of 1932 is no doubt the leading instance. Others seem to play a ratifying role: They bring about coalitional shifts that are sometimes mistakenly seen as major causes of policy

122. William Gillette, *Retreat from Reconstruction, 1869–1879* (Baton Rouge: Louisiana State University Press, 1979), chaps. 7–12, 15, quotation at p. 368. See also Eric Foner, *Reconstruction: America's Unfinished Revolution, 1863–1877* (New York: Harper and Row, 1988), pp. 524–34.

123. Schlesinger assigns considerable weight to such leadership. "Cycles of American Politics," pp. 31–34.

124. See also Albert O. Hirschman, *Shifting Involvements: Private Interest and Public Action* (Princeton, N.J.: Princeton University Press, 1982).

125. On 1937–38: Polenberg, "Decline of the New Deal," pp. 255–56. On the late 1970s see, for example, Otten, "Tilting Right?" p. 12; Wattenberg, "Second Shoe Falls," pp. 4–5.

change, whereas in fact they just reflect mood shifts that have already occurred. Thus the relation between Woodrow Wilson's last years and the Republican "normalcy" landslide of 1920: "Many months before Wilson and his party were repudiated in the election of 1920 the reaction had begun under Wilson's own administration."[126] "The progressive Wilson himself, not Harding, initiated the postwar conservatism."[127] Thus also the connection between 1937–38 and the election of 1938 when the Republicans gained eighty House seats—a swing unmatched since. That was a largely a ratifying event; the New Deal program had run into increasing trouble during 1937–38.[128] In other instances, mood shifts have taken place without much in the way of consonant electoral swings. The election of 1904 is not ordinarily seen as a mandate for national Progressivism, nor are those of 1906 and 1908 much help.[129] The mood swing under Carter lacked anything like clear origins in the election of 1976, although perhaps the 1980 election can be said to have ratified it. Of course, it does not require electoral revolutions for governments to stay in touch with their constituencies: Alert incumbent politicians, if they sense a mood shift, can shift too.

It will be evident that "public moods" are wispy phenomena that have unclear boundaries and fugitive causes. One might think that changes in mood, at least, would be trackable in mass opinion data. If one examines data for the 1960s and 1970s, a few promising correspondences appear.[130] Support for welfare spending dropped sig-

126. Hofstadter, *Age of Reform*, pp. 282–83.

127. Burner, "1919: Prelude to Normalcy," p. 5.

128. "By the end of 1938, even its supporters sensed that much of the impetus of the New Deal had died." Leuchtenburg, *Franklin D. Roosevelt and the New Deal*, p. 265.

129. Some political scientists look for the origins of the Progressive era in the electoral realignment of the 1890s. That does not seem a promising idea. For a skeptical view, see McCormick, "Walter Dean Burnham and 'the System of 1896,' " pp. 257–58. If preceding events are required, it evidently makes more sense to see the onset of Progressivism as a reaction to the consolidation of nationwide corporations that took place during a few years around 1900. See, for example, Faulkner, *Quest for Social Justice*, pp. 110–11.

130. The most useful sources were Benjamin I. Page and Robert Y. Shapiro, "Changes in Americans' Policy Preferences, 1935–1979," *Public Opinion Quarterly* 46 (1982), 24–42; Page and Shapiro, "Effects of Public Opinion on Policy," *American Political Science Review* 77 (1983), 175–90; Tom W. Smith, "America's Most Important Problem—A Trend Analysis, 1946–1976," *Public Opinion*

nificantly, for example, in the mid-1970s.[131] But in general the effort does not succeed. One reason is that appropriate questions have not been asked often enough. But beyond that, it is doubtful that moods can be captured very well by assuming that every person has a view and counting all views equally.[132] Moods seem to overrepresent elite views and to give great weight to opinion intensity and citizen action. They have a profile, in short, that is more likely to engage politicians than designers of surveys. Politicians have to dwell on whatever might be electorally consequential. Mass opinion is hardly irrelevant, but angry questions or letters, fed-up constituents, shifts in newspaper editorial opinion, reports of cracker-barrel judgments back home, real collective acts such as Proposition 13, and perhaps above all, any effective moves to organize appreciable numbers of voters can count for a great deal.[133]

Notwithstanding their wispiness, "public moods" can be ignored only at a cost. Consider the following account by David Vogel:

> From 1969 through 1972 [under Nixon], Congress enacted the most pro-gressive tax bill in the postwar period, reduced the oil-depletion allowance, imposed price controls on oil, transferred the primary authority for the regulation of both pollution and occupational health and safety from the states to the federal government, established the Consumer Product Safety Commission, and banned the advertising of cigarettes from radio and tele-vision. In a comparable span of four years—1978 through 1981—Congress defeated labor-law reform, voted against the establishment of a Consumer Protection Agency, restricted the power of the Federal Trade Commission, deregulated oil prices, delayed the imposition of automobile-emission stan-dards, reduced price controls on natural gas, and enacted two tax bills, the first of which primarily benefited the wealthy and a second which re-

Quarterly 44 (1980), 164–80; and Richard G. Niemi, John Mueller, and Tom W. Smith, *Trends in Public Opinion: A Compendium of Survey Data* (New York: Greenwood Press, 1989), chaps. 1, 3, 4.

131. Page and Shapiro, "Changes in Americans' Policy Preferences," p. 38.

132. For a discussion of the lack of a clear relation between "national moods" and mass opinion, see Kingdon, *Agendas*, pp. 155–56.

133. For a study of "activist opinion" conveyed to Capitol Hill by phone calls and mail during Reagan's budget campaign in 1981, see Darrell M. West, "Activists and Economic Policymaking in Congress," *American Journal of Po-litical Science* 32 (1988), 662–80. Those calls and letters evidently made a difference.

duced corporate taxes to their lowest level since the Second World War.[134] [All but the last of the conservative moves took place under Carter.]

Here we have items from the Nixon phase of the legislative "surge" of the 1960s and 1970s, then items from the political climate under Carter and Reagan. There is a striking difference. How do we deal with it? Moods and mood changes offer the beginning of an answer. At least they correspond to a certain kind of reality. In the 1960s and 1970s and the earlier eras, they offer a way to illuminate legislative and investigative "surges." We might not know that such "surges" existed—let alone how to explain them—if we restricted ourselves to the standard equipment of political science: election returns, realignment theories, mass survey data, and summary roll-call data. In particular, these approaches or sources do not supply either useful indicators or plausible explanations of the policy turnaround in the 1970s outlined in the quotation above. They largely miss it. Explanation seems to have to start elsewhere.

The reason for introducing "public moods" in this chapter was to explore a source of *alternative variation*. The particularly intense legislating of the 1963 through 1975–76 "surge" years seemed to call for that. But not everything that we might want to designate a "public mood" has been associated with intense legislating. Two other "moods" of the 1946–90 period are worth noting. As was discussed earlier, an anti-government mood set in during the mid- and late 1970s that featured, as citizen action, strenuous mobilizing efforts by the business community and the New Right.[135] Accordingly, the volume of major national lawmaking fell as its conservative content rose.

And McCarthyism, the anti-Communist alarm around 1950, had the trappings of a "mood." It engaged a sector of the public intensely, it led to passionate citizen action, it came and went, it lasted for years, and contemporary observers had no doubt about its existence. It failed to register well in mass survey data, but that scarcely mattered. It prompted some laws—the Internal Security Act of 1950, the security provisions of the McCarran-Walter Act of 1952, and the Communist Control Act of 1954. It inspired that era's remarkable loyalty inves-

134. Vogel, *Fluctuating Fortunes*, p. 13.

135. On the business community's mobilizing efforts in the mid- and late 1970s, for example in opposing the creation of a consumer protection agency, see Vogel, *Fluctuating Fortunes*, chaps. 7, 8; Vogel, "Power of Business;" John-

tigations. And in a sequence of background circumstances extending from 1948 through 1954, it was powerful enough to infuse governmental processes under Republicans and Democrats who held power alone or shared it. It was another source of *alternative variation*.

---

son, *In the Absence of Power*, pp. 233–41; Neil Ulman, "Companies Organize Employees and Holders into a Political Force," *Wall Street Journal*, August 15, 1978, pp. 1, 35. But it is by no means clear that business mobilization is needed to provoke a conservative "mood" or its legislative results. The Business Roundtable, the corporate world's instrument of the mid–1970s, does not seem to have had an analogue in 1937–38. A conservative mood set in anyway. Business money had gone into the anti–New Deal Liberty League in 1934–36, but that counter-mobilization failed badly. Evidently it was too early; Roosevelt was not vulnerable yet. In general, business mobilization may be more of an indicator than a cause of political change.

7 ◆ CONCLUSION

There is no way to assign numbers on a scorecard to the various explanations that have been presented in chapters 5 and 6. But a brief discussion that juxtaposes them may be useful. Table 7.1 lists them, along with an item that was mentioned: norms.

To summarize the points about investigations, it seems plausible to conclude that norms, electoral incentives, and perhaps events contribute to *constancy* (see the categories in table 7.1). They impinge on members of Congress year in and year out, or at least events such as outbreaks of executive-branch corruption do so often and perhaps randomly. So there is cause for investigations to occur constantly or at least randomly and often. But the high-profile national-security probes of 1948–54 and 1966–75 seem to call for factors that can account for *alternative variation*.[1] Viewed from one standpoint, these probes were arguably spurred by the anti-Communist "mood" of around 1950 and the liberal anti-establishment "mood" of the 1960s and 1970s. But viewed otherwise, they were assisted by opinion cleavages that cut across party lines: Senators McCarran in 1951–52, McCarthy in 1953–54, and Fulbright in 1966–68 all spoke for opinion publics that existed partly within their own parties as they targeted presidential administrations of their own parties. Either a mood or an important crosscutting cleavage might be expected to generate a pattern of *alternative variation*.

On the lawmaking side, one way to try to bring some order to table 7.1's entries, notwithstanding the softness of the data, is through regression analysis. Accordingly, table 7.2 reports the results of an

1. Note that no simple relation exists between wars and these sequences of probes. The probes of the Hiss-through-McCarthy period were well under way before the Korean war began. It may make more sense to claim that that era's anti-Communist mood shaped the conduct of the Korean war—consider MacArthur's aims and actions, his contacts on Capitol Hill, and his free rein given by the Truman administration—than to claim that the war caused or affected very much that mood.

TABLE 7.1
Factors That May Help to Overcome Expected Differences between
Unified and Divided Party Control

	Via compensation effects	By thrusting toward constancy	By producing alternative variation
In investigating			
Norms		xxxx	
Electoral incentives		xxxx	
Events		xxxx	
Cross-party opinion cleavages			
—on national security			xxxx
Public moods			xxxx
In lawmaking			
Norms		xxxx	
Electoral incentives			
—to stay in Congress		xxxx	
—aiming for the Senate		xxxx	
—aiming for White House	xxxx		
—party rivalry	xxxx?	xxxx	
Presidential leadership			
—different presidents			xxxx
—early vs. late in term			xxxx
Broad roll-call majorities			
—in problem solving		xxxx	
—to aggregate support		xxxx	
Events		xxxx	
Cross-party opinion cleavages		xxxx	
Public moods			xxxx

equation in which the number of important laws passed per Congress, for each of the twenty-two Congresses from 1946 through 1990 (see table 4.1), is the dependent variable. The values in question range from five enactments in 1959–60 through twenty-two in 1965–66, 1969–70, and 1973–74, with a mean of 12.1. The equation's independent variables are UNIFIED CONTROL as well as three others that might be thought to have produced *alternative variation*. BUDGETARY SITUATION, included out of respect for the idea that ambitious lawmaking might arise from the slack allowed by budgetary prosperity, washes out; surplus or deficit conditions had little or no effect. START OF TERM, representing the idea that more laws are likely to pass

TABLE 7.2
Variables Explaining Numbers of Important Laws Enacted Per Congress,
1946–1990

Variable	Coefficient	Standard error	t value
UNIFIED CONTROL—coded 1 for a time of unified party control, zero for a time of divided control	−.59	1.12	−.53
START OF TERM—coded 1 for first two years of a presidential term, zero for last two years	3.47	1.07	3.24*
ACTIVIST MOOD—coded 1 for Congresses from 1961 through 1976, zero for the rest	8.52	1.12	7.61**
BUDGETARY SITUATION—for any Congress, budget surplus or deficit as a percentage of government outlays; the figure is an average across the two years. Values range from −24% in 1983–84 to +21% in 1947–48, with a mean of −6.8%.	.053	.056	.96
INTERCEPT	7.90	1.01	7.85**

Notes: Dependent variable = number of important laws enacted during a
Congress, as recorded in table 4.1.
Number of cases = 22 (the 22 Congresses during 1946–1990)
Adjusted R-square = .756
*p less than .01
**p less than .001

during the first half of a four-year presidential term than during the
second half, works nicely. All else equal during 1946–90, 3.47 more
laws could be expected to pass during the first two years. ACTIVIST
MOOD, coded so as to make Schlesinger's "public purpose" and Huntington's "creedal passion" eras match as well as they could a sequence
of whole Congresses, which means 1961 through 1976, works exceptionally well. All else equal, the presence of that mood was worth some
8.5 laws per Congress. Moods remain elusive, but this quantitative
result accords with the discussion of chapter 4: In lawmaking, nothing
emerges more clearly from a postwar analysis than that something
special was going on from the early or mid-1960s through the mid-
1970s.

The UNIFIED CONTROL variable washes out. It produces an unstable coefficient that even has the wrong—that is, theoretically unexpected—sign. All else equal, in short, unified party control contributes nothing to volume of important enactments. The two Congresses whose values the equation predicts least well are those of 1961–62 under Kennedy (a large negative residual) and of 1987–88 under the fading Reagan and Speaker Wright (a large positive residual). Kennedy's first Congress, if one accepts the coding judgment that the activist mood of the 1960s and 1970s had already set in in 1961, "underproduced" laws. Reagan's last Congress "overproduced" them.[2]

Compensation effects cannot be tested for in any such equation. If existent, what they would do is to depress the coefficient of the UNIFIED CONTROL variable, since that registers the *net* effects of having unified as opposed to divided party control. That is, it picks up both deadlock kinds of effects as well as ones that might mitigate deadlock. From reading the equation, there is no telling whether such compensation took place during 1946–90. But perhaps it did. In particular, following the argument of chapter 5, lawmaking drives by out-party presidential candidates during times of divided party control—the

2. A PRESIDENTIAL LEADERSHIP variable coded high for Johnson and Reagan might have been entered as one more candidate for *alternative variation*. I did not do that. There are two problems. First, it is not clear which Congresses to attach the high readings to. Johnson in 1965–66, to be sure, but in 1967–68? In 1963–64, which was half his? Reagan beyond 1981–82? Second, the dependent variable truly breaks down in 1981–82. Counting Reagan's tax and expenditure cuts as each only one law greatly underassesses them. With this as a dependent-variable problem, it is hard to give a fair trial to an independent variable for PRESIDENTIAL LEADERSHIP. It is worth reporting that in the equation presented here and in other similar ones experimented with, the Congress of 1965–66 always produced a fairly sizable positive residual; this may show partly a Johnson leadership effect. I did run a series of equations in which some of the 267 laws underpinning the dependent variable were weighted at greater than one: Reagan's two 1981 measures were weighted at 5, and the other 17 laws capitalized in table 4.1 because contemporaries rated them as exceptionally important (such as the 1965 VRA) were weighted at 3. With this formulation (though still with no independent variable for PRESIDENTIAL LEADERSHIP), the Congresses of 1965–66 and 1981–82 always turned up large positive residuals, perhaps showing exceptional presidential leadership. But these results are shakily artifactual. In no equation using such a weighted dependent variable, it might be noted, did UNIFIED CONTROL exhibit any life as an independent variable.

Taft-Johnson-Muskie phenomenon—might have shaved the UNIFIED CONTROL coefficient.

Factors pushing toward lawmaking *constancy* had to leave any traces in the equation's intercept term, which proves to be impressively stable as well as high in magnitude. Appropriately interpreted, that term suggests that a Congress conducted under divided party control, against an average budgetary background, during the last two years of a presidential term, and without benefit of an activist mood, would have been expected to pass approximately 7.5 important laws anyway. That is a lot. It is only about 5 under the enactment average of 12.1 for the twenty-two postwar Congresses. There is no way to unpack the equation's intercept to find out just what factors might have structured it. But some promising candidates discussed earlier appear in table 7.1's *constancy* list: norms, external events, various electoral incentives, cross-party opinion cleavages, problem-solving propensities, and an arguably constant element of ease or difficulty associated with putting together winning Capitol Hill coalitions. Evidently, some such mix of factors keeps the legislative process moving along rather evenly regardless of patterns of party control or other transient circumstances.

That is the story for high-publicity investigations and important laws. By now, after several chapters addressed to non-patterns in those spheres, the reader may have entered a "nonetheless" frame of mind. Even if the analysis is convincing, are there not other ways in which unified as opposed to divided party control might make a significant difference?

There are. In closing, five such ways will be introduced here by posing questions and speculating briefly about what their answers might be. In all instances the speculation ends in skepticism: Unified versus divided control has probably *not* made a notable difference during the postwar era. The arguments stop short of systematic analysis and are thus inconclusive. But they point to relevant kinds of evidence and, perhaps as important, they make a case that evidence is relevant. It is an empirical matter, finally, whether conditions of party control make a difference—regardless of the aspect one is considering. One really does have to look and compare over time. It is not enough, as is often done, to single out some governmental pathology of the 1970s or 1980s, note that party control was divided, set out a plausible connecting logic, and declare divided control to be the culprit.

The first question is: Even if important laws win enactment just as often under conditions of divided party control, might they not be *worse* laws? Isn't "seriously defective legislation" a likelier result?[3] That is sometimes alleged, and if true it would obviously count heavily. The subject is murky, even if kept free of ideological tests of "worseness," but the case seems to have a two-pronged logic. First, enacting coalitions under divided control, being composed of elements not "naturally" united on policy goals, might be less apt to write either clear ends or efficient means into their statutes. Second, such coalitions, absolved from unambiguous "party government" checks by the electorate down the line, might worry less about the actual effects of laws.

For an example, consider the Energy Policy and Conservation Act of 1975, which was voted by a Democratic Congress and signed by Ford but "satisfied no one."[4] It was an awkwardly stitched-together compromise; many others could be cited from times of divided control. Lack of regard for effects—namely, long-run costs—is said to have been exhibited in the immense expansion of entitlements by Democratic Congresses under Nixon. Promises were just wantonly written into law.[5] In light of the savings-and-loan scandal, it may be worth noting that the Garn-St. Germain Depository Institutions Act, which has been called "perhaps the single most ill-conceived piece of domestic legislation in modern times," was enacted under divided control in 1982.[6] It took the constraints off loans that thrifts could make.

These are reasonable enough logics and instances, but the overall case is dubious. At least as convincing is the logic that enacting co-

3. The term is from John B. Gilmour, "Bargaining between Congress and the President: The Bidding-Up Phenomenon" (Paper presented at the 1990 Annual Meeting of the American Political Science Association), p. 25.

4. Richard H. K. Vietor, *Energy Policy in America since 1945: A Study of Business-Government Relations* (New York: Cambridge University Press, 1984), pp. 249–58, quotation at p. 249.

5. On entitlements expansion as a growing problem of budgetary "uncontrollability" in the years around 1970, see John W. Ellwood, "The Great Exception: The Congressional Budget Process in an Age of Decentralization," chap. 14 in Lawrence C. Dodd and Bruce I. Oppenheimer, eds., *Congress Reconsidered*, 3d ed. (Washington, D.C.: Congressional Quarterly Press, 1985), pp. 322–25.

6. John Kenneth Galbraith, "The Ultimate Scandal," *New York Review of Books*, January 18, 1990, p. 16.

alitions are hard to assemble even if party control is unified; awkwardly stitched-together compromises can occur anyway. In current scholarship, a favorite instance is the Natural Gas Policy Act of 1978—a "convoluted measure" of which "unintended consequences" have been a "hallmark" since its passage.[7] "Because assembling a centrist majority coalition in a polarized ideological conflict depended heavily on granting special favors to narrow groups, the bill created a bizarre and implausible regulatory scheme."[8] That happened in a Democratic Congress under Carter (UNI). Other instances could be cited from times of unified control.

Another consideration is that district-oriented distributive politics can intrude into lawmaking at any time. That is a particular coalition-building tendency that transcends conditions of party control. For example, the "demonstration cities" act of 1966 (UNI) began as a Johnson administration plan to fund some five to ten cities as showcases of urban reform, but the list expanded to 120 to 150 cities in order to assemble a congressional majority for passage. The result was a kind of legislative failure: no showcases, no planned experimentation, just another way of doling out small amounts of money widely.[9]

Unified party control, moreover, can foster a pathological enactment logic all its own. Anyone who witnessed the Great Society will remember Johnson's frenzied drive to pass as many bills as he could while his mandate and sizable Democratic congressional majorities lasted. It was a "politics of haste" in which "solutions were often devised and rushed into law before the problems were understood." "Pass the bill now, worry about its effects and implementation later—this was the White House strategy."[10] That strategy had its chief work-

7. Paul J. Quirk, "Regulatory Policy Making in the New Congress: Deregulation Revisited" (Paper presented at the Conference on the New Politics of Public Policy, Brandeis University, April 1990), pp. 24–29, first quotation at p. 25; John E. Chubb, "U.S. Energy Policy: A Problem of Delegation," in Chubb and Paul E. Peterson, eds., *Can the Government Govern?* (Washington, D.C.: Brookings Institution Press, 1989), pp. 73–76, other quotations at p. 74. Technically, the Natural Gas Policy Act of 1978 was a component of the omnibus energy measure enacted that year.

8. Quirk, "Regulatory Policy Making," p. 28.

9. R. Douglas Arnold, *Congress and the Bureaucracy: A Theory of Influence* (New Haven and London: Yale University Press, 1979), pp. 165–69.

10. Doris Kearns, *Lyndon Johnson and the American Dream* (New York: Harper

out in 1965 after the 1964 election generated a rare two-to-one Democratic edge in the House, but it figured also in 1964 as Johnson manipulated Democratic majorities in the aftershock of Kennedy's assassination. James L. Sundquist has written of that year's anti-poverty program: "Rarely has so sweeping a commitment been made to an institution so little tested and so little understood as the community action agency [the most prominent creation of the program]. And no time was accorded Congress to find out.... On some of the most important sections of the act, little legislative history was written or none at all."[11] Ingenious as the maneuvering to pass it might have been, the anti-poverty program was a "hastily packaged" product that, once enacted, soon lost popular and Capitol Hill support and sowed what Daniel Patrick Moynihan later termed "maximum feasible misunderstanding."[12]

As for reckless expansion of entitlements, that is a question of fact, and the record does not seem to favor unified party control. How about, for example, the expansion during the Great Society (UNI)? In fact, the enacters of Medicare and Medicaid in 1965 greatly underestimated the long-run costs of the former and scarcely gauged those of the latter at all. "Lyndon Johnson's decision not to run for president in 1967 may have been a wiser one than he realized, for, beyond his troubles with the Vietnam War, he had helped to open the flood gates of public programs without controls.... Medicare and Medicaid expenditures were greatly in excess of expectations."[13] It is interesting

and Row, 1976), pp. 216–18, quotations at pp. 216, 218. "There seemed to be few among the principal officers of government who were trying to determine how the programs could be made actually to work. The standard of success was the passage of the law" (p. 218). These statements refer to the Eighty-ninth Congress, elected in 1964.

11. James L. Sundquist, *Politics and Policy: The Eisenhower, Kennedy, and Johnson Years* (Washington, D.C.: Brookings Institution Press, 1968), p. 151.

12. See Jeffrey K. Tulis, *The Rhetorical Presidency* (Princeton, N.J.: Princeton University Press, 1987), pp. 161–72, first quotation at p. 172; Daniel P. Moynihan, *Maximum Feasible Misunderstanding: Community Action in the War on Poverty* (New York: Free Press, 1969), chap. 5.

13. Odin W. Anderson, *Health Services in the United States: A Growth Enterprise since 1875* (Ann Arbor, Mich.: Health Administration Press, 1985), pp. 201–02. See also Herbert Stein, *Presidential Economics: The Making of Economic Policy* (New York: Simon and Schuster, 1985), p. 116. On Medicaid: James T. Patterson, *America's Struggle against Poverty, 1900–1985* (Cambridge: Harvard University Press, 1986), p. 169; Robert Stevens and Rosemary Stevens, *Welfare*

to note the degree to which criticism of American political institutions lurches from era to era making time-bound diagnoses of what went wrong. As of the 1930s, for example, the leading kind of entitlements pathology was thought to be the veterans bonus bill enacted by a craven Congress over a right-thinking president's veto. That happened at least five times under Coolidge, Hoover, and Franklin Roosevelt between 1924 and 1936, all during times of unified party control.[14] And in the realm of savings-and-loan legislation, the Garn-St. Germain Act of 1982 was in fact the second shoe to drop. The first was the Depository Institutions and Monetary Control Act of 1980 (UNI), which raised interest rates that thrifts could pay and more than doubled federal deposit insurance to $100,000 per account. These were evidently imprudent moves.[15]

A democracy's laws, Tocqueville wrote, "are almost always defective or untimely."[16] That makes a search for "seriously defective legislation" easy. In fact, of course, a great deal of legislation is not seriously defective. At least by the tests of clear ends, effective means, and longevity, the postwar era presents such success stories as the Taft-Hartley Act of 1947, the National Defense Education Act of 1958, the Voting Rights Act of 1965, and the Food Stamp Acts of 1964 and 1970. Lawmaking can obviously work. But whatever the tests, it seems unlikely that divided party control lowers the quality of statutes. As suggestive additional evidence, one can read dozens of legislative his-

---

Medicine in America: A Case Study of Medicaid (New York: Free Press, 1974), pp. 51–53, 68–69.

14. See the data in V. O. Key, Jr., "The Veterans and the House of Representatives: A Study of a Pressure Group and Electoral Mortality," *Journal of Politics* 5 (1943), 28–30. See also E. Cary Brown, "Fiscal Policy in the 'Thirties: A Reappraisal," *American Economic Review* 46 (1956), 863–69.

15. According to one recent account, these statutory changes "guaranteed that the Savings and Loans . . . would engage in a binge of blue-sky financing and outright thievery." George P. Brockway, "Who Killed the Savings and Loans?" *New Leader*, September 3, 1990, p. 16. On raising the deposit insurance ceiling from $40,000 to $100,000: "No hearing was held on this move; there was no debate. It now seems clear that, at the time, most of the legislators had no idea of what they were doing." L. J. Davis, "Chronicle of a Debacle Foretold: How Deregulation Begat the S&L Scandal," *Harper's*, September 1990, p. 53.

16. Alexis de Tocqueville, *Democracy in America* (Garden City, N.Y.: Doubleday Anchor, 1969), p. 232. See also pp. 248–50.

tories by policy-area specialists and not come across judgments that it does; it if did, such analysts would probably notice.

The second question is: Even if important individual statutes can win enactment regardless of conditions of party control, how about programmatic "coherence" across statutes? Isn't that a likelier outcome under unified party control? The argument is sometimes made.[17] Confronted by this claim, one's first response is to note that "coherence" exists in the eyes of beholders, that beholders differ in what they see, and in any event, why is "coherence" necessary or desirable? Democracy, according to some leading models, can function well enough as an assortment of decentralized, unconnected incursions into public affairs. Interests, ideas, and causes disjointedly intrude into governmental processes and win victories in Charles E. Lindblom's *Intelligence of Democracy*.[18] "Minorities rule" in Robert A. Dahl's *Preface to Democratic Theory*.[19] Nothing requires the imposition or perception of any kind of cognitive order across governmental activities in general.

Still, widespread agreement does exist about the features and importance of at least two patterns of coherence across statutes, and those should be considered. One is *ideological coherence*, for which an argument might go as follows. To permit broad-ranging change of the sort recommended by ideologies that arise now and then, and to provide a graspable politics to sectors of the public who might be interested in such change, a system needs to allow ideological packaging. That is, it needs to allow, at least sometimes, the enactment of rather large collections of laws thrusting in the same ideological direction. But such packaging has already been discussed. The postwar American system has accommodated it under circumstances of both unified and divided party control—notably in the successfully enacted presidential programs of Johnson (UNI) and Reagan (DIV), and in the liberal legislative surge of 1963 through 1975–76 (UNI then DIV). Presidential programs, given their properties as drama, can probably

17. See, for example, James P. Pfiffner, "Divided Government and the Problem of Governance," chap. 3 in James A. Thurber, ed., *Divided Democracy: Cooperation and Conflict between the President and Congress* (Washington, D.C.: Congressional Quarterly Press, 1991), p. 48.

18. Charles E. Lindblom, *The Intelligence of Democracy: Decision Making through Mutual Adjustment* (New York: Free Press, 1965).

19. Robert A. Dahl, *A Preface to Democratic Theory* (Chicago: University of Chicago Press, 1956), chap. 5.

reach the general public more effectively, but ideological surges arising from "moods" can unquestionably engage appreciable sectors of the public.

Then there is *budgetary coherence*—that is, a match between revenue and expenditure across all government programs. Whether such a match occurs is of course ultimately a matter of statutes, including appropriations bills. It goes without saying that the federal government's immense deficits have daunted and preoccupied the country's political elite as much as anything during the last decade. For some observers, the deficits have also posed a clear test of divided party control, which it has flunked. A single ruling party would have done better, the argument goes, for reasons either of ideological uniformity or electoral accountability. Lloyd N. Cutler made the latter argument in 1988: "If one party was responsible for all three power centers [House, Senate, and presidency] and produced deficits of the magnitude in which they have been produced in recent years, there would be no question of the accountability and the responsibility of that party and its elected public officials for what had happened."[20]

Is this a valid case, finally, against divided party control? That has to remain an open question, since not much scholarship has yet appeared about the history of budgeting as it may have been affected by conditions of party control; also, highly relevant events will no doubt continue to take place. But the case is considerably less compelling than it may first look. For one thing, there is evidently no statistical relation between divided party control and deficit financing over the two centuries of American national history, or more specifically since World War II.[21] That recent period includes the 1950s, it is useful to remember, when Eisenhower, who faced Democratic Congresses for six years, fought major political battles and drew much criticism from liberal intellectuals because he would *not* accept unbalanced budgets. Taking into account size of deficit or surplus, what the postwar pattern does show is a "sudden break" under Reagan.[22]

20. Lloyd N. Cutler, "Some Reflections about Divided Government," *Presidential Studies Quarterly* 18 (1988), 489.

21. James E. Alt and Charles H. Stewart III, "Parties and the Deficit: Some Historical Evidence" (Paper prepared for the Conference on Political Economics, National Bureau of Economic Research, February 1990), pp. 6–7, 18–19, and tables 2 and 6.

22 Andre Modigliani and Franco Modigliani, "The Growth of the Federal Deficit and the Role of Public Attitudes," *Public Opinion Quarterly* 51 (1987),

Deficits "blossomed suddenly in 1981."[23] A time series of federal debt as a percentage of gross national product falls almost monotonically from 1946 through 1974, holds more or less steady until 1981, and then surges.[24] The 1980s are the problem.

An explanation that seems to fit this pre-1980 versus post-1980 experience involves not conditions of party control but rather individual presidents' policies. At least since World War II, according to Paul E. Peterson, Congress "has generally followed the presidential lead on broad fiscal policies."[25] Overall congressional appropriations—that is, for each year the total across all programs—have ordinarily come quite close to overall presidential spending requests.[26] Changes in total revenue generated by congressional tax enactments have ordinarily approximated those proposed by presidents.[27]

Sometimes these results have not come easily. It required a year to enact the Kennedy tax cut proposed in 1963 (UNI). Johnson's tax surcharge, a deficit-reduction measure proposed in August 1967 (UNI), won enactment only after ten months of deadlock and a "battle of the titans" between the president and Ways and Means chairman Wilbur Mills.[28] The encounter is instructive. At the low point, in May 1968, Johnson accused Ways and Means of "blackmail" and was reported to be "in a mood of despair, fearing that the tax bill may be dead," although "some lawmakers [were] still clinging to hope that

470. "To summarize, the great deficits that began in 1982 are something altogether unparalleled in the fiscal history of the United States, except during major wars and depressions" (p. 473).

23. Paul E. Peterson, "The New Politics of Deficits," chap. 13 in John E. Chubb and Peterson, eds., *The New Direction in American Politics* (Washington, D.C.: Brookings Institution Press, 1985), pp. 365–70, quotation at p. 366.

24. Ibid., p. 369.

25. Ibid., p. 366. For a general discussion, see pp. 370–82. "Throughout the postwar period Congress has operated within a budget framework initially specified by the president.... However much Congress may modify the details of that policy, it seems to have accepted the executive's prerogative to define the budget's general contours" (p. 379).

26. Ibid., pp. 372–79. The data are for 1947 through 1984.

27. Ibid., pp. 380–82. "On tax matters, Congress also mainly follows the presidential lead" (p. 381). The data are for 1948 through 1984.

28. See the account in Lawrence C. Pierce, *The Politics of Fiscal Policy Formation* (Pacific Palisades, Calif.: Goodyear Publishing, 1971), pp. 7–8, 146–72, quotation at p. 146.

the threatened deterioration of the U.S. economic position, domestically and internationally, will yet compel the warring politicians to compromise."[29] The basic problem was that congressional conservatives would vote for a tax increase only if it was accompanied by substantial expenditure cuts. House Republicans warned that they would not supply needed votes unless the president and a majority of House Democrats publicly backed such a package. Johnson finally capitulated. A centrist, cross-party House coalition approved a compromise plan in mid-June; many anti-tax Republicans and liberal Democrats (notably most members from the Detroit and New York City areas) opposed it.

This was a success story, of sorts. And in general, presidents have ended up winning the overall tax and spending contours they asked for, or close to them, regardless of conditions of party control.[30] Under divided control, that held true for Nixon in 1969–74, although the ultimate mix of defense as opposed to domestic spending during those years did not satisfy him.[31] It held for Eisenhower, who guarded his budgets as effectively from a Democratic spending drive in 1957–60 as he had from Republican tax-cutting pressure in 1953.[32] It finally held for Bush in the fall of 1990, when he won "the biggest deficit reduction legislation in history."[33] The circumstances were unusually

29. Ibid., p. 155 (first quotation); Edwin L. Dale, Jr., "Johnson Demands Increase in Taxes Despite Election," *New York Times*, May 4, 1968, p. 16 (second quotation); Norman C. Miller and Richard F. Janssen, "Tax Chances Seen Further Dimmed by Johnson Talk, But Economic Aides No Longer Fear Fiscal 'Shambles,' " *Wall Street Journal*, May 6, 1968, p. 3 (third quotation).

30. "Even during the Carter administration—when, surprisingly enough, the fiscal differences between the executive and legislative branches were the largest—congressional appropriations differed from presidential requests by less than 0.7 percent of GNP." Paul E. Peterson and Mark Rom, "Macroeconomic Policymaking: Who Is in Control?" in Chubb and Peterson, eds., *Can the Government Govern?* p. 166.

31. Peterson, "New Politics of Deficits," pp. 375, 381; Stein, *Presidential Economics*, chap. 5.

32. Herbert Stein, *The Fiscal Revolution in America* (Chicago: University of Chicago Press, 1969), chaps. 11–14; Iwan W. Morgan, *Eisenhower Versus "the Spenders": The Eisenhower Administration, the Democrats, and the Budget, 1953–60* (London: Pinter, 1990), Conclusions; Dwight D. Eisenhower, *The White House Years*, vol. 2, *Waging Peace, 1956–1961* (Garden City, N.Y.: Doubleday, 1965), pp. 377–81, 385–88.

33. David E. Rosenbaum, "House and Senate Pass Budget Bill; Bush Is 'Pleased,' " *New York Times*, October 28, 1990, p. I:1.

adverse: A fall election approached, primary electorates had shown a surly anti-incumbent mood, a recession was setting in, and Bush had just confused the electorate and his own party by abandoning his "Read my lips" no-tax pledge of the 1988 campaign. The result came after five months of haggling, a temporary no-funds shutdown of the Washington Monument, public outcries against government disorder, and a desertion by House Republicans that shifted the final package in a Democratic direction. But a five-year $490 billion plan did pass. In a perhaps unparalleled test, during prewar times, the generalization held in 1932 when Hoover sought a major tax increase from a Democratic House during an election year at the depth of the depression. He got it—if only after, as discussed earlier, backbench Democrats and progressive Republicans rebelled against party leaders and wrote their own brand of provisions.[34]

And the generalization held for Reagan in 1981 (DIV). Though he made unusual requests, he got largely what he asked for.[35] His basic mix of a severe tax cut, heavy cuts in domestic spending, but increased defense spending and hands off Social Security was ratified by Congress and paved the way for the deficits of the 1980s.[36] The program's enactment owed partly to Reagan's and David Stockman's inventive arithmetic, but there was support from economists. These included supply-side theorists, a fringe of the profession, but also the Reagan coalition's monetarists who had come to question the relevance of deficits to prices, income, or growth (at least in the short run).[37] This

34. See Jordan A. Schwarz, *The Interregnum of Despair: Hoover, Congress, and the Depression* (Urbana: University of Illinois Press, 1970), chap. 5. It would be interesting to do a comparative analysis of the deficit-reduction enterprises of 1932, 1968, and 1990.

35. On the Reagan tax cut: "The bill that passed cut taxes by about as much as the President had proposed. This should not have been a surprise. There is usually little Congressional motivation to cut taxes less than a President says is prudent." Stein, *Presidential Economics*, p. 272.

36. At a rhetorical level, the president did keep asking for deeper domestic spending cuts than Congress gave him in 1981, but evidently he had no better idea than anyone else where those might come from. See David A. Stockman, *The Triumph of Politics: How the Reagan Revolution Failed* (New York: Harper and Row, 1986), pp. 91–92, 128–33, 274–76, 344–46, 356–60.

37. Peterson, "New Politics of Deficits," pp. 382–97; James D. Savage, *Balanced Budgets and American Politics* (Ithaca, N.Y.: Cornell University Press, 1988), pp. 209–22; Hugh Heclo and Rudolph G. Penner, "Fiscal and Political Strategy in the Reagan Administration," chap. 2 in Fred I. Greenstein, ed.,

was a rationale for deficits, or at least for a lack of concern about them. True, some vigorous logrolling took place on Capitol Hill in 1981 as White House agents conceded tax breaks to advance the president's tax bill and reprieved targeted programs to enact Gramm-Latta II (the expenditure cuts).[38] Both sorts of bargaining added to future deficits. But these actions came at the margin and in the service of a cause.[39] As much as anything, Reagan's 1981 victories seem to have been a triumph of ideas—a low-tax, low-spend doctrine that at once had the backing of some respectable economists and was saleable in simple form to a mass public. Of course the effort required a good salesman.

In fiscal affairs, Paul E. Peterson and Mark Rom argue, the apt analogy is between Reagan and Franklin Roosevelt (who always faced Congresses of his own party): "Deficit politics has proven to be a winning strategy for two popular presidents, both of whom had controversial agendas that shifted American policy in a new direction." "Overall, deficit politics became a vital component of the two strongest, most dramatic presidencies of the twentieth century."[40] In both cases, deficit financing seemed to work. That is, the electorate, reacting as customary to macroeconomic indicators, rewarded the party in control

---

The Reagan Presidency: An Early Assessment (Baltimore: Johns Hopkins University Press, 1983), pp. 21–26.

38. See Stockman, *Triumph of Politics*, chaps. 8, 9; R. Douglas Arnold, *The Logic of Congressional Action* (New Haven and London: Yale University Press, 1990), pp. 208–09.

39. To draw an analogy, one of the classic exercises of congressional logrolling took place during passage of the Smoot-Hawley tariff of 1930, which, from the standpoint of the world economy, may have been the most unfortunate statute enacted by the U.S. government during the twentieth century. (Note that it passed at a time of unified party control.) But Robert Pastor has convincingly argued that, notwithstanding the logrolling, a doctrine of protectionism shared by President Hoover and congressional Republicans was essential to the act's passage. Take that away, as happened in the next important consideration of foreign trade under the Democrats in 1934, and the cross-industry logrolling disappeared also. Doctrines dominated deals. The argument here is that Reaganite ideology comparably legitimized the logrolling of 1981. See Robert A. Pastor, *Congress and the Politics of U.S. Foreign Economic Policy, 1929–1976* (Berkeley: University of California Press, 1980), pp. 77–84. On Smoot-Hawley, see E. E. Schattschneider, *Politics, Pressures, and the Tariff: A Study of Free Private Enterprise in Pressure Politics, as Shown in the 1929–1930 Revision of the Tariff* (Hamden, Conn.: Archon Books, 1963).

40. Peterson and Rom, "Macroeconomic Policymaking," pp. 179, 180.

of the presidency.[41] In the 1980s that meant Republican victories in 1984 and 1988 (times of prosperity) although losses in 1982 (a recession year).[42] That, in the economic sphere, is the kind of "accountability" that the American system offers.

It is entirely possible, of course, that the immense deficits of the 1980s would have been avoided if one party had controlled the government. But it is an act of faith to suppose so. Party-centered accountability would scarcely have done the trick: Nothing we know about electoral behavior suggests that American voters, whatever the circumstances of party control, will reward a government for balancing budgets. Beyond this, perhaps the key decision in conjuring up counterfactual replays of the 1980s is whether to allow the intrusion of a captivating low-tax ideology into the system. If the answer is yes, budgets come under pressure. Given that pressure, imagine for example a Republican government in control of all three branches led by Reagan, Bush, Howard Baker, Bob Dole, Robert Michel, and Newt Gingrich. Would it have balanced its budgets? Recall that much of the actual budgetary disagreement during the 1980s took place *within* the Republican party.

On the Democratic side, to envision a post-Carter ruling combination in control of all three branches is not that easy. But Democrats have not proven immune to low-tax pressure. Developments at the state level are suggestive, although, for constitutional reasons, budgetary disorder has to assume forms there other than deficits. In California, an all-Democratic government was bowled over by Proposition 13 in 1978. In Massachusetts, an all-Democratic government virtually disintegrated in 1989–90 as a result of low-tax, low-spending sentiment exhibited in opinion polls and primaries. How would a Democratic government at the national level have managed such demands?

41. The standard source is Gerald H. Kramer, "Short-Term Fluctuations in U.S. Voting Behavior, 1896–1964," *American Political Science Review* 65 (1971), 131–43. For an analysis that covers the post–World War II era, see Robert S. Erikson, "Economic Conditions and the Presidential Vote," *American Political Science Review* 83 (1989), 567–73.

42. On the 1984 election, see D. Roderick Kiewiet and Douglas Rivers, "The Economic Basis of Reagan's Appeal," chap. 3 in Chubb and Peterson, eds., *New Direction in American Politics*; Donald R. Kinder, Gordon S. Adams, and Paul W. Gronke, "Economics and Politics in the 1984 American Presidential Election," *American Journal of Political Science* 33 (1989), 491–515.

That seems to be the appropriate question. "Party government" does not provide a refuge from them.

The third question is: Doesn't government administration suffer as a result of divided party control? Doesn't exaggerated pulling and hauling between president and Congress undermine the implementation of laws and, in general, the functioning of agencies and the administration of programs? High-publicity Capitol Hill investigations, which have been discussed, are relevant to an answer, but the subject is broader than that. It is also vaguer and quite difficult to address. The strategy here will be to present a plausible case *for* an instance of such undermining of administration and then draw a historical comparison. This will scarcely exhaust the topic, but the instances to be compared are important in their own right as well as suggestive about conditions of party control in general.

The plausible instance is Congress's thrust toward "micro-managing" the executive branch in recent decades.[43] That is, Congress has greatly increased its staff who monitor administration, multiplied its days of oversight hearings, greatly expanded its use of the legislative veto (until a federal court ruled that device unconstitutional in 1983), taken to writing exceptionally detailed statutes that limit bureaucratic discretion (notably in environmental law), and tried to trim presidential power through such measures as the War Powers Act of 1973 and the Budget and Impoundment Act of 1974.[44] Whether these moves have helped or harmed the system can be argued either way, but let us stipulate for the moment that they have undermined administration.

Has "micro-management" resulted, at least partly, from divided party control of the government? That too can be argued either way. An abundant list of alternative causes includes public and congressional reaction to the Vietnam war (as conducted by both Johnson

43. The term appears in, for example, James Q. Wilson, *Bureaucracy: What Government Agencies Do and Why They Do It* (New York: Basic Books, 1989), pp. 241–44.

44. See Joel D. Aberbach, *Keeping a Watchful Eye: The Politics of Congressional Oversight* (Washington, D.C.: Brookings Institution Press, 1990), pp. 34–46; William T. Gormley, Jr., *Taming the Bureaucracy: Muscles, Prayers, and Other Strategies* (Princeton, N.J.: Princeton University Press, 1989), pp. 56–59 and chap. 8.

and Nixon) and the public's rising distrust of bureaucracy.[45] But let us hypothesize that divided party control is at least partly the cause. Here is the argument. Rather than appearing gradually, "micro-management" came into its own rather quickly under Nixon and Ford in the 1970s—especially during the Nixon-Ford term of 1973–76. To cite some quantitative evidence, days spent per year on congressional oversight hearings, and average number of pages per enacted law (an indicator of statutory detail), achieved *most* of the considerable increase they showed from 1961 through 1984 during just the four years of 1973–76.[46]

That was during a period of divided party control. Obviously, micro-management has not flashed on whenever party control became divided (as under Eisenhower) or flashed off whenever it became unified (as under Carter). Much of it, at least, came in under Nixon-Ford and stayed. One might say that those years saw the initiation of a "regime" of micro-management—that is, a durable set of views and institutionally located practices geared to that end. Once in place, those views and practices could survive the transition to Carter and then to Reagan. Their origin is what counts. To implicate divided party control plausibly, one has to argue that two conditions were necessary for this "micro-management regime" to come into existence. First, party control had to be divided: Congress would not have inaugurated such a regime otherwise. Second, there had to occur some unusual shock to the system such as Watergate, Nixon's conduct of the war, or simply Nixon's aggressive presidency: Divided control would not have engendered such a regime otherwise. Divided control, that is, was a necessary *part* of the causal structure that triggered the regime.[47]

That is a plausible, particular argument. Can it be generalized? The broader case would be that members of a relevant class of congressional regimes that includes the micro-management one—that is, regimes that can reasonably be alleged to undermine administration—can be expected to arise under the same circumstances. That is, they

45. See Aberbach, *Keeping a Watchful Eye*, pp. 26–28, 39–46, 48–73, 191–93, and Gormley, *Taming the Bureaucracy*, pp. 32–35.

46. Aberbach, *Keeping a Watchful Eye*, pp. 38, 44.

47. To put it another way, and to generalize, the key causal variable is an interaction term whose components are a relevant kind of shock and the circumstance of divided party control.

require some similar shock to the system plus a background of divided party control.

Has any other such regime ever existed? As it happens, what looks like a particularly good instance of one originated in 1938 and led a vibrant life through 1954. It was that era's "loyalty regime"—the brilliant innovation of Democratic Congressman Martin Dies of Texas, founder of the House Un-American Activities Committee. Dies pioneered a formula that carried through the Hiss, McCarran, Army-McCarthy and other investigations after the war.[48] It was a low-cost, high-publicity, committee-centered way of waging a congressional opposition against the New Deal, the Truman administration, and then Eisenhower. Its chief technique was the hearing where someone could accuse members of the executive branch of being disloyal to the United States. No one should be surprised that that evidently had a pronounced effect on administration. Beyond its effects on the targeted personnel, it could demoralize agencies, preoccupy the White House, put a chill on unorthodox policy options, and even exile whole schools of thought from the government (as with China specialists after 1949).

It seems a good bet that this loyalty regime made as much of a mark on administration—to be sure, its own kind of mark—as has Congress's more recent micro-management regime. Compare, for example, the "Who lost China?" inquiries that dogged Truman's China policy with the Boland amendments aimed at micro-managing Reagan's Central America policy. But of course the loyalty regime began, led nearly all its existence, and ended during times of unified party

48. Although 1948 through 1954 seems to have been the peak period for this regime, at least as regards the executive branch (the investigators did have other targets), HUAC also made a significant impact earlier. Between 1938 and 1947, the committee pursued alleged disloyalty in the WPA's Federal Theatre and Writers Project, the National Labor Relations Board, the National Youth Administration, the Tennessee Valley Authority, the Office of Price Administration, the Federal Communications Commission, the Office of Civil Defense, the Board of Economic Warfare, the War Production Board, and the Departments of Labor, State, and Interior. The Department of Justice came under fire for allegedly disregarding disloyalty elsewhere. See Walter Goodman, *The Committee: The Extraordinary Career of the House Committee on Un-American Activities* (New York: Farrar, Straus and Giroux, 1964), pp. 29, 35, 42–48, 55, 69–75, 100, 104–13, 124–28, 131–52, 171–72, 203–07. Almost all of this took place while the Democrats controlled both the presidency and Congress—that is, before the 1946 election. Dies chaired HUAC through 1944.

control.[49] Nothing is more striking than the inventiveness of the lop-sidedly Democratic Congress of 1937–38. Not only did it originate HUAC—"the outstanding political show of 1938."[50] It also generated a House Rules Committee regime that, although not involved in administration, gave conservatives a cross-party location for blocking or delaying liberal legislative proposals between 1937 and 1961.[51] Under Democratic presidents, those were often White House pro-posals. The options of loyalty probes and Rules Committee vetoes helped to insure that, for a generation, government would proceed largely through open contention among officials operating from sep-arate executive and congressional power bases.

The analogy here is between Congress's loyalty and micro-management regimes. The former shows at least that regimes af-fecting—and arguably undermining—administration *can* materialize and thrive during times of unified party control. That is the narrow claim. It does not rule out the possibility that such regimes have been less common or consequential during times of unified control—al-though to demonstrate that would require evidence and it is not clear what it would be. In the instances of the loyalty and micro-management regimes—and also the Rules Committee one—one cred-ible and parsimonious account of at least their origins has nothing to do with conditions of party control. Instead it would emphasize the extraordinary disruption caused to the system by Roosevelt and Nixon around the time they were winning landslide re-elections and entering

49. Or receded into insignificance if not exactly ended. No loyalty investi-gation had much impact on the executive branch after 1954.

50. Ibid., p. 54. On the origins of HUAC, see ibid., chaps. 1, 2; Richard Polenberg, "The Decline of the New Deal, 1937–1940" in John Braeman, Robert H. Bremner, and David Brody, eds., *The New Deal: The National Level* (Columbus: Ohio State University Press, 1975), pp. 257–58; William E. Leu-chtenburg, *Franklin D. Roosevelt and the New Deal, 1932–1940* (New York: Har-per and Row, 1963), pp. 280–81. "Ostensibly nonpartisan, the Dies Committee served the purposes of those who claimed that the New Deal was a Red strat-agem" (p. 281). Nothing may index better the demise of the New Deal than the switch of public and media attention from La Follette's pro-union hearings in 1937 to Dies's anti-Communist investigation of 1938.

51. The Rules Committee's move into that role during 1937–38 is discussed in Patterson, *Congressional Conservatism*, pp. 53, 167–68, 176–77, 179–83, 186, 193–94, 225–29, 243–44, 247.

their second terms.[52] Roosevelt forged an alliance with the new CIO, built a WPA patronage organization deployable in national elections, introduced his controversial court-packing and executive reorganization plans, and ultimately tried to purge House and Senate Democrats in the 1938 primaries.[53] Nixon conducted the Indochina war in his memorable way, hatched internal security schemes, aggressively impounded Capitol Hill appropriations, advanced a plan (which resembled Roosevelt's) to centralize control of the administrative branch, and finally brought on Watergate.[54] Given the way American politics works, it would have been surprising in either president's case if an alarmed Congress had *not* undertaken serious countermoves.

The fourth question is: Does the conduct of foreign policy suffer under divided party control? That might be a special concern, since "coordination" is often held to be central to effective foreign policymaking. Perhaps an excess of "deadlock" or "non-coordination" occurs under conditions of divided control. But of course such disorderliness, looked at from the other side as by opponents of Truman's China policy or Reagan's Central America policy, figures as a healthy exercise of checks and balances. Foreign policy is often a fighting matter at home. There does not seem to be any way around this. "Coordination," however much sense it may seem to make, does not and cannot dominate every other value.[55]

Yet once past that realization, it is not clear what standards to apply. None will be proposed here. But let the reader try the following thought experiment. Choose *any* plausible set of standards and, using them, scan through the history of American foreign policymaking since World War II. Here is a prediction of what most readers will conclude: In general, the record was no worse when the two parties shared power. Any appraisal has to accommodate or steer around, for example, the Marshall Plan, which owed to bipartisan cooperation

52. To put it another way, as earlier, the interaction term drops its divided-control component and becomes just a shock variable.

53. See for example Sidney M. Milkis, "Franklin D. Roosevelt and the Transcendence of Partisan Politics," *Political Science Quarterly* 100 (1985), 479–504.

54. Richard P. Nathan draws the analogy between Roosevelt's and Nixon's executive reorganization drives in *The Plot That Failed: Nixon and the Administrative Presidency* (New York: John Wiley and Sons, 1975), pp. 87–89.

55. For a relevant discussion, see Larry N. George, "Tocqueville's Caveat: Centralized Executive Foreign Policy and American Democracy," *Polity* 22 (1990), 419–41.

during a time of divided control; the Kennedy-Johnson intervention in Indochina, which, whatever else may be said about it, scarcely took its shape because of a lack of coordination; Nixon's openings to China and the Soviet Union, which were maneuvered with little Capitol Hill dissent during a time of divided control; and Bush's liberation of Kuwait in 1990–91. Given just these items, many readers may agree, considerable ingenuity would be needed to concoct a verdict spanning the four and a half decades that favors unified party control. As argued in chapter 4, the same lack of pattern appears in foreign policy areas requiring legislative action across several Congresses—foreign aid, foreign trade, and treaty ratifications. There too the record does not seem to have differed or suffered under divided control.[56]

The fifth question: Are the country's lower-income strata served less well under divided party control? One can assemble a theory that they might be, assuming for a moment that "serve" refers to direct government action rather than, say, encouragement of long-term economic growth. Separation of powers biases the American regime toward the rich, Progressive theorists used to argue at the outset of the twentieth century. The rich profit when the government does nothing, whereas the non-rich require concerted public action that can all too easily be blocked somewhere in the system's ample array of veto-points. An obvious remedy would be a constitution allowing strict majority rule.[57] But lacking that, according to a conventional argument of political science, much depends on political parties. Their distinctive role is to impose on the country's collection of government institutions a kind of order that serves majority interests. In principle, that might be done by one party embodying the views and experiences of the non-rich (a socialist sort of argument) or by two parties bidding for the votes of the non-rich (a Downsian sort of argument). Either way, unified control is needed to deliver the goods. It allows action, rules out buck-passing, fixes responsibility, permits accountability.

56. Foreign trade policy can be said to require its own special brand of "coherence." Often that is not forthcoming, but in one recent review of U.S. trade policy since the 1930s there is no suggestion that divided party control has caused any distinctive problems. See David B. Yoffie, "American Trade Policy: An Obsolete Bargain?" pp. 100–38 in Chubb and Peterson, eds., *Can the Government Govern?*

57. For the Progressive case, see J. Allen Smith, *The Spirit of American Government: A Study of the Constitution; Its Origin, Influence, and Relation to Democracy* (New York: Macmillan, 1907).

That is a plausible line of argument, and the Great Society as well as the New Deal might be said to bear it out. But altogether too much of the record since World War II does not. What were the origins of the "social safety net" that the Reagan administration—during a time of divided control, for what that is worth—succeeded in widening the holes of?[58] In fact, that net owed much of its weaving to the Nixon and Ford years—also a time of divided control. That period was the source of EEA and CETA jobs, expanded unemployment insurance, low-income energy assistance, post–1974 housing allowances, Pell grants for lower-income college students, greatly multiplied food-stamps assistance, a notable progressivizing of tax incidence, Supplementary Security Income for the aged, blind, and disabled, and Social Security increases that cut the proportion of aged below the poverty line from 25 percent in 1970 to 16 percent in 1974.[59] The laws just kept getting passed. The Reaganite assault against both the Great Society and the 1970s pitted era against era and mood against mood. But it did not pit divided party control against unified party control or even all that clearly Republicans against Democrats.

These five questions are not the only additional ones that might be asked about unified as opposed to divided party control.[60] This work

58. On the safety net, see for example Peter Passell, "Forces in Society, and Reaganism, Helped Dig Deeper Hole for Poor," *New York Times*, July 16, 1989, p. I:1.

59. See Patterson, *America's Struggle against Poverty*, chap. 10 (on Social Security expansion at p. 158), and pp. 197–98, 200; Timothy Conlan, *New Federalism: Intergovernmental Reform from Nixon to Reagan* (Washington, D.C.: Brookings Institution Press, 1988), pp. 81–82; R. Allen Hays, *The Federal Government and Urban Housing* (Albany: State University of New York Press, 1985), pp. 145–51; Robert X. Browning, *Politics and Social Welfare Policy in the United States* (Knoxville: University of Tennessee Press, 1986), pp. 84–90, 95, 107–14, 120–21, 141–48, 161–62. Largely at Democratic behest, shifts of tax law in a progressive direction took place under Nixon in 1969 (DIV) and also under Hoover in 1932 (DIV) and Bush in 1990 (DIV).

60. A topical one concerns appointments to the Supreme Court. At three junctures since World War II, presidents who undertook to move the Court in a liberal or conservative direction have had their appointments blocked by the Senate. Not confirmed were Johnson nominees Abe Fortas (for elevation to Chief Justice) and Homer Thornberry in 1968 (UNI), Nixon nominees Clement Haynsworth and G. Harrold Carswell in 1969–70 (DIV), and Reagan nominees Robert Bork and Douglas Ginsburg (who withdrew) in 1987 (DIV). If one takes into account who finally won the vacant positions, then in an ideological sense Johnson's campaign can be said to have failed (Warren

skirts, moreover, the separate and obviously important question of whether the American system of government, with its separation-of-powers features, has been functioning adequately in recent times. Some analysts, for example John E. Chubb and Paul E. Peterson, say no: "When governments of quite different political combinations [that is, unified as well as divided control] all fail to perform effectively, it is worth considering whether the problem is the government itself and not the people or parties that run it."[61] Energy and budgetary policies have been creaking. Each of the last two decades has ended with a riveting spectacle of government inefficacy or disorder—Carter's "malaise" crisis in 1979 and Bush's budget wrangle in 1990. Otherwise, the country is faced with declining voter turnout as well as a rise in election technologies and incumbent-serving practices that seem to be delegitimizing elected officials.[62]

There is no end of taking steps to reform American political institutions, or of good reasons for it. But short of jettisoning the separation-of-powers core of the Constitution—an unlikely event—it would probably be a mistake to channel such concern into "party government" schemes. This work has tried to show that, surprisingly, it does not seem to make all that much difference whether party control of the American government happens to be unified or divided. One reason we assume it does is that "party government" plays a role in political science somewhere between a Platonic form and a grail. When we reach for it as a standard, we draw on abstract models, presumed European practice, and well-airbrushed American experience, but we seldom take a cold look at real American experience.

Burger became Chief Justice), Nixon fared indifferently (the position went to Harry Blackmun), and Reagan succeeded (the position went to Anthony Kennedy).

61. John E. Chubb and Paul E. Peterson, "American Political Institutions and the Problem of Governance," in Chubb and Peterson, eds., *Can the Government Govern?* p. 1. See also Terry M. Moe, "The Politics of Bureaucratic Structure," in ibid.

62. It has been alleged that divided party control *causes* lower turnout, or at least has done so recently, by confusing voters and muffling choice. The record of the past century and a half does not bear out the idea. Note that the mid-1870s through the mid-1890s was at once the country's golden age of voter turnout and an era of usually divided government. Turnout began its twentieth-century plunge, for whatever reasons, after 1896, when party

We forget about Franklin Roosevelt's troubles with HUAC and the Rules Committee, Truman's and Kennedy's domestic policy defeats, McCarthy's square-off against Eisenhower, Johnson versus Fulbright on Vietnam, and Carter's energy program and "malaise."

Political parties can be powerful instruments, but in the United States they seem to play more of a role as "policy factions" than as, in the British case, governing instruments. A party as policy faction can often get its way even in circumstances of divided control: Witness the Taftite Republicans in 1947, congressional Democrats under Nixon, or the Reaganites in 1981. How, one might ask, were these temporary policy ascendancies greatly different from that of the Great Society Democrats in 1964–66?

To demand more of American parties—to ask that they become governing instruments—is to run them up against components of the American regime as fundamental as the party system itself. There is a strong pluralist component, for example, as evidenced in the way politicians respond to cross-cutting issue cleavages. There is a public-opinion component that political science's modern technologies do not seem to reach very well. The government floats in public opinion; it goes up and down on great long waves of it that often have little to do with parties. There is the obvious structural component—separation of powers—that brings on deadlock and chronic conflict, but also nudges officials toward deliberation, compromise, and super-majority outcomes. And there is a component of deep-seated individualism among American politicians, who build and tend their own electoral bases and maintain their own relations of responsibility with electorates. This seems to be a matter of political culture—perhaps a survival of republicanism—that goes way back. Unlike most politicians elsewhere, American ones at both legislative and executive levels have managed to navigate the last two centuries of history without becoming minions of party leaders. In this complicated, multi-component setting, British-style governing by party majorities does not have much of a chance.

control returned to unified. See Walter Dean Burnham, "The Changing Shape of the American Political Universe," *American Political Science Review* 59 (1965), 11.

EPILOGUE ◆ THE RECORD DURING 1991–2002

Since 1990, the study of U.S. lawmaking has mushroomed in both volume and variety. One leading question has been: How should we think about legislative productivity? In conceptual terms, there has emanated a two-pronged fork. On one prong are what might be called *denominator* or *ratio* studies — that is, analyses that feature "some actually-did-pass numerator over some all-that-were-possibilities-for-passage denominator."[1] In recent years, several authors have contributed excellent work by deploying various denominators — for example, proposals on which presidents take a stand,[2] pledges in party platforms,[3] and policy issues discussed in *New York Times* editorials.[4] For any Congress it can be asked what proportions of such lists of items end up being enacted. To what degree do various stipulated agendas, to put it another way, become law?

On the other prong are what might be called *numerator* studies, or, in a mode influenced by economics, *move away from policy stability* studies.[5] To this way of thinking, agendas and denominators are not all that interesting or important. In the final analysis, what matters is whether the government actually does something new. Does it move away from existing policy?

In this book I have opted for prong two.[6] That is for at least three

1. See page 34.

2. George C. Edwards III, Andrew Barrett, and Jeffrey Peake, "The Legislative Impact of Divided Government," *American Journal of Political Science* 41 (1997), 545–63.

3. Terry J. Royed and Stephen A. Borrelli, "Political Parties and Public Policy: Social Welfare Policy from Carter to Bush," 29 *Polity* (1997), 539–63.

4. Sarah A. Binder, *Stalemate: Causes and Consequences of Legislative Gridlock* (Washington, D.C.: Brookings Institution Press, 2003).

5. Keith Krehbiel, *Pivotal Politics: A Theory of U.S. Lawmaking* (Chicago: University of Chicago Press, 1998).

6. See pages 34–37.

reasons. First, I have particular doubts about using presidential positions or proposals as a decisive denominator. We have a sprawling separation-of-powers regime. Legislative proposals can emanate from Capitol Hill as well as from the White House. In recent years, consider the McCain-Feingold drive to reform campaign finance. Probably no one would study parental influence on children by investigating just fathers. Similarly, presidential success scores may make sense as calibrators of presidencies,[7] but they pose problems as calibrators of the whole government or the regime.

Second, assume a solution to the above. Assume that both White House and Capitol Hill proposals can somehow be blended into an overall policy agenda—a generous hybrid denominator. That can be done, for any Congress. Items that meet some threshold of prominence can be identified. But in this circumstance a troublesome endogeneity problem can arise—at least for purposes of analyzing unified versus divided control. Any party controlling any institution has a shot at manufacturing prominence for its ideas. Consider Newt Gingrich as an agenda setter when he became Speaker of the House in 1995. Two parties rather than one at the various institutional helms—that is, in a condition of divided control as opposed to unified control—may make for a bigger overall agenda. Does this agenda expansion happen? Charles R. Shipan argues that it does.[8] Beyond this, it is also possible that on balance a larger agenda will make for a lower overall success rate. For one thing, processes can get overloaded. In short, endogeneity can cloud the analysis.

Third and most important, why should we pay so much attention to policy proposals? They can be a kind of vapor that surrounds real legislative action. Politicians are always making proposals. Parties are always making proposals. That is what politicians and parties are supposed to do. But such offerings are often vague, shifting, infeasible, or otherwise

7. Note, however, that presidents can play games. They can run up their scores. We are finding that out with Bush 43, who has seemed to follow a strategy of endorsing whatever grand compromises Congress comes up with and vetoing nothing.

8. Charles R. Shipan, "Does Divided Government Increase the Size of the Legislative Agenda?" in Scott Adler and John Lapinski (eds.), *The Macro-Politics of Congress* (forthcoming). Originally presented at the Conference on the Macro-Politics of Congress, Boulder, Colo., June 2001. In Binder's study of lawmaking success from 1947 through 2000, where a posited agenda for any Congress is the number of policy issues discussed during it in *New York Times* editorials, agenda size averaged 107 items under circumstances of unified control, but 123 items under circumstances of divided control. See Binder, *Stalemate*, p. 38.

insubstantial. In general, a sensible public will discount all of them at a very high rate. Actual government production is arguably the news worth paying attention to. Does it really happen that taxes are raised, tariffs are cut, wars are declared, treaties are ratified, highways are financed, pollutants are banned, behaviors are criminalized, airlines are deregulated, or prescription drugs are funded? Changes like that can matter. To be sure, legislative enactments themselves can be vaporous achievements, since implementation is yet to come. But enactments ordinarily possess a certain solidity. To me, they seem to be the items worth documenting.

Continuing in that spirit, I present here a list of important laws enacted during the six Congresses from 1991 through 2002. Again, that span amounts to a Bush-Clinton-Bush sandwich — the last two years of the George H. W. Bush (Bush 41) presidency, the full eight years of the Clinton presidency, and the first two years of the George W. Bush (Bush 43) presidency.[9] Certainty, I should emphasize once again, is not a possible guide in compiling such a list of laws. Judgments need to be made. The documentary sources can be elusive and exasperating — notably during these years, as it happens, for the Congress of 1999–2000. In addition, the decade of the 1990s, like the 1980s, featured certain big-bang omnibus enactments — the deficit-reduction deals of 1993 and 1997, resembling the 1990 deal that just squeezed into the 1991 edition of this book — that seemed to dwarf most everything else and that render any simple counting up of laws precarious.[10]

In general, I use here the same methodology to count laws as I did in chapter 3, but with three amendments.[11] First, this is entirely a "Sweep

9. The list for 1991–92 supersedes that presented as an "Epilogue" on page 200 of the 1993 paperback edition of *Divided We Govern*.

10. On the problem of accommodating omnibus enactments, see Glen S. Krutz, "Getting Around Gridlock: The Effect of Omnibus Utilization on Legislative Productivity," *Legislative Studies Quarterly* 25 (2000), 533–49.

11. Since the early 1990s, I have been posting a list of important laws for each Congress as soon as I could after it adjourned. The site is *http://pantheon.yale.edu/dmayhew/data3.html.* In preparing an overall six-Congress dataset for the new edition of this book, I took a new synoptic look at the stacks of documentary evidence for those twelve years. That resulted in a few changes to what I had posted earlier. For the record, I added two marginal laws (abortion clinic access in 1994, 100,000 new teachers in 1998), subtracted one marginal law (bioterrorism defense in 2002), added one joint resolution (the Persian Gulf Resolution of 1991; see the discussion above), added and subtracted a few newspaper sources,

One" enterprise. All the sources are newspaper (or in a few cases, magazine) wrap-up stories written at the closes of congressional sessions. A mammoth additional project would be needed to bring "Sweep Two" up to date, and that would probably entail revising judgments in the original text. With regrets, I have left "Sweep Two" alone. Second, I have used journalistic sources beyond the *New York Times* and the *Washington Post*.[12] In recent times a few other publications have been offering decent congressional wrap-up stories, at least sporadically, and I have taken advantage. This can be a help especially when the *Times* falls short, which it sometimes does.

Third, this time I have included joint resolutions, which can be important legislative instruments in the foreign policy area. In the original edition, I identified three such resolutions but left them all out,[13] even though I did include treaty ratifications. Now I regret that omission. It is very difficult to size up the enactment interaction (let us call it that) between Congress and the presidency during the Bush years—both Bushes—without coming to grips with joint resolutions. What is a joint resolution? In process and legal terms, according to Walter J. Oleszek, "There is no significant difference between a bill and a joint resolution."[14] Both instruments require a majority in each house and a president's signature. Both can be vetoed by presidents.[15] Both have the force of law. With help,[16] to clean up the record, I have gone back and canvassed the relevant sources between 1947 and 1990 to make sure which joint resolutions I *should* have included the first time around if I *had* in principle accommodated them. There were three under Eisenhower and Johnson. Also, there was the War Powers Resolution of 1973, which as it happens I *did* include on the first round (it is often called the War Powers *Act,* which likely led me on). Now we have three major joint resolutions

---

and overhauled my earlier decisions for 1999 through 2002 about capitalizing laws for being especially important. The website now has the new material.

12. See Appendix C for a complete list of sources for 1991–2002.

13. See pp. 40–42.

14. Walter J. Oleszek, *Congressional Procedures and the Policy Process* (Washington, D.C.: Congressional Quarterly Press, 1978), p. 224.

15. Congress also uses joint resolutions to propose amendments to the Constitution. But those endeavors require two-thirds in both houses, and the president plays no role.

16. Thanks to Matthew Glassman.

under the Bushes. That makes for seven in all during 1947 through 2002, of which six have been crisis instruments awarding military authority to presidents who claimed they needed it. The War Powers Resolution of 1973 certainly did not do that, but in process terms it is a sibling. See table E.1 for the full list. In the original edition of this book, an inclusion of the Formosa Resolution of 1955, the Middle East Resolution of 1957, and the Tonkin Gulf Resolution of 1964 (which helped to legitimize the Vietnam War for awhile) would have raised the total law count from 267 to 270.[17] In this epilogue, the Persian Gulf Resolution of 1991, the Use of Force Resolution of 2001 (centering on Afghanistan), and the Iraq Resolution of 2002 are accommodated.

For the full new list covering all major enactments from 1991 through 2002, see table E.2. This is a continuation of table 4.1 in chapter 4.[18] Like that table, this one sorts the entries into columns according to conditions of party control, it tags Sweep One items (which means all entries this time) with an asterisk, and it capitalizes the enactments that the sources seemed to size up as extraordinarily important. Deciding on the capitalizations was very difficult for 1999 through 2001. Overall, I settled on the two deficit-reduction deals of 1993 and 1997, the three war-authorizing resolutions of 1991, 2001, and 2002, NAFTA in 1993, welfare reform in 1996, telecommunications reform in 1996, the Bush tax cut in 1991, the

17. Sweep One would have picked up all three resolutions of 1955, 1957, and 1964. Sweep Two as executed would have picked up just the middle of these three, but that is a complicated matter. If the three had appeared in Sweep One, I might have recognized them, so to speak, for purposes of Sweep Two by crafting a suitable "policy area" that might in turn have accommodated them. For the relevant methodology, see pp. 44–47. Note that the 1955 and 1957 resolutions were approved during divided party control, the 1964 resolution during unified party control.

18. There are anomalies here, as in the earlier list covering 1947 through 1990. See p. 40n17. College loan reform in 1993 passed as part of the Clinton deficit-reduction package (which is also listed). Welfare reform in 1996 passed as part of a budget reconciliation measure. The line item veto passed in 1996, on the House side, as part of a debt limit extension rule. Immigration reform in 1996, public housing reform in 1998, the 100,000 new teachers guarantee in 1998, the Community Renewal and New Markets Act of 2000, and the $40 billion emergency spending in 2001 ended up piggybacking on appropriations bills. The creation of the commission to investigate the September 11 attack passed as part of an intelligence authorization bill. The balance-the-budget deal of 1997 actually passed as *two* bills — the Tax Reconciliation Act of 1997 and the Spending Reconciliation Act of 1997. But the press discussed that deal as *one* item, and following earlier custom I have therefore listed it as one enactment here.

TABLE E. 1

Major Joint Resolutions in the Area of Foreign Policy Enacted during 1947–2002

Year	Context	Subject	House vote		Senate vote	
1955	Eisenhower D Cong	*Formosa Resolution.* Authorized president to use force to defend Formosa and Pescadores.	Dem Rep Total	255–1 185–2 410–3	Dem Rep Total	42–2 43–1 85–3
1957	Eisenhower D Cong	*Middle East Resolution.* *Eisenhower Doctrine.* Authorized president to block Communist expansion in the Middle East.	Dem Rep Total	186–33 164–27 350–60	Dem Dem Total	30–16 42–3 72–19
1964	Johnson D Cong	*Tonkin Gulf Resolution.* Authorized president to use all necessary means to block aggression in Southeast Asia.	Dem Rep Total	241–0 175–0 416–0	Dem Rep Total	56–2 32–0 88–2
1973	Nixon D Cong	*War Powers Resolution.* Curbed president's authority to commit U.S. troops in combat. Over Nixon's veto.	Dem Rep Total	198–32 86–103 284–135	Dem Rep Total	50–3 25–15 75–18
1991	Bush 41 D Cong	*Persian Gulf Resolution.* Authorized president to roll back Iraqi invasion of Kuwait.	Dem Rep Total	86–179 164–3 250–183	Dem Rep Total	10–45 42–2 52–47
2001	Bush 43 D Senate R House	*Use of Force Resolution.* After September 11, authorized president to use all necessary force against terrorism, notably in Afghanistan.	Dem Rep Total	204–1 214–0 420–1	Dem Rep Total	50–0 47–0 98–0
2002	Bush 43 D Senate R House	*Iraq Resolution.* Authorized president to use force against Iraq, regardless of U.N. view.	Dem Rep Total	81–126 215–6 296–133	Dem Rep Total	29–21 48–1 77–23

USA Patriot Act of 2001, and the creation of the new Homeland Security Department in 2002.[19] Probably missing from table E.2, let it be noted, are an unknown number of substantial enactments that the end-of-session wrap-up stories, for whatever reasons, missed but that some future Sweep Two–type analysis might pick up. Three candidates for such notice might be the Nunn-Lugar Act of 1991 aimed at dismantling the ex-Soviet nuclear arsenal, the Helms-Burton Act of 1996 discouraging trade with Cuba, and the Defense of Marriage Act (DOMA) of 1996 banning federal recognition of gay marriages. Wrap-up coverage has its limits.

In all, sixty-six enactments are listed in table E.2 for 1991–2002. In three quick statistical respects, the pattern matches that for earlier times. The recent six Congresses varied a good deal in overall volume — from a high of sixteen laws in 2001–02 and fifteen in 1995–96 through a low of six in 1999–2000. On average, the first halves of the presidential terms (that is, Clinton's during 1993–94 and 1997–98 and Bush 43's during 2001–02)

19. The launching of that department has been called the "biggest reorganization of government since World War II." "Politics, Security Shape Agenda," *Congressional Quarterly Almanac 2002* (Washington, D.C.: Congressional Quarterly Press, 2003), pp. 1–3. For Clinton's first two Congresses the question of what to capitalize was aided by two well-grounded comparative judgments in 1996: "Of the four most significant legislative acts of the Clinton presidency, only one — the 1993 budget and economic plan, which has cut the deficit by more than half — came with solid Democratic support overcoming unanimous Republican opposition. The second, the Telecommunications Act of 1996, was a bipartisan measure, crafted in a Republican Congress after a similar bill died when the Democrats were in control. Third, the North American Free Trade Agreement [of 1993], was passed with Republican majorities supporting Clinton against the strenuous opposition of the top Democratic leaders and most Democratic members. And the fourth, the welfare bill, also was opposed by the Democratic leadership and never would have become law if Republicans had not persevered and produced big majorities." David S. Broder, "Hanging Together," *Washington Post National Weekly Edition,* September 2–8, 1996, p. 4. "The result is that Mr. Clinton's record of achievement so far looks better than that of his Democratic presidential predecessor, Jimmy Carter. Three big pieces of legislation stand out. True, two of them — the passage of the North Atlantic Free-Trade Agreement (NAFTA) in 1993 and the recent welfare reform ("ending welfare as we know it") — were Republican-inspired and involved the president in an agonizing confrontation with his own political supporters. But it took Mr. Clinton to deliver enough Democratic votes for these measures, much as it took Nixon to go to China. The third, the budget battle of 1993, Mr. Clinton won by the thinnest possible margin against unified Republican opposition." "Second-Term Clinton? Modesty Ablaze," *The Economist,* August 1996, pp. 15–17.

narrowly beat out the second halves of the terms (that is, Bush 41's during 1991–92 and Clinton's during 1995–96 and 1999–2000). The averages on this are respectively, for what it is worth, twelve and ten. And the uniquely low value for 1999–2000 replicates a familiar seventh-year lawmaking sag for second-term presidents, regardless of conditions of party control.[20]

But on the major question at issue, it is not easy to put a feather between the system's performance during 1991–2002 under unified as opposed to divided party control. To be sure, only six Congresses appear in table E.2, only one operated fully under unified control, the omnibus measures rise above the rest, and Senator Jeffords, by defecting in May 2001, administered a major setback to simple Congress-by-Congress analysis. On the UNI-DIV front, how is 2001–02 to be scored? Although any solution is a stretch, one obvious move is to allocate, say, the first four months of the time span of 2001–02 to unified control and the remainder of the twenty-four months to divided control.[21] With that Solomonic judgment as a background, the system produced thirteen laws during the two years and four months of unified control during 1991–2002, and fifty-three laws during the nine years and eight months of divided control. That comes down to a tie—eleven laws per Congress under either condition. This may be getting a little silly, but an eyeball test directed to table E.2 will probably generate a similar conclusion. Possibly the best case for unified control is that three of the eleven capitalized items appear on its watch. (That is, unified control brought 27 percent of the capitalized laws while prevailing during only 19 percent of the dozen-year span.) But we are not seeing differences here to get excited about.

In simple descriptive terms, what is at the back of this *non*-difference? High volume in 2001–02 after the Jeffords switch (to DIV) is one answer— that is, the various post–September 11 measures but also enactments under Bush 43 addressing education, campaign finance, corporate responsibility, agriculture, election reform, and fast-track trade authority.

20. See pp. 118n40, 149n31, 157n62.

21. It is an obvious move that raises obvious questions. During the first four months of a Congress, bills are ordinarily in the exploration stage. Enactment comes later. On the other hand, the first four months of a Congress under unified party control (which early 2001 was) are often exactly the time when favored bills are rushed through quickly. That famously happened in 1965, and there are instances in 1993. Indeed, the Bush 43 tax cut is an instance in 2001.

TABLE E.2

Lists of Important Enactments by Congress, 1991–2002

Divided party control	Unified party control
1991–92	**1993–94**
Bush 41	Clinton
D Cong	D Cong
*PERSIAN GULF RESOLUTION. To roll back Iraqi invasion of Kuwait. 1991.	*OMNIBUS DEFICIT REDUCTION ACT. $496 billion savings over 5 years; top tax bracket to rise to 36% plus 10% surcharge; hike in Earned Income Tax Credit. 1993.
*Surface transportation act (ISTEA). $151 billion for highways, mass transit. 1991.	*NORTH AMERICAN FREE TRADE AGREEMENT (NAFTA) APPROVED. Mexico and Canada. 1993.
*Civil Rights Act of 1991. To allow lawsuits against job discrimination.	*Family and Medical Leave Act of 1993. Mandated 12 weeks of unpaid leave for family emergencies.
*Omnibus energy act. To restructure electricity industry, spur conservation, encourage new fuels. 1992.	
*Strategic Arms Reduction Treaty ratified. 1992.	
*Economic aid package for ex-Soviet republics. 1992.	
*Cable-TV regulation. To impose new rate and service requirements. Over Bush's veto. 1992.	
*California water policy. To switch water from agri-business to cities and environment. 1992.	

TABLE E.2 (continued)

Divided party control	Unified party control
	* *Motor Voter act.* To spur voter registration through use of driver, welfare, military-recruitment offices. 1993.
	* *National Service act.* "AmeriCorps" plan to offer college money in exchange for community service work. 1993.
	* *Reform of college-student loan financing.* Money to be provided directly rather than through banks. 1993.
	* *Brady bill.* To require 5-day waiting period for purchase of handguns. 1993.
	* *Goals 2000.* To establish national education goals. 1994.
	* *Omnibus crime act.* Ban on assault weapons; expansion of death penalty; new prison construction, police officers, prevention programs. 1994.
	* *California desert protection.* To create largest wilderness area outside Alaska. 1994.
	* *Abortion clinic access.* Criminal penalties to combat violence at abortion clinics. 1994.
	* *General Agreement on Tariffs and Trade (GATT) approved.* To lower tariffs among 124 nations and create World Trade Organization (WTO). 1994.
1995–96 Clinton R Cong	* *Curb on unfunded mandates.* New protection for state and local governments. 1995.
	* *Congressional Accountability Act.* Federal labor laws to apply to Congress itself. 1995.
* *Lobbying reform.* New disclosure requirements. 1995.	

TABLE E.2 (*continued*)

Divided party control	Unified party control
* *Curb on shareholder lawsuits.* To curb frivolous suits against flagging firms. Over Clinton's veto. 1995.	
* *WELFARE REFORM.* End of 61-year welfare guarantee to low-income women and children; block grants and regulatory leeway to states instead. 1996.	
* *TELECOMMUNICATIONS REFORM.* To spur competition in telephone, video, data services; to break up local telephone and cable-TV monopolies. 1996.	
* *Agriculture deregulation.* To undo farm subsidies and move the industry toward free market. 1996.	
* *Line-item veto.* By statute, empowered president to kill individual spending items. (Later struck down by the judiciary.) 1996.	
* *Anti-terrorism act.* New controls on borders, funds of suspected groups; curbs on death-row appeals. 1996.	
* *$24 billion spending cuts in budget deal for fiscal 1996.* Ending the shut-down-the-government crisis. 1996.	
* *Health insurance portability act.* Kassebaum-Kennedy Act. Insurance to be portable across jobs. 1996.	
* *Minimum wage hike.* From $4.25 to $5.15. Bundled with tax breaks for business. 1996.	
* *Overhaul of pesticides regulation.* 1996.	
* *Overhaul of safe drinking water legislation.* 1996.	
* *Immigration reform.* To cut illegal immigration through border controls, deportation, workplace ID's. 1996.	

TABLE E.2 (*continued*)

Divided party control	Unified party control
1997–98 Clinton R Cong	*DEAL TO BALANCE THE BUDGET BY 2002. $263 billion in spending cuts; $95 billion in tax cuts; $33 billion for new children's health insurance; new $500 child tax credit. 1997.*	
* *Chemical Weapons Convention ratified.* 1997.	
* *Overhaul of Food and Drug Administration. To expedite approval of new drugs.* 1997.	
* *Adoption of foster children. To ease the process.* 1997.	
* *Transportation construction act. $218 billion for highways and mass transit.* 1998.	
* *Overhaul of Internal Revenue Service. More rights and protections to taxpayers.* 1998.	
* *NATO expansion ratified. To add Poland, Hungary, the Czech Republic.* 1998.	
* *Reform of public housing. New decision-making leeway to local authorities.* 1998.	
* *100,000 new school teachers. A Clinton plan.* 1998.	
1999–2000 Clinton R Cong	* *Banking reform. Authorized cross-ownership of banks, brokerages, insurance companies.* 1999.	
* *Y2K planning. To limit firms' liability for new-millennium computer mixups.* 1999.	
* *Ed-flex program. New state leeway in spending federal education money.* 1999.	

TABLE E.2 (continued)

Divided party control	Unified party control

Divided party control:

* *Permanent Normal Trading Relations (PNTR) with China.* 2000.
* *Florida Everglades restoration act.* 2000.
* *Community Renewal and New Markets Act.* $25 billion over 10 years for development in poor locales. 2000.

2001–02
Bush 43
D Senate
(after
May 01)
R House

* *USE OF FORCE RESOLUTION.* After September 11, authorized president to use all necessary force against terrorism, notably in Afghanistan. 2001.
* *USA PATRIOT ACT.* Broad new authority to president to track, arrest, and prosecute domestic terrorists. 2001.
* *Airline bailout.* $15 billion to help stabilize the industry after September 11. 2001.
* *Airline security.* New government program to hire 30,000 airport screeners. 2001.
* *$40 billion emergency spending.* For defense, domestic security, recovery of New York.
* *Education reform.* To require annual student testing; $263 billion in new funds. 2001.

Unified party control:

2001–02
Bush 43
R Cong
(early 2001)

* *BUSH TAX CUT.* $1.35 trillion over 10 years; rate cuts; phaseout of estate tax; ease of marriage penalty; expansion of child tax credit. 2001.

TABLE E.2 (continued)

Divided party control	Unified party control
* *IRAQ RESOLUTION*. Authorized use of U.S. force against Iraq, regardless of U.N. view. 2002.	
* *NEW HOMELAND SECURITY DEPARTMENT*. Combined parts of 22 existing agencies. 2002.	
* *Campaign finance reform*. To ban soft money and certain pre-election ads. 2002.	
* *Agriculture subsidies*. $180 billion over 10 years. A rollback of 1996 deregulation. 2002.	
* *Corporate Responsibility Act*. To regulate the accounting industry and crack down on corporate fraud. After the collapse of Enron. 2002.	
* *Fast-track trade authority*. New authority to president to negotiate foreign trade deals. 2002.	
* *Election reform*. New nationwide standards; $3.9 billion to help the states meet them. 2002.	
* *Terrorism insurance*. $100 billion back-up guarantee against future attacks; to aid insurance and real estate industries. 2002.	
* *Commission created to investigate September 11 attacks*. 2002.	

High volume in 1995–96 (DIV) is another answer.[22] Yes, the Republicans' Program deriving from their 1994 midterm victory largely fizzled, but the party's congressional wing and the Clinton White House found it mutually advantageous to craft some legislative compromises in the run-up to the 1996 election. Both sides had too much recent failure on their blotters (in 1994 and 1995). Onto the books in 1996 went welfare reform, telecommunications reform, a minimum-wage hike, immigration reform, the Kassebaum-Kennedy health-insurance portability act, and other measures.

Modest volume in 1993–94 (UNI) is another answer.[23] Clinton's first year was reasonably impressive—the White House budget package, NAFTA, and middle-bore Democratic party favorites such as the Family Leave Act, the Motor Voter Act, the National Service Act, and the Brady bill requiring a waiting period to buy handguns. But 1994 was a lean legislative year. True, it is hard to discuss it without getting into denominators. The Clinton health-care drive that convulsed the country for months ended in nothing.[24] Other majority-party aims that foundered included welfare reform, a ban on replacement workers in strikes, campaign finance reform, lobbying reform, and an assortment of environmental updates in the areas of clean water, safe drinking water, pesticides, hazardous waste, endangered species, Superfund, and mining law.[25] A Democratic crime bill fell apart in August 1994. Bipartisan aims such as product liability reform and telecommunications reform, and conservative aims such as

22. For an interesting comparison between lawmaking in 1995–96 under Clinton and in 1947–48 under Truman—both the aftermaths of Republican midterm surges—see Richard S. Conley, "Divided Government and Democratic Presidents: Truman and Clinton Compared," *Presidential Studies Quarterly* 30 (2000), 222–44.

23. On the Congress of 1993–94, see James P. Pfiffner, "President Clinton and the 103rd Congress: Winning Battles and Losing Wars," chap. 9 in James Thurber, ed., *Rivals for Power: Presidential-Congressional Relations* (Washington, D.C.: Congressional Quarterly Press, 1996); David R. Mayhew, "Clinton, the 103rd Congress, and Unified Party Control: What Are the Lessons?" chap. 10 in John G. Geer, ed., *Politicians and Party Politics* (Baltimore: Johns Hopkins University Press, 1998).

24. See Haynes Johnson and David S. Broder, *The System: The American Way of Politics at the Breaking Point* (Boston: Little, Brown, 1996).

25. Legislative casualties for the Democrats in calendar 1993 had included a Clinton economic stimulus plan, a BTU energy tax, a "freedom of choice" charter for women, and statehood for the District of Columbia.

term limits and a balanced budget amendment, failed also.[26] The *Washington Post*'s sendoff to the 103rd Congress in October 1994 went as follows: "This will go into the record books as perhaps the worst Congress — least effective, most destructive, nastiest — in 50 years."[27]

As in 1947 through 1990, a dog was not barking to expectations during these recent six Congresses — or at least was not barking very much. On the lean evidence, unified party control was not a superior supplier of legislative volume. In more general theoretical terms, why is that? To draw on the analysis offered in chapters 5 and 6, it seems to me that three of the six accounts that I presented there are particularly relevant here.

First, there is the factor of *cross-cutting issue cleavages*.[28] Possibly no issue in American history has exemplified that pattern better than foreign trade in recent times. Both of today's parties are split, although the Republicans lean more heavily to the free-trade side than the Democrats do to the protectionist side. During 1991–2002, hard-fought victories for free trade occurred under both conditions of party control. In 1993 (UNI) the winning formula for NAFTA was the Clinton White House plus Republican majorities in both houses against Democratic majorities in both houses. In 2000 (DIV), the formula for Permanent Normal Trading Relations with China (PNTR) was the Clinton White House plus Republican majorities in both houses and a Democratic majority in the Senate (they signed on this time) against a Democratic majority in the House. In 2002 (DIV), the formula for new fast-track authority to the president was the Bush 43 White House plus Republican majorities in both houses

26. See Mayhew, "Clinton, the 103rd Congress, and Unified Party Control," p. 269.

27. "Perhaps the Worst Congress" (editorial), *Washington Post*, October 7, 1994. *Congressional Quarterly* came up with unusually high "presidential support scores" for both 1993 and 1994. Those scores measure the proportion of House and, separately, Senate roll calls on which the president's side wins, from among those on which the White House takes a position. Again, scores like these do not plausibly measure system success, even if they may work for White House success. But even allowing just the latter, a high score for 1994 is very dubious. Health-care reform never figured in any roll calls at all in the House — no version of the president's plan ever made it to the floor — and only four minor ones in the Senate. A presidential yardstick for 1994 that does not reach health-care reform is not much of a yardstick. It is like, say, a yardstick for economic performance that omits readings for 1929. See Steve Langdon, "Clinton's High Victory Rate Conceals Disappointments," *Congressional Quarterly Weekly Report*, December 31, 1994, pp. 3619–20. Langdon was quite aware of the difficulty the index ran into in 1994.

28. See chap. 6.

against Democratic majorities in both houses.[29] In this policy area, a lens only into conditions of party control has not been very helpful recently.

Second, there is the factor of *necessary broad majorities*[30] — at least outside the realm of budgets and few other subjects. With congressional bills often needing a two-thirds vote to survive presidential vetoes or a three-fifths vote to survive Senate filibusters, rule by narrow majorities is not easy.[31] These two blockade points can amount to powerful equalizers across conditions of party control. One relevant crunch time during 1991–2002 was the 103rd Congress of 1993–94, when the Democrats controlled all three elective institutions but fell short of sixty members in the Senate. Forty-one determined Republicans could conduct or threaten filibusters, and sometimes they did that. In at least five instances- Clinton's economic stimulus plan, product liability, striker replacement, lobbying reform, and campaign finance reform, Senate filibustering was at least the proximate cause of a major bill's defeat during 1993–94, and other bills sagged before such threats.[32] In short, in terms of enactment volume, the Senate filibuster option helped cut the 103rd Congress down to size. Formal Democratic control of all three institutions was not enough.

This having been said, one has to be careful not to blame the filibuster, or the potential of it, for everything that dies. Some Democratic projects in 1993–94 could not a command House floor majority — for example, the "freedom of choice" charter, District of Columbia statehood, and the party's crime bill. That was spectacularly true of Clinton's evolving health-care plan, about which Speaker Tom Foley later reflected: "There

29. On these three measures, House Republicans voted respectively 132–43, 164–57, and 190–27. Senate Republicans voted 34–10, 46–8,and 43–5. House Democrats voted 102–156, 73–138, and 25–183. Senate Democrats voted 27–28, 37–7, and 20–29. There was one other important trade enactment during 1991–2002. In a lame-duck session in late 1994 (UNI), the GATT accord was approved by large majorities of both parties in both houses.

30. See chap. 5.

31. See Krehbiel, *Pivotal Politics;* David W. Brady and Craig Volden, *Revolving Gridlock: Politics and Policy from Carter to Clinton* (Boulder, Colo.: Westview, 1998).

32. See Adam Clymer, "Having 'Done Enough Harm,' Senate Inches to Adjournment," *New York Times,* October 5, 1994; Daniel Wirls, "Unified Government, Divided Congress? The Senate and the Democratic Agenda in the 103rd Congress," paper presented at the annual conference of the American Political Science Association, Chicago, 1995. In the case of product liability, it was Democrats, not Republicans, who blocked cloture and thus killed the bill.

wasn't anything out there they wanted to vote for. We weren't close to a majority on any specific health care plan."[33] In a Gallup poll in April 1994, two-thirds of respondents thought that "quality of care would decline and they would be worse off" if Clinton's plan passed.[34] With numbers like these, congressional floor majorities are unlikely and the filibuster potential is probably irrelevant.

Third, there is the factor of *external events*.[35] What induces Congress to enact laws? A powerful rival to any consideration having to do with parties, elections, or conditions of party control is simply events. As a commonsensical as well as a theoretical matter, members of Congress previously satisfied with the status quo in some policy area may change their minds if jolted by an event. With a big enough jolt and enough changed minds, all the impediments to action, including filibusters and presidential vetoes, can crumble away. Events do much of their causal work on Capitol Hill *between* elections rather than at or on them. On December 8, 1941, for example, the day after the Japanese attack on Pearl Harbor and near the midpoint of the 77th Congress, all but one member of Congress opted to reject the American status quo policy of *not* fighting a war against Japan, and war was declared.[36]

Events left a mark on the statute books during 1991–2002. The Persian Gulf Resolution of 1991 answered the invasion of Kuwait. The Corporate Responsibility Act of 2002 followed the collapse of Enron. Election reform in 2002 followed the mess in Florida. But obviously, exhibit A for the events argument is the explosion of eight major enactments — nine if the Iraq resolution of October 2002 is included — that were triggered by the terrorist attack of September 11, 2001. (See table E.2.) As a dislodger of status quo policies in several areas, including civil liberties by way of the USA Patriot Act, that attack is hard to top.

But hold on for a moment, it might be objected. Should a congressional spasm like that after September 11 really count as "lawmaking"? Isn't that cheating somehow? What does it have to do with enacting party programs? Isn't lawmaking supposed to center on familiar and agreeable agendas like education, the environment, government spending, and

33. Johnson and Broder, *The System*, p. 509.

34. Ibid., p. 371.

35. See chap. 6; Krehbiel, *Pivotal Politics*, p. 78.

36. In the terms of Krehbiel's analysis in *Pivotal Politics*, this country's status quo policy toward Japan came to lie outside the "gridlock interval" once Congress and the White House heard about Pearl Harbor.

welfare provision? Well, in a world sealed off from time, contingency, and calamities, that view might suffice, but in the real world it falters. Reacting to emergencies is as enduring a theme of congressional lawmaking as anything else. In lawmaking terms, the best analogues to the Congress of 2001–02 are probably those of 1861–63 during the Civil War, 1917–18 during World War I, and 1941–42 and 1943–44 during World War II. Issuing from those past high-volume Congresses were laws providing for immense spending, taxing, and regulation that had supremely important short-term effects, and in some cases long-term ones: As a revenue initiative of lasting consequence, for example, probably nothing in American history excels the shift to income tax broadening and withholding during World War II.[37] Another candidate for a good analogue is Franklin Roosevelt's first Congress during its "hundred days" phase of early 1933. Although the New Deal is ordinarily discussed under "party programs," this was an emergency session. Most of its laws were emergency laws.[38] The country's banking system was collapsing — an *inter*-election event in the sense that it was occurring *during* Hoover's last few months in one of the long post-election lameduck expanses of those times.[39] In short, in the congressional lawmaking realm, the autumn of 2001 had basic properties in common with such past seasons, now vanishing from memory as living Americans dwindle who could make the comparisons, as the spring of 1933 and the winter of 1941–42.[40]

37. "The country emerged from the war with a completely different revenue structure, one that has remained largely in place until the present." John Joseph Wallis, "American Government Finance in the Long Run: 1790 to 1990," *Journal of Economic Perspectives* 14 (2000), 61–82, at p. 73. The Current Tax Payment Act of 1943 was a key ingredient.

38. John Frendreis, Raymond Tatalovich, and John Schaff, "Predicting Legislative Output in the First One Hundred Days, 1897–1995," *Political Research Quarterly* 54 (2001), 853–70, at pp. 867–68. "The significant enactments of the Roosevelt One Hundred Days of 1933 were driven by the exigencies of the Great Depression, crisis economic conditions that were uniquely traumatic to the nation" (p. 868).

39. "But in March [1933], the country was gripped by financial disaster crowning three years of deepening depression. Banks were failing on every hand. Desperate depositors were losing their life's savings. Desperate businesses were short of cash. Roosevelt at once took executive measures, but he needed legislative authority for more and so called the new Congress into special session." Richard E. Neustadt, "*The Contemporary Presidency:* The Presidential 'Hundred Days': An Overview," *Presidential Studies Quarterly* 31 (2001), 121–25, at p. 122.

40. Across American history, it is a fair question whether inter-election events have surpassed election verdicts in boosting status quo policies outside the con-

In terms of the analysis in chapters 5 and 6, two of the factors discussed here, cross-cutting cleavages and the need for broad majorities, probably helped along lawmaking *constancy* across the six Congresses during 1991–2002. The other factor, external events, owing to the crowd-up of enactments after September 11, 2001, made for a potent source of *alternative variation* in lawmaking during the twelve years — that is, alternative to any pattern hinging on unified versus divided control.

That seems to be the story for lawmaking volume during 1991–2002. How about other respects in which party control might have made a difference? I close by discussing three such patterns briefly here.

---

gressional "gridlock interval." Trophies for the former impulse might include, for example, the Alien and Sedition Acts of 1798, the Embargo Act of 1807, the establishment of the Second National Bank in 1816, the Force Bill of 1833 (reining in the South Carolina nullifiers), the Legal Tender Act of 1862, the establishment of the Freedmen's Bureau in 1865, the First Reconstruction Act of 1867, the First Ku Klux Klan Act of 1870, the repeal of the Silver Purchase Act in 1893, the Foraker Act establishing civil government in Puerto Rico in 1900, the Pure Food and Drug Act of 1906, the Aldrich-Vreeland Currency Act of 1908, the style-setting Revenue Act of 1916, the Espionage Act of 1917, the Sedition Act of 1918, the Esch-Cummins Transportation Act of 1920, the Flood Control Act of 1928, the Reconstruction Finance Corporation Act of 1932, the high-tax Revenue Act of 1932, the Emergency Banking Relief Act of 1933, the Wealth Tax Act of 1935, the Food, Drug, and Cosmetic Act of 1938, the relaxation of the Neutrality Act in late 1939, the Alienation Registration Act (the Smith Act) of 1940, the Burke-Wadsworth Selective Service Training Act of 1940, the Lend Lease Act of 1941, the Emergency Price Control Act of 1942, the Current Tax Payment Act of 1943, the GI Bill of Rights in 1944, the Bretton Woods Agreement Act of 1945, the Atomic Energy Act of 1946, the National Security Act of 1947, the Marshall Plan in 1948, the Displaced Persons Act of 1948, the McCarran Internal Security Act of 1950, the Mutual Security Act of 1951, the National Aeronautics and Space Administration Act of 1958, the National Defense Education Act of 1958, the Civil Rights Act of 1964, the Omnibus Crime Control and Safe Streets Act of 1968, the Open Housing Act of 1968, the Economic Stabilization Act of 1970, the War Powers Resolution of 1973, the Emergency Petroleum Allocation act of 1973, the Federal Election Campaign Act of 1974, the bailout of New York City in 1975, the bailout of the Chrysler Corporation in 1979, and the bailout of the savings and loan industry in 1979. At least in these cases and many others, it is a good bet that interelection events were *necessary* causes of the legislative enactments that occurred. In the tricky case of the First Reconstruction Act of 1867, which was enacted on March 2 at the end of a lame-duck session of Congress, certain events during the months *after* the midterm election of November 1866 seem to have spurred it. See David Donald, *The Politics of Reconstruction, 1863–1867* (Baton Rouge: Louisiana State University Press, 1965), pp. 56–57; Eric L. McKitrick, *Andrew Johnson and Reconstruction* (Chicago: University of Chicago Press, 1960), pp. 455–60.

The *content* of legislation is of course a feature all by itself. In this book I have not made any systematic effort to code enactments by, for example, whether they lean to the left or the right.[41] Off the top, however, during 1991 through 2002, no one would be astonished to find a liberal drift under the Democrats in 1993–94 (UNI), a conservative drift under the Republicans in early 2001 (UNI), and a middling record otherwise (DIV). There is evidence for that case. In particular, the size of the Democratic tax hike of 1993 as well as the Republican tax cut of 2001 almost certainly owed to unified party control. Those were major legislative moves. The Family Leave and Motor Voter acts of 1993 (UNI) were quick achievements of unified party control (Bush 41 had vetoed both during the previous Congress).

But that is just about it. Otherwise, in content terms there seems to have been a good deal of commonality across the six Congresses — or seven Congresses, if Bush 41's first Congress of 1989–90 (DIV) is roped into the comparison, as might usefully be done here.[42] From 1989 through 1997, under all conditions of party control, one motif in the actual enactments was deficit reduction — that is, the major omnibus instruments of 1990 (DIV), 1993 (UNI), and 1997 (DIV).[43] Another was at least modest welfare state expansion — a minimum-wage hike in 1989 (DIV), the Americans with Disabilities Act (ADA) of 1990 (DIV), a $12.4 billion hike in the Earned Income Tax Credit (EITC) as part of the deficit-reduction deal of 1990 (DIV), a $20.8 billion EITC hike as part of the deficit-reduction deal of 1993 (UNI), the Family Leave Act of 1993 (UNI), another minimum-wage hike in 1996 (DIV), the Kassebaum-Kennedy health portability insurance act of 1996 (DIV), and the new Children's Health Insurance Program (CHIP) as part of the deficit-reduction deal of 1997 (DIV). To be sure, there was a significant *contraction* through welfare reform in 1996 (DIV), but the general motif was expansion.[44]

41. That is nicely done in Robert S. Erikson, Michael B. MacKuen, and James A. Stimson, *The Macro Polity* (New York: Cambridge University Press, 2002), chap. 9.

42. In legislative productivity taken alone, Bush 41's first Congress of 1989–90 was in retrospect quite impressive. See John Maggs, "41, Reconsidered," *National Journal*, July 20, 2002, pp. 2156–64.

43. For a comparison of the 1990 and 1993 instruments, see Mayhew, "Clinton, the 103rd Congress, and Unified Party Control," p. 271.

44. As in 2003, with the Republicans' Medicare prescription drugs program. As instances of welfare-state expansion here I have included enactments that lodge costs against private profit and nonprofit organizations as well as against taxpayers.

Beyond this, my guess is that fifty years from now anyone weighing the importance of laws enacted from 1991 through August 2001 (until the attacks on the Pentagon and the World Trade Center) will emphasize the deregulation of the economy—the electricity industry in 1991 (DIV), telecommunications in 1996 (DIV), and banking in 1999 (DIV), as well as the approval of NAFTA in 1993 (UNI), GATT in 1994 (UNI), PNTR in 2000 (DIV), and fast-track trade authority in 2002 (DIV). (To dismantle barriers to foreign trade is arguably a kind of deregulation.) In this broad area of deregulation, as in deficit reduction and welfare state expansion, conditions of party control do not offer a very reliable guide to these recent Congresses. In terms of directional content, the best case for the importance of which party runs the government has probably been tax hikes and tax cuts.

Richer pay dirt appears for 1991-2002 regarding the *level of conflict* exhibited in enacting major laws. There the difference between unified and divided party control scored dramatically. In chapter 5, in tracking enactments from 1947 through 1990, I probed for the proportions of major laws that were approved by two-thirds majorities in one or both houses, and, separately, by bipartisan majorities in one or both houses. See tables 5.2 and 5.3.[45] Divided party control had an edge in both categories, but it was not a huge edge. Broad majorities tended to occur under both conditions. Not so during the recent Congresses. See the updated statistics in tables E.3 and E.4.[46] Now the patterns of conflict differ starkly.[47] In particular, virtually nothing of importance cleared the Congress of 1993-94 (UNI) or the early all-Republican phase of the Congress of 2001 backed by broad majorities.[48] Under unified party control

45. Fuller information on these roll calls than appears in this book is posted at *http://pantheon.yale.edu/dmayhew/data3.html.*

46. Three of the enactments represented in the tables were treaty ratifications that involved only the Senate — those on strategic arms reduction in 1991, chemical weapons in 1997, and NATO expansion in 1998. Majorities of both parties as well as the required two-thirds of the members signed on in all three cases.

47. For an analysis along this line, see Gregory R. Thorson and Tasina Nitzschke, "Politics and Policy in the 103rd and 104th Congresses: Evaluating the Effects of Divided Government in the Postreform Era," *Congress & the Presidency* 27 (spring 2000), 1–24.

48. The decisive approval of GATT in 1994 is the chief exception to this generalization. To be sure, NAFTA passed in 1993 courtesy of a *wrong* narrow majority, so to speak, since Republican majorities carried it for Clinton against Democratic opposition during a Democratic-controlled Congress.

TABLE E.3
Important Laws Passed by Two-thirds Majorities, 1991–2002

	During divided control			During unified control		
	⅔ in both houses	⅔ in one house	⅔ in neither house	⅔ in both houses	⅔ in one house	⅔ in neither house
1991–92	6	1	1			
1993–94				2	3	7
1995–96	14	1				
1997–98	9					
1999–2000	5	1				
early 2001						1
2001–02	11	1	3			
Total	45	4	4	2	3	8
Percent	85	8	8	15	23	62

during these recent times, successful lawmaking came to be extremely partisan — a result of course evident in the political atmosphere of this era as well as in these numbers. No other Congress since at least World War II had exhibited anything like the narrow-based lawmaking of 1993–94 and early 2001.

As a side note, notice in tables E.3 and E.4 the consistently broad majorities marshaled recently under divided party control. In fact, twenty-one of the forty-five laws enacted under this condition won at least *nine-to-one* support on final passage in *both* houses. In political science, there is a tendency to dismiss results like this as "hurrah" votes as classically instanced by a resolution declaring national marigold week. How can something be important if almost nobody was against it? Worse yet, how can near-unanimous results fit into serious roll call analysis? Throw them out. I believe that this dismissiveness is a mistake. In 2002, the Corporate Responsibility Act passed by 423–3 in the House and 99–0 in the Senate. In 2001, the Use of Force Resolution passed by 420–1 in the House and 98–0 in the Senate — thus duplicating exactly, as it happens, the pattern of dissent in the declaration of war against Japan in 1941. How can results like these be considered unimportant? Their very lopsidedness was a loud statement. To ignore unanimous or near-unanimous roll calls seems to me to buy into a theory of conflict, not one of lawmaking or policymaking. On balance, it also probably tends to downplay legislative results under conditions of divided party control.

TABLE E.4
Important Laws Passed with the Support of Majorities of Both Democrats and
Republicans, 1991–2002

	During divided control			During unified control		
	D+R in both houses	D+R in one house	D+R in neither house	D+R in both houses	D+R in one house	D+R in neither house
1991–92	6	1	1			
1993–94				1		11
1995–96	11	2	2			
1997–98	9					
1999–2000	5	1				
early 2001						1
2001–02	9	4	2			
Total	40	8	5	1	0	12
Percent	75	15	9	8	0	92

Finally, there is the subject of *high-publicity congressional investigations of the executive branch*.[49] In chapter 2, analyzing 1947 through 1990, I concluded that such probes were just about as prominent under conditions of unified control as under divided control. See table 2.1.[50] Does that conclusion hold up for 1991 through 2002? Well, not really. See table E.5, which employs the same coding rules as earlier. Yes, there are blanks for the divided-control Congresses of 1991–92, 1999–2000, and 2001–02. Yes, a Senate run by Democrats sustained a damaging probe of Clinton's Whitewater involvements in 1993–94 (UNI). But the Congress of 1997–98 (DIV) outprobed all the rest during 1991–2002. Republican investiga-

49. Interesting new work is under way on this subject: Jonathan P. Kastellac, "Congressional Investigations and Divided Government," course paper at Columbia University, 2003; David C. W. Parker and Matthew M. Dull, "Divided We Quarrel: Institutional Conflict Beyond the Legislative Arena," paper presented at the annual meeting of the American Political Science Association, Philadelphia, August 2003.

50. I have posted a list of *dates* of the *New York Times* front-page stories that generated the dataset for table 2.1, as well as now for table E.5. The site is again *http://pantheon.yale.edu/dmayhew/data3.html.* Also posted here are marginal corrections to some of the days-on-the-front-page counts for 1947 through 1990. Although these corrections may be of interest to specialists, they do not cause trouble for the original analysis in chapter 2, and I have not entered them into the prose or tables of this new edition of the book.

TABLE E.5

Congressional Investigations Critical of the Executive Branch that Generated
New York Times Front-page Stories on Twenty or More Days, 1991–2002

	Divided party control		Unified party control	
	N days of NYT stories	The charges and the investigations	N days of NYT stories	The charges and the investigations
1991–92 Bush 41 D Cong	None			
1993–94 Clinton D Cong			22	*Improper White House behavior regarding past Whitewater investments.* Senate Banking Committee. Chaired by Don Riegle, D-MICH. Featured alleged improper contacts with regulators, evasive testimony, resignation of Deputy Treasury Secretary Roger C. Altman. 1993–94.
1995–96 Clinton R Cong	24	*Improper White House behavior regarding past Whitewater investments.* Senate Special Committee on Whitewater. Chaired by Alphonse D'Amato, R-NY. Featured James and Susan McDougal, circumstances of Vincent Foster's death, White House documents, alleged Hillary Clinton stonewalling. 1995–96.		

	Divided party control	Unified party control
1997–98 Clinton R Cong	59	*Clinton administration's shady campaign finance practices during 1996.* Special Senate panel chaired by Fred Thompson. R-TENN; House Government Reform Committee chaired by Dan Burton, R-IND; and other panels. Featured dodgy Asian financier, Buddhist nuns, White House coffees, alleged sale of Lincoln bedroom. 1997.	
	52	*Perjury and obstruction of justice by President Clinton in Monica Lewinsky coverup.* House Judiciary Committee. Chaired by Henry Hyde, R-ILL. Featured prosecutor Kenneth Starr, secretary Betty Currie, Lewinsky, grand-jury tape, blue dress, gifts. Resulted in committee vote to impeach Clinton. 1998.	
1999–2000 Clinton R Cong	None		
2001–02 Bush 43 R Cong (until May 01)			None

TABLE E.5 (*continued*)

	Divided party control	Unified party control
2001–02 Bush 43 D Senate (after May 01) R House	None	

tors had a field day with Clinton's edgy campaign finance practices, and then came the House Judiciary Committee's impeachment hearings — certainly one of the political highlights of the decade. The latter enterprise has to weigh especially heavily on the scales, and like the Watergate probes of 1973–74 it implicates divided party control. It is hard, if not quite impossible, to imagine a Democratic House impeaching Clinton.

For 1991–2002, the overall verdict on differences between conditions of party control seems to be: no on legislative volume, somewhat on legislative content, decisively yes on levels of conflict, and yes on investigations.

APPENDIX A ◆ SOURCES

FOR SWEEP ONE

(CONTEMPORARY JUDGMENTS

ABOUT IMPORTANT

ENACTMENTS)

1947–48

New York Times, July 27, 1947, p. IV:3; July 28, 1947, p. 10; June 21, 1948, p. 8; August 8, 1948, p. I:1.

Washington Post, July 27, 1947, p. 1B; June 21, 1948, p. 6A.

Robert J. Donovan, *Conflict and Crisis: The Presidency of Harry S Truman, 1945–1948* (New York: W. W. Norton, 1977), chaps. 30, 32, 33.

Harold F. Gosnell, *Truman's Crises: A Political Biography of Harry S Truman* (Westport, Conn.: Greenwood Press, 1980), chaps. 26–28.

Susan M. Hartmann, *Truman and the Eightieth Congress* (Columbia: University of Missouri Press, 1971).

William Frank Zornow, *America at Mid-Century* (Cleveland: Howard Allen, 1959), pt. 1, *The Truman Administration*, chaps. 2–4.

1949–50

New York Times, October 20, 1949, pp. 1, 6, 28; October 21, 1949, p. 24; October 23, 1949, p. IV:3; September 10, 1950, p. IV:12; September 24, 1950, p. I:94; December 24, 1950, p. IV:2; January 2, 1951, p. 22; January 3, 1951, pp. 1, 19.

Washington Post, October 20, 1949, pp. A1, A3; September 25, 1950, p. 8A.

Robert J. Donovan, *Tumultuous Years: The Presidency of Harry S Truman, 1949–1953* (New York: W. W. Norton, 1982), chaps. 4, 11, 24, 28.

David R. Kepley, *The Collapse of the Middle Way: Senate Republicans and the*

Bipartisan Foreign Policy, 1948–1952 (Westport, Conn.: Greenwood Press, 1988), chaps. 2–6.

Richard S. Kirkendall, ed., *The Truman Period as a Research Field* (Columbia: University of Missouri Press, 1967), essays by Barton J. Bernstein ("Economic Policies"), Richard O. Davies ("Social Welfare Policies"), and William C. Berman ("Civil Rights and Civil Liberties").

Zornow, *America at Mid-Century*, pt. 1, *Truman Administration*, chaps. 4, 5, 7.

1951–52

New York Times, October 21, 1951, pp. I:1, 55, IV:2; July 6, 1952, pp. 34, IV:4.

Washington Post, October 21, 1951, p. 1B; July 6, 1952, p. 6M.

Donovan, *Tumultuous Years*, chap. 34.

Gosnell, *Truman's Crises*, chap. 37.

Alonzo L. Hamby, *Beyond the New Deal: Harry S Truman and American Liberalism* (New York: Columbia University Press, 1973), chaps. 20, 22.

Zornow, *America at Mid-Century*, pt. 1, *Truman Administration*, chap. 7.

1953–54

New York Times, August 4, 1953, pp. 1, 13; August 21, 1954, pp. 1, 8, 9; August 22, 1954, pp. IV:1, 6.

Washington Post, August 4, 1953, p. 4; August 22, 1954, p. 4B.

Gary W. Reichard, *The Reaffirmation of Republicanism: Eisenhower and the Eighty-third Congress* (Knoxville: University of Tennessee Press, 1975), chaps. 3–7.

1955–56

New York Times, August 3, 1955, p. 14; August 7, 1955, p. IV:1; July 28, 1956, pp. 1, 35; July 29, 1956, pp. I:1, 50, IV:2.

Washington Post, August 2, 1955, p. 22; July 29, 1956, pp. A1, A15.

Robert J. Donovan, *Eisenhower: The Inside Story* (New York: Harper and Brothers, 1956), chap. 23.

Rowland Evans, Jr., and Robert Novak, *Lyndon B. Johnson: The Exercise of Power* (New York: New American Library, 1966), chaps. 6, 8.

Elmo Richardson, *The Presidency of Dwight D. Eisenhower* (Lawrence: Regents Press of Kansas, 1979), chap. 5.

Zornow, *America at Mid-Century*, pt. 2, *Eisenhower Administration*, chap. 6.

1957–58

New York Times, August 25, 1957, p. IV:7; August 31, 1957, pp. 1, 8; August 24, 1958, pp. I:1, 56, 57, IV:3; August 25, 1958, pp. 1, 7.

Washington Post, August 30, 1957, p. A1; August 24, 1958, pp. A1, A2.

Stephen E. Ambrose, *Eisenhower*, vol. 2, *The President* (New York: Simon and Schuster, 1984), chaps. 17–19.

Evans and Novak, *Lyndon B. Johnson*, chaps. 7–9.

Richardson, *Presidency of Dwight D. Eisenhower*, chaps. 6, 7.

Zornow, *America at Mid-Century*, pt. 2, *Eisenhower Administration*, chap. 8.

1959–60

New York Times, September 14, 1959, pp. 1, 24; July 3, 1960, pp. IV:5, 6; September 2, 1960, p. 10.

Washington Post, September 16, 1959, pp. A1, A2, A16; September 2, 1960, p. A14; September 4, 1960, pp. E1, E5.

Evans and Novak, *Lyndon B. Johnson*, chap. 10.

Alfred Steinberg, *Sam Johnson's Boy: A Close-Up of the President from Texas* (New York: Macmillan, 1968), chaps. 53, 54, 56.

1961–62

New York Times, September 28, 1961, p. 32; October 14, 1962, pp. I:1, 65, IV:8; October 15, 1962, p. 23.

Washington Post, September 28, 1961, pp. A1, A2; October 14, 1962, p. E1.

Marian D. Irish, "The Kennedy Administration: Appraisal at the Halfway Mark," chap. 2 in Jack W. Peltason, ed., *1963–64 American Government Annual* (New York: Holt, Rinehart and Winston, 1963).

Louis W. Koenig, "Kennedy and the 87th Congress," chap. 5 in Ivan Hinderaker, ed., *1962–63 American Government Annual* (New York: Holt, Rinehart and Winston, 1962).

Herbert S. Parmet, *JFK: The Presidency of John F. Kennedy* (New York: Dial Press, 1983), chaps. 4, 9.

1963–64

New York Times, December 22, 1963, pp. I:27, IV:2; January 5, 1964, p. IV:8; October 4, 1964, pp. I:1, 79; October 5, 1964, pp. 1, 24.

Washington Post, October 4, 1964, pp. A1, A8.

Jack Bell, *The Johnson Treatment: How Lyndon B. Johnson Took Over the Presidency and Made It His Own* (New York: Harper and Row, 1965), chaps. 3, 5, 9, 10.

Evans and Novak, *Lyndon B. Johnson*, chaps. 17, 19.

Mark F. Ferber, "The Second Session of the 88th Congress," chap. 4 in Donald G. Herzberg, ed., *1965–66 American Government Annual* (New York: Holt, Rinehart and Winston, 1965).

Parmet, *JFK*, chap. 13.

Philip S. Wilder, Jr., "Congress, 1963—The Transitional Session," chap. 4 in Donald G. Herzberg, ed., *1964–65 American Government Annual* (New York: Holt, Rinehart and Winston, 1964).

1965–66

New York Times, October 23, 1965, pp. 1, 28; October 24, 1965, p. IV:1; October 25, 1965, pp. 40, 41; October 23, 1966, p. IV:8; October 24, 1966, pp. 1, 34, 35.

Washington Post, October 23, 1966, pp. A1, A14, A16.

Evans and Novak, *Lyndon B. Johnson*, chap. 22.

Steinberg, *Sam Johnson's Boy*, chap. 71.

1967–68

New York Times, December 16, 1967, pp. 1, 20; December 17, 1967, pp. I:65, IV:2, 10; October 15, 1968, pp. 1, 35, 46.

Washington Post, December 16, 1967, pp. A1, A4; December 17, 1967, pp. C1, C2, C3.

1969–70

New York Times, December 24, 1969, pp. 1, 10, 24; January 1, 1971, pp. 1, 10, 11; January 3, 1971, p. IV:2; January 4, 1971, p. 26.

Washington Post, December 24, 1969, pp. A1, A4; January 3, 1971, pp. A1, A3.

Rowland Evans, Jr., and Robert D. Novak, *Nixon in the White House: The Frustration of Power* (New York: Random House, 1971), chaps. 5, 7.

A. James Reichley, *Conservatives in an Age of Change: The Nixon and Ford Administrations* (Washington, D.C.: Brookings Institution Press, 1981), chaps. 5, 6, 10.

1971–72

New York Times, December 19, 1971, pp. I:50, IV:10; October 19, 1972, pp. 1, 28; October 20, 1972, pp. 1, 24, 42.

Washington Post, December 18, 1971, p. A2; October 15, 1972, pp. A1, A18.

Reichley, *Conservatives in an Age of Change*, chap. 8.

1973–74

New York Times, December 25, 1973, p. 14; December 21, 1974, pp. 1, 28; December 22, 1974, pp. I:1, 27; December 23, 1974, p. 20.

Washington Post, December 23, 1973, p. A2; December 26, 1973, p. A18; December 21, 1974, pp. A1, A6.

Reichley, *Conservatives in an Age of Change*, chaps. 15, 17.

1975–76

New York Times, December 21, 1975, p. I:30; December 23, 1975, p. 22; October 2, 1976, p. 7; October 3, 1976, pp. I:1, 20, IV:4.

Washington Post, December 21, 1975, p. A2; October 2, 1976, pp. A1, A5.

Gerald R. Ford, *A Time to Heal: The Autobiography of Gerald R. Ford* (New York: Harper and Row, 1979), pp. 224–25, 227, 258–59, 338–41.

Reichley, *Conservatives in an Age of Change*, chaps. 15, 17, 18.

1977–78

New York Times, December 18, 1977, pp. I:1, 38, IV:2; October 16, 1978, pp. 6, 7, 8; October 17, 1978, pp. 51, 56; November 6, 1978, p. 51; November 12, 1978, pp. 1, 79.

Washington Post, December 16, 1977, pp. A1, A14; October 16, 1978, pp. A1, A8.

Jimmy Carter, *Keeping Faith: Memoirs of a President* (New York: Bantam Books, 1982), pp. 84, 91–111, 152–78.

Haynes Johnson, *In the Absence of Power: Governing America* (New York: Viking, 1980), pp. 187–93, 221–25, 231–41, 250–55.

1979–80

New York Times, December 22, 1979, p. 38; December 17, 1980, p. A30.

Washington Post, December 21, 1979, pp. A1, A3, A4; December 14, 1980, p. A2.

Carter, *Keeping Faith*, pp. 180–85, 193, 261–65, 320, 581–83.

1981–82

New York Times, December 19, 1981, p. 14; December 22, 1982, p. A22; December 23, 1982, p. B6; December 25, 1982, pp. 1, 5; December 26, 1982, p. IV:4.

Washington Post, December 17, 1981, p. A2; December 22, 1982, pp. A1, A6.

Congressional Quarterly Weekly, 1981, pp. 331, 443, 499, 602, 783, 839, 891, 1127, 1167, 1323, 1431–33, 1463–64, 1659, 1819, 1943, 2105, 2215, 2271, 2430.

Laurence I. Barrett, *Gambling with History: Ronald Reagan in the White House* (Garden City, N.Y.: Doubleday, 1983), chaps. 9, 10, 20, 24.

Lou Cannon, *Reagan* (New York: G. P. Putnam's Sons, 1982), chap. 20.

1983–84

New York Times, August 9, 1983, p. A18; November 20, 1983, pp. I:1, 38; October 14, 1984, pp. I:1, 32, IV:22.

Washington Post, November 20, 1983, pp. A1, A6, A7; October 12, 1984, pp. A1, A4.

1985–86

New York Times, December 21, 1985, pp. 1, 12; December 22, 1985, pp. I:1, 26, IV:1, 4; October 18, 1986, pp. 1,8; October 19, 1986, pp. I:1, 30, 31.

Washington Post, December 19, 1985, pp. A1, A8; December 22, 1985, p. C6; October 19, 1986, pp. A1, A16, A17.

1987–88

New York Times, December 23, 1987, pp. A1, B8; December 27, 1987, p. IV:4; October 24, 1988, pp. A1, B7.

Washington Post, December 23, 1987, pp. A1, A6; October 23, 1988, pp. A4, A5, A6, C6.

1989–90

New York Times, November 19, 1989, p. IV:1; November 24, 1989, pp. A1, B22; October 28, 1990, pp. I:1, 27; IV:1; October 29, 1990, pp. A1, B9.

Washington Post National Weekly Edition, December 4–10, 1989, p. 13; November 5–11, 1990, pp. 8, 27.

Los Angeles Times, October 28, 1990, pp. A1, A24.

APPENDIX B ◆ SOURCES
FOR SWEEP TWO
(SPECIALISTS IN
POLICY AREAS)

The works listed under each policy area are the ones that were used to prepare that area's Sweep Two list of enactments. The numbers appearing just after the name of a policy area tell which enactments ended up on the area's Sweep Two list. The numbers refer back to table 4.1. The first two digits of an entry refer to a year, and the one or two digits after the dash identify a law enacted during that year. Thus 47–1 refers to the Taft-Hartley Act, which is the first law listed in table 4.1 among the six enacted in 1947. The entry 48–4 refers to the Hope-Aiken Act, which appears last among the four laws enacted in 1948. The entry 70–14 refers to the Economic Stabilization Act of 1970—the fourteenth in table 4.1's list of laws passed in that year. In any Congress's full list in table 4.1, the entries for the odd year always precede the entries for the even year, so there is no problem having a numbering code here that goes by year rather than by full two-year Congress.

Agriculture 48–4, 49–5, 54–6, 54–8, 56–1, 58–6, 61–6, 64–7, 65–15, 70–11, 73–3, 77–5, 81–3.

Willard W. Cochrane and Mary E. Ryan, *American Farm Policy, 1948–1973* (Minneapolis: University of Minnesota Press, 1976), chaps. 2, 3.

D. Gale Johnson, Kenzo Hemmi, and Pierre Lardinois, *Agricultural Policy and Trade: Adjusting Domestic Programs in an International Framework* (New York: New York University Press, 1985), pp. 60–66.

Kenneth J. Meier, *Regulation: Politics, Bureaucracy, and Economics* (New York: St. Martin's Press, 1985), chap. 5.

Luther G. Tweeten, "Agriculture Policy: A Review of Legislation, Programs, and Policy," in Conference on Food and Agricultural Policy, *Food and Agricultural Policy* (Washington, D.C.: American Enterprise Institute, 1977), pp. 29–42.

U.S. Department of Agriculture, Economic Research Service, *History of Agricultural Price-Support and Adjustment Programs, 1933–84: Background for 1985 Farm Legislation*, Agriculture Information Bulletin #485 (Washington, D.C.: U.S. Government Printing Office, 1984), pp. 17–44.

Graham K. Wilson, *Special Interests and Policymaking: Agricultural Policies and Politics in Britain and the United States of America, 1956–70* (New York: John Wiley and Sons, 1977), pp. 60–72.

Arms control 63–1, 69–5, 72–7.

John Lewis Gaddis, *Russia, the Soviet Union, and the United States: An Interpretive History* (New York: John Wiley and Sons, 1978), chaps. 7, 9.

William G. Hyland, *Mortal Rivals: Superpower Relations from Nixon to Reagan* (New York: Random House, 1987).

Alan F. Neidle, "The Rise and Fall of Multilateral Arms Control: Choices for the United States," in Edward C. Luck, ed., *Arms Control: The Multilateral Alternative* (New York: New York University Press, 1983), pp. 8–16.

Chalmers M. Roberts, "The Road to Moscow," chap. 1 in Mason Willrich and John B. Rhinelander, eds., *SALT: The Moscow Agreements and Beyond* (New York: Free Press, 1974).

Arts and humanities 65–9.

Kenneth Goody, "Arts Funding: Growth and Change between 1963 and 1983," *Annals of the American Academy of Political and Social Science* 471 (January 1984), 144–57.

Campaign finance 72–1, 74–3.

Gary C. Jacobson, *Money in Congressional Elections* (New Haven and London: Yale University Press, 1980), chap. 6.

Cities 48–3, 49–1, 54–7, 56–3, 64–2, 64–4, 65–4, 65–11, 66–7, 68–4, 72–3, 74–11, 75–3.

Charles N. Glaab and A. Theodore Brown, *A History of Urban America*, 3d ed. (New York: Macmillan, 1983), chap. 14.

Jon C. Teaford, *The Twentieth-Century American City: Problem, Promise, and Reality* (Baltimore.: Johns Hopkins University Press, 1986), chaps. 5–7.

Civil rights 57–1, 60–1, 64–1, 65–2, 68–1, 70–3, 72–9, 75–2, 82–4.

Theodore Eisenberg, *Civil Rights Legislation: Cases and Materials* (Indianapolis, Ind.: Bobbs-Merrill, 1981), pp. 1–3.

Hugh Davis Graham, *The Civil Rights Era: Origins and Development of National Policy, 1960–1972* (New York: Oxford University Press, 1990), pp. 3–5 and chaps. 5, 6, 10, 14, 17.

Gary Orfield, *Congressional Power: Congress and Social Change* (New York: Harcourt Brace Jovanovich, 1975), chaps. 5, 6.

James L. Sundquist, *Politics and Policy: The Eisenhower, Kennedy and Johnson Years* (Washington, D.C.: Brookings Institution Press, 1968), chap. 6.

Abigail M. Thernstrom, *Whose Votes Count? Affirmative Action and Minority Voting Rights* (Cambridge: Harvard University Press, 1987).

Civil service 78–4.

Patricia W. Ingraham and Carolyn Ban, eds., *Legislating Bureaucratic Change: The Civil Service Reform Act of 1978* (Albany: State University of New York Press, 1984), Introduction.

Consumer protection 58–9, 62–4, 66–4, 67–4, 68–9, 72–8, 74–8.

Meier, *Regulation*, chap. 4.

Peter Temin, *Taking Your Medicine: Drug Regulation in the United States* (Cambridge: Harvard University Press, 1980), chaps. 1, 6. (This source obviously deals with just drug legislation, a subset of the category here.)

Copyright 76–2.

Neil Boorstyn, *Copyright Law* (Rochester, N.Y.: Lawyers Cooperative Publishing, 1981), Preface.

Criminal code 84–1.

Congressional Quarterly, *Congress and the Nation, 1981–1984* (Washington, D.C.: Congressional Quarterly Press, 1985), pp. 698–701.

DOD reorganization 47–4, 86–7.

Congressional Quarterly, *Congressional Quarterly Almanac, 1986* (Washington, D.C.: Congressional Quarterly Press, 1987), pp. 455–59.

Deregulation (covers some earlier regulatory acts also—ones being dismantled). 70–4, 72–2, 73–11, 75–1, 75–6, 76–5, 77–6, 77–7, 78–2, 78–5, 80–1, 80–2, 80–3, 80–4, 82–6, 84–4.

Martha Derthick and Paul J. Quirk, *The Politics of Deregulation* (Washington, D.C.: Brookings Institution Press, 1985), chap. 1.

Meier, *Regulation*, chap. 3 (specifically on banks).

Leonard W. Weiss and Michael W. Klass, eds., *Regulatory Reform: What Actually Happened* (Boston: Little, Brown, 1986), pp. 9–13 and cases 1–6 and 9.

Education 50–3, 57–1, 58–3, 60–1, 63–2, 64–1, 65–3, 65–10, 72–11.

Orfield, *Congressional Power*, chaps. 7, 8.

Lawrence E. Gladieux and Thomas R. Wolanin, *Congress and the Colleges: The National Politics of Higher Education* (Lexington, Mass.: D. C. Heath, 1976), pp. xi–xiii, chap. 1, p. 252.

Joel Spring, *The Sorting Machine: National Educational Policy since 1945* (New York: David McKay, 1976), chaps. 2–6.

Sundquist, *Politics and Policy*, chap. 5.

Employment 61–4, 62–2, 64–2, 64–3, 65–5, 67–1, 71–4, 73–4, 74–1, 77–2, 78–1, 82–2, 82–7.

Donald C. Baumer and Carl E. Van Horn, *The Politics of Unemployment*

(Washington, D.C.: Congressional Quarterly Press, 1985), chap. 1. Note table 1.1 at pp. 10–13.

Janet Wegner Johnston, "An Overview of U.S. Federal Employment and Training Programmes," chap. 4 in Jeremy Richardson and Roger Henning, eds., *Unemployment: Policy Responses of Western Democracies* (Beverly Hills, Calif.: Sage Publishing, 1984).

Sar A. Levitan, Peter E. Carlson, and Isaac Shapiro, *Protecting American Workers: An Assessment of Government Programs* (Washington, D.C.: Bureau of National Affairs, 1986), pp. 46–49.

Orfield, *Congressional Power*, chaps. 10–11.

Sundquist, *Politics and Policy*, chap. 3.

Employment opportunity 63–6, 64–1, 67–6, 72–9.

Levitan, Carlson, and Shapiro, *Protecting American Workers*, chap. 4.

Energy 69–6, 70–4, 73–11, 75–1, 75–5, 77–4, 78–2, 80–4, 80–5.

Richard H. K. Vietor, *Energy Policy in America since 1945: A Study of Business-Government Relations* (New York: Cambridge University Press, 1984).

Environment 47–6, 48–3, 63–5, 64–5, 65–7, 65–13, 65–14, 66–2, 69–6, 70–4, 72–2, 72–6, 76–3, 76–8, 77–6, 77–7, 80–7.

James P. Lester and Ann O'M. Bowman, eds., *The Politics of Hazardous Waste Management* (Durham, N.C.: Duke University Press, 1983), chaps. 2, 3.

Meier, *Regulation*, chap. 6.

Sundquist, *Politics and Policy*, chap. 8.

Federalism 69–6, 70–4, 70–15, 72–2, 72–3, 72–10, 74–9, 74–11, 81–1, 81–2, 82–7, 85–1.

Timothy Conlan, *New Federalism: Intergovernmental Reform from Nixon to Reagan* (Washington, D.C.: Brookings Institution Press, 1988), chaps. 3–5, 7, 8.

Food stamps 64–6, 70–15, 73–3, 77–5.

Robert X. Browning, *Politics and Social Welfare Policy in the United States* (Knoxville: University of Tennessee Press, 1986), pp. 95, 110–11, 142–48.

Conlan, *New Federalism*, p. 82.

Foreign aid 47–2, 48–1, 49–4, 50–1, 51–1, 54–8, 61–8, 61–9, 73–8.

Elliott R. Morss and Victoria A. Morss, *U.S. Foreign Aid: An Assessment of New and Traditional Development Strategies* (Boulder, Colo.: Westview Press, 1982), chap. 2.

Robert A. Pastor, *Congress and the Politics of U.S. Foreign Economic Policy, 1929–1976* (Berkeley: University of California Press, 1980), chap. 9.

Foreign trade 51–2, 55–1, 58–4, 62–1, 74–1, 79–2, 84–3.

Stephen L. Lande and Craig VanGrasstek, *The Trade and Tariff Act of*

1984: Trade Policy in the Reagan Administration (Lexington, Mass.: D. C. Heath, 1986), chap. 1.

Pastor, *Congress and the Politics of Foreign Economic Policy*, chaps. 3–6.

Robert Pastor, "The Cry-and-Sigh Syndrome: Congress and Trade Policy," chap. 6 in Allen Schick, ed., *Making Economic Policy in Congress* (Washington, D.C.: American Enterprise Institute, 1983).

Health 60–2, 63–3, 63–4, 65–1, 71–3, 73–10, 74–9.

Odin W. Anderson, *Health Services in the United States: A Growth Enterprise since 1875* (Ann Arbor, Mich.: Health Administration Press, 1985), chaps. 12, 13, 16.

Joseph P. Morrissey and Howard H. Goldman, "Care and Treatment of the Mentally Ill in the United States: Historical Developments and Reforms," *Annals of the American Academy of Political and Social Science* 484 (March 1986), 12–27. (This obviously addresses a subcategory, not health in general.)

Mark E. Rushefsky, *Making Cancer Policy* (Albany: State University of New York Press, 1986), pp. 71–72. (Also addresses a subcategory.)

Sundquist, *Politics and Policy*, chap. 7.

Housing 49–1, 54–7, 61–1, 65–11, 66–7, 68–2, 72–3, 74–11, 81–2.

R. Allen Hays, *The Federal Government and Urban Housing: Ideology and Change in Public Policy* (Albany: State University of New York Press, 1985), pp. xiii–xiv and chaps. 4–9.

Nathaniel S. Keith, *Politics and the Housing Crisis since 1930* (New York: Universe Books, 1973), chaps. 4, 5, 7–12.

Eugene J. Meehan, *The Quality of Federal Policymaking: Programmed Failure in Public Housing* (Columbia: University of Missouri Press, 1979), chap. 2.

Immigration 52–2, 65–8, 86–2.

Michael C. LeMay, *From Open Door to Dutch Door: An Analysis of U.S. Immigration Policy since 1820* (New York: Praeger, 1987), chaps. 5, 6.

Internal security 50–4.

Robert Justin Goldstein, *Political Repression in Modern America: From 1870 to the Present* (New York: Schenkman, 1978), chaps. 9, 11.

Labor-management relations 47–1, 59–1.

Julius G. Getman and Bertrand B. Pogrebin, *Labor Relations: The Basic Processes, Law and Practice* (Westbury, N.Y.: Foundation Press, 1988), pp. 1–4.

Betty W. Justice, *Unions, Workers, and the Law* (Washington, D.C.: Bureau of National Affairs, 1983), pp. 7–17.

Legislative-executive relations 73–1, 74–5.

James L. Sundquist, *The Decline and Resurgence of Congress* (Washington, D.C.: Brookings Institution Press, 1981), chaps. 8, 9.

Minimum wage 49–3, 55–2, 61–2, 66–6, 74–4, 77–3.

Levitan, Carlson, and Shapiro, *Protecting American Workers*, chap. 5, especially the charts on pp. 81 and 87.

Nuclear energy 54–5, 57–2, 74–7.

K. S. Shrader-Frechette, *Nuclear Power and Public Policy: The Social and Ethical Problems of Fission Technology* (Boston: D. Reidel Publishing, 1980), pp. 7–12.

Occupational safety 69–1, 70–7.

Levitan, Carlson, and Shapiro, *Protecting American Workers*, chap. 6.

Michael S. Lewis-Beck and John R. Alford, "Can Government Regulate Safety? The Coal Mine Example," *American Political Science Review* 74 (1980), 745–56.

Pensions (private) 74–2.

Levitan, Carlson, and Shapiro, *Protecting American Workers*, chap. 10.

Post office 70–2.

Roger Sherman, ed., *Perspectives on Postal Service Issues* (Washington, D.C.: American Enterprise Institute, 1980), pt. 1.

Poverty 50–2, 56–2, 58–7, 61–4, 62–2, 62–6, 64–2, 65–1, 67–1, 72–4, 72–10, 81–2.

James T. Patterson, *America's Struggle against Poverty, 1900–1985* (Cambridge: Harvard University Press, 1986), chaps. 5, 6, 8–14.

Sundquist, *Politics and Policy*, chap. 4.

Public lands 64–5, 69–6, 76–6, 76–7, 80–6.

Tom Arrandale, *The Battle for Natural Resources* (Washington, D.C.: Congressional Quarterly Press, 1983), pp. 7–12 and chap. 3.

Social Security 50–2, 56–2, 65–1, 69–2, 71–1, 72–4, 77–1, 83–2.

Paul Light, *Artful Work: The Politics of Social Security Reform* (New York: Random House, 1985).

Martha Derthick, *Policymaking for Social Security* (Washington, D.C.: Brookings Institution Press, 1979), pp. 47–48, 214–15, 238–44, 285–87, and chaps. 15–17, 19.

Soviet relations 47–2, 48–1, 49–2, 52–3, 63–1.

Gaddis, *Russia, the Soviet Union, and the United States*, chaps. 7, 9.

Space 58–2, 58–3, 58–5, 61–7, 62–3, 63–1, 67–5.

Walter A. McDougall, *The Heavens and the Earth: A Political History of the Space Age* (New York: Basic Books, 1985), chaps. 7, 16, 17, 20.

Taxes 48–2, 50–6, 50–7, 51–3, 54–1, 56–3, 62–5, 64–3, 65–12, 68–5, 69–4, 71–2, 75–5, 76–4, 77–2, 78–1, 80–4, 81–1, 82–2, 82–3, 84–2, 86–1.

Joseph A. Pechman, *Federal Tax Policy*, 5th ed. (Washington, D.C.: Brookings Institution Press, 1987), chap. 3. Note table 3.1 at pp. 40–41.

James M. Verdier, "The President, Congress, and Tax Reform: Patterns over Three Decades," *Annals of the American Academy of Political and Social Science* 499 (September 1988), 114–23.

John F. Witte, *The Politics and Development of the Federal Income Tax* (Madison: University of Wisconsin Press, 1985), chaps. 7–11.

Transportation 56–3, 58–8, 61–1, 64–4, 66–1, 70–8, 70–12, 70–13, 73–2, 73–7, 73–9, 74–10, 76–5.

Robert C. Lieb, *Transportation: The Domestic System* (Reston, Va.: Reston Publishing, 1978), chaps. 3–5, 13, 20.

James A. Dunn, Jr., "Railroad Policies in Europe and the United States: The Impact of Ideology, Institutions, and Social Conditions," *Public Policy* 25 (1977), 205–40. (This obviously addresses a subcategory, not the full area.)

Unemployment insurance 70–16, 76–1.

Browning, *Politics and Social Welfare Policy*, p. 161.

Congressional Quarterly, *Congress and the Nation, 1973–76* (Washington, D.C.: Congressional Quarterly Press, 1977), p. 709.

Levitan, Carlson, and Shapiro, *Protecting American Workers*, chap. 8. Note figure 10 on p. 165.

Wage and price controls 50–5, 70–14.

Hugh Rockoff, *Drastic Measures: A History of Wage and Price Controls in the United States* (New York: Cambridge University Press, 1984), chaps. 6, 7.

Water projects 56–4, 68–6.

Donald Worster, *Rivers of Empire: Water, Aridity, and the Growth of the American West* (New York: Pantheon, 1985), chap. 6.

Wild-card category 47–2, 50–3, 61–5, 63–1, 64–2, 65–1.

Nelson W. Polsby, *Political Innovation in America: The Politics of Policy Initiation* (New Haven and London: Yale University Press, 1984). This discusses a selection of important policy initiatives in a number of foreign and domestic areas from 1946 through 1965.

APPENDIX C ◆ SOURCES FOR

SWEEP ONE, 1991-2002

1991-92

Adam Clymer, "It Isn't Graceful, But the Laws Get on the Books," *New York Times*, August 4, 1991.

Adam Clymer, "Congress Does Something, But Mostly Just Stands There," *New York Times*, November 17, 1991.

Adam Clymer, "Tarnishment for Many at the End of Congress," *New York Times*, November 29, 1991.

Jeffrey H. Birnbaum and Jackie Calmes, "Congress, in a Late Sprint, Fulfills Most Vows, But Hurdles on Health, Taxes, Budget Lie Ahead," *Wall Street Journal*, November 29, 1991.

Helen Dewar, "Marching in Place While the Band Moves On," *Washington Post National Weekly Edition*, December 9–15, 1991.

Michael Ross, "Frustrations Linger as Congress Draws to Close," *Los Angeles Times*, October 8, 1992.

Adam Clymer, "Bills Sent to Bush as 102nd Congress Wraps Up Its Work," *New York Times*, October 9, 1992.

Adam Clymer, "The Gridlock Congress: The 102nd Will Be Remembered as Much for Its Embarrassments as Its Legislation," *New York Times*, October 11, 1992.

Helen Dewar, "Between Gulf War and Sniping, Legislative Casualties," *Washington Post*, October 11, 1992.

Beth Donovan and Congressional Quarterly Staff, "Partisanship, Purse Strings Hobbled the 102nd," *Congressional Quarterly Weekly*, October 31, 1992, pp. 3451–52.

1993-94

Jackie Calmes and John Harwood, "Congress Rushes to Close Book on One Busy Year, But Clinton Promises to Apply the Spurs in Next," *Wall Street Journal*, November 22, 1993.

Adam Clymer, "Sour End to Strong Year," *New York Times,* November 24, 1993.

Helen Dewar and Kenneth J. Cooper, "Dust Clears on a Fruitful Legislative Year; Clinton's First-Round Fight Record Is Rated Best Since Eisenhower's," *Washington Post,* November 28, 1993.

George J. Church, "The Gridlock Breakers; Passage of the Brady Bill Caps a Solid Season for the 103rd Congress," *Time,* December 6, 1993, pp. 32–33.

Michael Ross, "103rd Congress Grinding to a Halt amid Partisan Rage," *Los Angeles Times,* October 8, 1994.

Jill Zuckerman and John Aloysius Farrell, "Partisanship Derailed Congress' Fast Start," *Boston Globe,* October 9, 1994.

Adam Clymer, "Rancor Leaves Its Mark on 103rd Congress," *New York Times,* October 9, 1994.

Helen Dewar and Kenneth J. Cooper, "103rd Congress Started Fast But Collapsed at Finish Line," *Washington Post,* October 9, 1994.

"A Final Word on the 103rd," *U.S. News and World Report,* October 17, 1994, p. 20.

1995–96

Alan Murray, "As Historic Congress Breaks for Halftime, Its Goal Is in Sight But Remains Unmet," *Wall Street Journal,* August 11, 1995.

Helen Dewar, "Update on the Contract: Promises Waiting to Be Kept," *Washington Post National Weekly Edition,* August 21–27, 1995.

Helen Dewar, "Long on Talk, Short on Legislation: The First Session of the 104th Congress Was Marked By What Did Not Become Law," *Washington Post National Weekly Edition,* January 8–14, 1996.

Adam Clymer, "G.O.P. Revolution Hits Speed Bumps on Capitol Hill," *New York Times,* January 21, 1996.

Norman J. Ornstein, "Grading the 104th Congress," *Roll Call,* September 23, 1996, p. A-14.

Helen Dewar and Eric Pianin, "Concession Supersedes Revolution: GOP Attempts to Appease Voters," *Washington Post,* September 29, 1996.

David Rogers, "Spending Pact Marks Major Retreat by GOP Leaders," *Wall Street Journal,* September 30, 1996.

Janet Hook, "G.O.P. Congress Leaves Broad Imprint on U.S. Legislation; Conservative Swath Is Less Sweeping than Initial Agenda, But Probably More Durable, Experts Say," *Los Angeles Times,* October 1, 1996.

Chris Black, "GOP Firebrands Take More Moderate Tone," *Boston Globe,* October 1, 1996.

Adam Clymer, "Clinton and Congress: Partnership of Self-Interest," *New York Times,* October 2, 1996.

1997–98

Alison Mitchell, "Return of Partisanship to Capitol Hill," *New York Times,* November 14, 1997.

Helen Dewar and John E. Yang, "Tripped by the Big Issues: The Budget Agreement Is Just a Memory as Congress Wraps Up Its Session with a Wimper," *Washington Post National Weekly Edition,* November 24, 1997.

Helen Dewar and Juliet Eilperin, "Congress: Much Ado About Nothing?" *Washington Post National Weekly Edition,* August 17, 1998.

Katharine Q. Seelye, "As Congress Session Ends, a Question of Legacy," *New York Times,* October 18, 1998.

Sarah A. Binder and Thomas E. Mann, "The 105th: It Could've Been a Contender," *Washington Post,* October 18, 1998.

Janet Hook, " 'Do-Nothing Congress': One for History Books," *Los Angeles Times,* October 20, 1998.

Helen Dewar, "Capitol Tally: One Big Win But Many More Losses," *Washington Post,* October 23, 1998.

1999–2000

Alison Mitchell, "Underlying Tensions Kept Congress Divided to the End," *New York Times,* November 21, 1999.

Helen Dewar and Juliet Eilperin, "Tough Issues to Drift into Election Year," *Washington Post,* November 21, 1999.

David E. Rosenbaum, "Congress Leaves Business Groups Almost All Smiles," *New York Times,* November 26, 1999.

Major Garrett, "Congress to Voters: We're OK," *U.S. News and World Report,* November 29, 1999.

Mary Agnes Carey, "Parties' Ambitious Agendas Made Little Headway in 106th," *Congressional Quarterly Weekly,* December 16, 2000, pp. 2883–84.

Daniel J. Parks, "Omnibus Spending Deal Clears as White House Settles for Less," *Congressional Quarterly Weekly,* December 16, 2000, pp. 2857–59.

Eric Pianin and Dan Morgan, "Congress Ends Session with a Budget Deal," *Washington Post,* December 16, 2000.

Jim Abrams, "Grading of 106th Congress's Work Splits Along Party Lines," *Boston Globe,* December 17, 2000.

Adam Clymer and Lizette Alvarez, "With Minimal Fanfare, Congress Calls It Quits," *New York Times,* December 17, 2000.

"The Legacy of the 106th Congress," *National Journal,* December 23, 2000.

2001–02

Adam Clymer, "After Twists of a Novel, Congress Goes Home," *New York Times,* December 22, 2001.

Janet Hook, "New Realities to Confront Congress in Coming Year," *Los Angeles Times,* December 22, 2001.

Helen Dewar, "For Congress, Anything But Ordinary," *Washington Post,* December 23, 2001.

Susan Milligan, "Congress Runs Out of Bipartisanship," *Boston Globe,* December 23, 2001.

Alison Mitchell, "Daschle Takes Parting Shot as Congress Breaks," *New York Times,* October 19, 2002.

Janet Hook, "A Congress of Milestones Exits: In Spite of Partisanship, Legislators Head into the Election Having Passed Far-Reaching Bills on Issues from Campaign Finance to Agriculture," *Los Angeles Times,* October 20, 2002.

Helen Dewar, "Not One for the History Books: Stifled by Partisan Division, the 107th Congress Lurched from to Drama to Deadlock," *Washington Post National Weekly Edition,* October 28–November 3, 2002.

Jim Abrams, "Lame-Duck Congress Delivers Late Flurry," *Boston Globe,* November 16, 2002.

Carl Hulse, "Its Eyes Fixed on Terrorism, Congress Put Off Many Bills," *New York Times,* November 21, 2002.

Alan Fram, "107th Congress Nears End," *Los Angeles Times,* November 21, 2002.

Helen Dewar, "Congress Adjourns Officially," *Washington Post,* November 22, 2002.

"Politics, Security Shape Agenda," *Congressional Quarterly Almanac 2002* (Washington, D.C.: Congressional Quarterly Press, 2003), pp. 1.3–1.9.

APPENDIX D ◆ A DEFENSE
OF SWEEP TWO

Drawing from the original edition of *this volume*, several scholars have borrowed and used my list of laws from Sweep One,[1] but fewer have made use of Sweep Two. For identifying major laws, current judgments by wrapup journalists seem to be preferred over retrospective judgments by policy experts. In this edition of the book I have steered clear of a Sweep Two analysis myself. That may seem like a repudiation of the idea. It is not. Undertaking a retrospective sweep was not feasible this time. Yet valid by itself as a wrapup-type sweep may be, I continue to believe that, as a matter of both principle and practice, a wrapup sweep is ideally accompanied by something like my retrospective Sweep Two. That is for four reasons.

First, there is the basic reason I presented earlier.[2] Any society will be concerned with the *real downstream effects* of its legislative enactments, not just with the *estimated likely importance* of those enactments as gauged when they originally passed. Journalistic wrapup stories are a plausible guide to "estimated likely importance." That is more or less what the reporters look for. As an instance of this distinction, consider the National Environmental Policy Act of 1969, with its initially underappreciated requirement of "environmental impact statements." That law did not make much of a splash as it passed, but few environmental standards have affected American life in the long run more. Accordingly, Sweep One missed NEPA, but Sweep Two picked it up.

Second, a methodological point. Anyone undertaking a Sweep One–type analysis will come across question-mark cases in the journalistic wrapup stories — enactments that are vaguely or dissonantly or unsatisfactorily covered or are, even with crystal-clear coverage, borderline items. What to do? Judgments need to be made. Errors of inclusion or omission,

1. For example, see Robert S. Erikson, Michael B. MacKuen, and James A. Stimson, *The Macro Polity* (New York: Cambridge University Press, 2002), chap. 9.

2. See pp. 42, 44–45.

245

so to speak, are likely to result–even if it is not easy to envision an authoritative exogenous standard by which we would know that. One virtue of a Sweep Two analysis is that it can help rescue unfortunate *omissions* from a wrapup result. To be sure, a Sweep Two analysis cannot do anything to expel unfortunate *inclusions* from a wrapup result, but perhaps the omissions are worth rescuing.[3]

Third, even in the realm of enactments sized up by journalists as important, a Sweep One–type analysis probably undercounts a certain brand of enactment. At issue is when and where such a size-up occurs. Here I am thinking of a particular kind of bias that may occur indiscriminately across conditions of party control. In writing their end-of-session wrapup stories, journalists tend to center on the main programmatic aspirations of the White House or the congressional parties. Even if they know perfectly well that an enactment is important, and indeed have written stories at one time or another during the year sizing it up exactly that way, they may omit it from an end-of-session wrapup account if it is, so to speak, "off message." Consider the Helms-Burton Act of 1996, regarding relations with Cuba, and the Defense of Marriage Act of 1996, regarding gay marriages. Those enactments earned a good deal of ink at the dates they passed, but they were entrepreneurial efforts extraneous to presidential or party programs, and they tended to miss the wrapups. A future Sweep Two–type analysis might pick them up.

Fourth, in gathering the materials for *Divided We Govern* I came to suspect that Sweep One risked another kind of bias that Sweep Two might help to correct for.[4] Let us call it a "White House hype" bias. In a Sweep Two canvass, policy specialists sifting through laws enacted over several decades do not care much about the conditions of party control under which those laws were passed; they care about which laws were consequential. But wrapup journalists in a Sweep One canvass might be somewhat biased toward unified party control. To state the point as a counterfactual, they might judge enactments to be "important" under conditions of unified party control that they would hold back on, assuming exactly the same enactments, under conditions of divided party control. That is

3. On the unfortunate inclusion side, one small likely bias, so to speak, of a Sweep One–type analysis is to occasionally overinclude laws enacted during the last days of a Congress. Some of them may make it into wrapup stories for reasons of current vividness. Given another couple of months of reflection by the reporters, they might fall away.

4. See the discussions on pp. 89–91; David R. Mayhew, "Let's Stick with the Longer List," *Polity* 25 (1993), 485–88, at pp. 486–87.

because a "passing the president's program" script is very easy to reach for in the former case—as in Lyndon B. Johnson's legislative drive in 1965. Those Great Society enactments needed to be feted and savored one by one. But a "conflict between institutions" script tends to dominate in the circumstance of divided control, and real legislative achievements can get lost in the shuffle. For one thing, laws emanating from Capitol Hill rather than the White House can be discounted. For another, attention can center on the blood that preceded the compromises rather than on the often substantial ingredients of the compromises.

In this regard, consider some statistics drawn from the original Sweep One and Sweep Two datasets. Specifically, they are for the years 1947 through the end of Reagan's first term in 1984—up to the point where my Sweep Two sources were no longer reaching the bulk of newly enacted laws.[5] Included are nineteen Congresses—ten that operated under conditions of divided control, nine under unified party control. To be sure, any summary statistic built on numbers of enacted laws glides over the problem of extraordinarily important laws—notably Reagan's omnibus tax and expenditure cuts in 1981. But let that pass. For these thirty-eight years, the average Sweep One yield per Congress (this includes many items also validated by Sweep Two) was 10.8 enactments under unified control, 8.4 enactments under divided control. The average Sweep Two yield per Congress (this includes many items also validated by Sweep One) was 10.8 enactments under unified control, 10.2 enactments under divided control. For both sweeps, a small average edge went to unified party control, but the edge was larger for Sweep One (2.4 enactments) than for Sweep Two (0.6 enactments).

More specifically, how do these numbers play through the postwar history? See Figure D.1, where the average yields of Sweep One and Sweep Two per Congress are presented for each of four successive time spans—the presidencies of Truman and Eisenhower from 1947 through 1960, those of Kennedy and Johnson from 1961 through 1968, those of Nixon and Ford from 1969 through 1976, and those of Carter and Reagan from 1977 through 1984. First catching the eye is the now familiar "bulge" of lawmaking under especially Johnson and Nixon.[6] Yet beyond

5. For details on the reach of Sweep Two, see "Information on Sweeps One and Two" at *http://pantheon.yale.edu/dmayhew/data3.html.*

6. See William Howell, Scott Adler, Charles Cameron, and Charles Riemann, "Divided Government and the Legislative Productivity of Congress, 1945–94," *Legislative Studies Quarterly* 25 (2000), 285–312, at pp. 297–99.

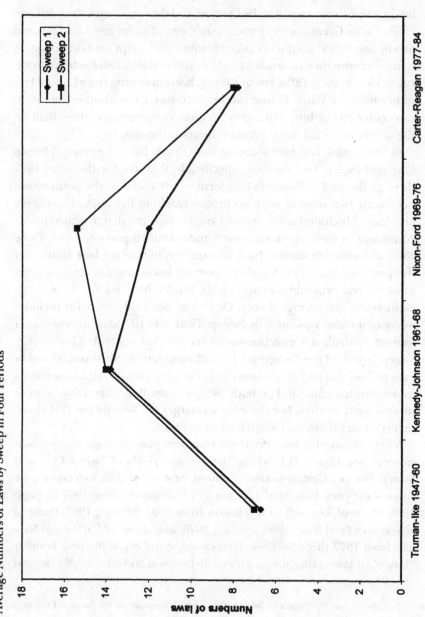

FIGURE D.1
Average Numbers of Laws by Sweep in Four Periods

Numbers of laws

Truman-Ike 1947-60 Kennedy-Johnson 1961-68 Nixon-Ford 1969-76 Carter-Reagan 1977-84

Sweep 1
Sweep 2

that, Sweep Two scores at least a small quantitative edge in every era, but most notably under Nixon and Ford. The single Congress with the largest Sweep Two edge (19 to 13) is that of 1973–74, which was dominated by the Watergate scandal.

It is not clear what to make of this Nixon/Ford pattern. Perhaps my Sweep Two instrument is at fault. It could be exhibiting a "recency bias" in the sense that the retrospective policy works I consulted, most of which were written in the 1980s, might have favored laws just recently passed. Yet the data for the Carter and Reagan presidencies do not bear out that idea.

Much else might have gone on also, but I favor the Sweep One bias idea. I would guess that the Nixon/Ford era, which offered divided party control and chronically bitter interbranch conflict from start to finish, is an all-time Exhibit A for the proposition that wrapup journalists can undermonitor, so to speak, important lawmaking. More generally, American society as a whole seems to have undermonitored the statutory harvest of that time, as we are seeing in a current round of Nixon "revisionism" that emphasizes the era's rich legislative record.[7]

Consider the following enactments of the Nixon/Ford era that Sweep One overlooked: the National Environmental Policy Act (NEPA) of 1969, with its environmental impact statements; the Economic Stabilization Act of 1970, which empowered Nixon to impose wage and price controls (he soon did); the Equal Employment Opportunity Act of 1972, which extended anti-discrimination law to public employers and educational institutions; Supplementary Security Income (SSI) in 1972 as a new entitlement for the aged, blind, and disabled; Pell grants in 1972 as an aid for lower-income college students; the Endangered Species Act of 1973; the Emergency Petroleum Allocation Act of 1973, which got the government into the business of allocating oil and petroleum products and created the Federal Energy Agency (FEA); the Housing and Community Development Act of 1974, which switched federal housing aid to block grants and direct rent subsidies; the Earned Income Tax Credit (EITC) in 1975 as a new kind of subsidy to the low-income employed; and the Resource Conservation and Recovery Act of 1976, which provided for cradle-to-grave regulation of hazardous wastes.[8]

7. See, for example, David Greenberg, *Nixon's Shadow: The History of an Image* (New York: W. W. Norton, 2003), chap. 8.

8. On NEPA, see Kenneth J. Meier, *Regulation: Politics, Bureaucracy, and Economics* (New York: St. Martin's, 1985), pp. 144–45; Richard H. K. Vietor, *Energy Policy in*

One can imagine the feting and savoring of these items if they had issued one by one from a Great Society–type menu. Among other things, three key ingredients of the modern entitlements regime — SSI, EITC, and Pell grants — are included. Conservatives have complained about the weaving of a "stealth" welfare state under Nixon and Ford, and, given the spotty press coverage, the charge becomes understandable.[9] For a case of conflict drowning out achievement, it would be hard to match the story of SSI in 1972: Overwhelmingly, journalists that year dwelt on the failure of Nixon's gargantuan Family Assistance Plan (FAP), apparently not seeing that the SSI entitlement enacted as a fallback called for its own headlines.

If a "White House hype" bias exists that favors unified party control,

---

America since 1945 (New York: Cambridge University Press, 1984), p. 229. On the Economic Stabilization Act: Hugh Rockoff, *Drastic Measures: A History of Wage and Price Controls in the United States* (New York: Cambridge University Press, 1984), chap. 7. On the Equal Employment Opportunity Act: Sar A. Levitan, Peter E. Carlson and Isaac Shapiro, *Protecting American Workers* (Washington, D.C.: Bureau of National Affairs, 1986), chap. 4; Gary Orfield, *Congressional Power: Congress and Social Change* (New York: Harcourt Brace Jovanovich, 1975), pp. 88–91. On SSI: Timothy Conlan, *New Federalism: Intergovernmental Reform from Nixon to Reagan* (Washington, D.C.: Brookings Institution Press, 1988), pp. 81–82; James T. Patterson, *America's Struggle Against Poverty, 1900–1985* (Cambridge: Harvard University Press, 1986), pp. 197–98, 200. On Pell grants: Lawrence E. Gladieux and Thomas R. Wolanin, *Congress and the Colleges: The National Politics of Higher Education* (Lexington, Mass.: D. C. Heath, 1976), pp. xi–xiii, chap. 1, p. 252. On the Emergency Petroleum Act: Vietor, *Energy Policy in America*, chap. 10. On the Housing and Community Development Act of 1974: R. Allen Hays, *The Federal Government and Urban Housing* (Albany: State University of New York Press, 1985), pp. xiii–xiv, chap. 6; Eugene J. Meehan, *The Quality of Federal Policymaking: Programmed Failure in Public Housing* (Columbia: University of Missouri Press, 1979), chap. 2. On the Resource Conservation and Recovery Act: Meier, *Regulation*, pp. 161–63; James P. Lester and Ann O'M. Bowman, eds., *The Politics of Hazardous Waste Management* (Durham, N.C.: Duke University Press, 1983), chaps. 1–3.

9. The Earned Income Tax Credit won birth as an ingredient of the Tax Reduction Act of 1975, which made it into Sweep Two but not Sweep One. In my Sweep One notes for 1975–76, I find some (although I thought insufficient) discussion of the Tax Reduction Act, but no mention of the EITC. One journalist's wrapup story, in discussing initiatives in the area of social policy during that Congress, concluded: "No innovative programs were enacted." David E. Rosenbaum, "Two-Year Ford-Congress Struggle Viewed as a Draw by Both Parties," *New York Times*, October 3, 1976, p. 20. For an account of the genesis of the EITC, see Christopher Howard, *The Hidden Welfare State: Tax Expenditures and Social Policy in the United States* (Princeton, N.J.: Princeton University Press, 1997), chap. 3.

has it been constant in size or force over time? I would guess not. I would guess that it peaked exactly during the Nixon/Ford era. As it happens, it was during that time that the numbers of staff members of congressional committees historically mushroomed—more than doubled. This was a one-time, record-setting explosion of bureaucratic capacity on Capitol Hill.[10] No doubt the institution's lawmaking capacity grew also. As one indicator, the new laws winning enactment became a great deal thicker (that is, more pages per law)[11] during these years, yet as that happened the enactments possibly also became more complex and confusing, for journalists and everybody else. Here is a perfect recipe for journalistic confusion: individual House and Senate members surprisingly and un-precedentedly empowered by new staff resources to write complex and confusing laws in a context of divided party control dominated by the Vietnam War, Watergate, and soaring interbranch conflict. That seems to be what happened. Since the 1970s wrapup journalists seem to have adapted better to the realities of divided party control and congressional initiatives. Certainly they had little trouble following the fortunes of the "Contract with America" in 1995–96.

As a concluding note, I should say that Sweep Two as I devised and administered it is a good ways short of a surefire back-stop detector of every historically important law. Whatever the ultimate yardstick for iden-tifying such measures might be, I have stumbled across certain laws through casual reading since 1991, or else given new thought to certain laws I already knew about back then, that eluded both my original Sweep One and Sweep Two and that now look like good candidates. I regret missing the Displaced Persons Act of 1948 (DIV), which seems to have been a truly important initiative. I missed the Celler-Kefauver Act of 1950 (UNI), which barred vertical and horizontal mergers by firms and is said to have had a "profound effect on the American economy."[12] I missed the Endangered Species Act of 1973 (DIV).[13] That is because I had trouble dealing with the regulatory statutes passed during the Nixon/Ford years.

10. See Joel D. Aberbach, *Keeping a Watchful Eye: The Politics of Congressional Over-sight* (Washington, D.C.: Brookings Institution Press, 1990), pp. 43–44.

11. Ibid., p. 38.

12. Bill Luchansky and Jurg Gerber, "Constructing State Autonomy: The Fed-eral Trade Commission and the Celler-Kefauver Act," *Sociological Perspectives* 36 (1993), 217–240, quotation at p. 219.

13. Of the measures listed in the text earlier, this is the only one missed by Sweep Two.

There were dozens.[14] Sweep Two, as I crafted it, could not accommodate them all. I missed the important Government Ethics Act of 1978 (UNI), probably because the newspaper coverage of it was confusing. I caught the revision of the tax code enacted in 1978 (UNI), but I had no idea that the initiation of 401(k) retirement plans, an underpublicized move, was an ingredient of it.[15] Every now and then one comes across a claim like the following: "Possibly the most inspired piece of legislation to be enacted in America over the past half-century was the Bayh-Dole Act of 1980" (UNI). This measure opened to the public "all the inventions and discoveries that had been made in laboratories throughout the United States with the help of taxpayers' money." Those inventions and discoveries had been sitting on shelves, it is said. The result was to convert universities into "hotbeds of innovation" and to help "reverse America's precipitous slide into industrial irrelevance."[16] Perhaps all that is correct. I missed the Bayh-Dole Act, too.

14. See Murray K. Weidenbaum, *Business, Government, and the Public* (Englewood Cliffs, N.J.: Prentice Hall, 1981), pp. 8–11; Richard A. Harris, "A Decade of Reform," chap. 1 in Harris and Sidney M. Milkis, eds., *Remaking American Politics*, (Boulder, Colo.: Westview, 1989), p. 6.

15. See Michael Barone, "Changes for the Better," *U.S. News & World Report*, April 28, 2003, p. 32. This is about important but unnoticed laws.

16. "Innovation's Golden Goose," *The Economist*, December 14, 2002, p. 3 (Opinion).

INDEX